MEMORY IMPROVED: Reading and Memory Enhancement Across the Life Span Through Strategic Text Structures

MEMORY IMPROVED:
Reading and Memory Enhancement Across the Life Span Through Strategic Text Structures

Bonnie J. F. Meyer
University of Washington
Carole J. Young
Grand Canyon College
Brendan J. Bartlett
Brisbane College of Advanced Education

1989

LAWRENCE ERLBAUM ASSOCIATES, PUBLISHERS
Hillsdale, New Jersey   Hove and London

Lawrence Erlbaum Associates, Inc., Publishers
365 Broadway
Hillsdale, New Jersey 07642

Library of Congress Cataloging-in-Publication Data
Memory improved.
Bibliography: p.
Includes indexes.
1. Memory in old age.   2. Reading comprehension in old
age.   3. Reading—Ability testing.   4. Aging—Psychologi-
cal aspects.   I. Meyer, Bonnie J. F.   II. Young,
Carole J.   III. Bartlett, Brendan J.
BF724.85.M45M45   **1989**   155.67   88-16367
ISBN 0-8058-0111-1

Printed in the United States of America
10   9   8   7   6   5   4   3   2   1

Contents

Acknowledgments

Preparation of this research was supported in part by National Institute of Aging grant AG03438. The authors wish to thank the older adult assistants, Jack Gleason and Alden Ryan, whose help in running this study was invaluable. In addition, the conscientious efforts of Bonnie Gray were very helpful in recruiting and working with the subjects. Assistance in conducting the study was appreciated from Betsy Rice, Shirley Rees-McGee, Geraldine Ellison, Ann Chan, and Alice Christie. Also, we are extremely grateful to our participants; they were a delightful group whose commitment and strenuous work enabled us to complete this study.

*This book is dedicated to our families
and the Creator of the family.*

1 Introduction and Rationale for the Study

PURPOSE OF THE BOOK AND STUDY

The overall goal of the research presented in this book was to determine if instruction focusing on an effective prose learning strategy could improve the reading comprehension and memory of young and older adults. The reading strategy examined teaches readers to utilize the writing plans or top-level structures in texts to facilitate encoding and retrieval. We identified this strategy by examining what more than 1000 adults recalled in writing after they read short magazine articles. Successful readers at all ages appear to search out and follow the text's superordinate relational structure and focus on the text's message and how it relates to supporting major details. They approach text with knowledge about how texts are conventionally organized and with a strategy to seek and use the top-level structure in a particular text as an organizational framework to facilitate encoding and retrieval.

The training program taught learners to employ a deliberate strategy for remembering what they read. In reading, they were taught to choose the organizational plans used by writers to organize information. In remembering, they were taught to use the same organizational plan. A key phrase in the instructional program was to CHOOSE IT, USE IT OR LOSE IT. The strategy enables readers to discriminate main ideas versus trivia in terms of its importance to an author's message. It also enables readers to systematically search their memory for information stored from an article. This strategy was called the plan strategy by the participants in the study and will be referred to by this name throughout the book; prior research has indicated its effectiveness with children and young

1

adults (e.g., Bartlett, 1978; Carrell, 1985; Meyer, Brandt, & Bluth, 1980; Reutzel, 1985; Slater, Graves, & Piche, 1985; Taylor & Beach, 1984).

Generally, older adults (62 and older) do not remember as much as young adults (18—32) from their reading (Meyer, 1987). Two theories exist to explain this poorer performance. One states that, with aging, people remember less due to irreversible cell loss and less efficient cell functioning in the central nervous system. In contrast, the other theory focuses on experience. One version of the experiential model explains that older people remember less because in their everyday life they are not practicing reading and remembering information as much as younger people, who are involved in school or job related reading and remembering. The other version states that a specific type of practice is missing for older adults; that is, practice with an efficient prose learning strategy. Older adults deficient in remembering what they read either did not learn such effective strategies in school decades ago or fail to use them now due to lack of use.

Our past studies with about 600 young, middle-age, and older adults revealed a subgroup of older adults that remember about as much as young adults. This subgroup of older adults had important characteristics in common; they were frequent readers, had acquired at least one college degree, attained extremely high scores on vocabulary tests, and could use the top-level structure in reading materials to guide their learning and memory.

This research posed the question: Can instruction aimed at teaching the plan strategy improve the reading comprehension of high school educated older adults with average to high average vocabulary scores? Adults with these characteristics have been shown to exhibit large age deficits in using the top-level structure of texts and signals in text that cue readers to this organization (e.g., "in contrast," "as a result"). The intervention program directly taught these skills in which these older adults are deficient.

For the current study we screened out adults who were using the strategy on the pretest. Thus, the instruction was aimed at adults who were not using the reading strategy and as a result could most benefit from the instruction. Eliminated from the sample were 12% of the older adults and 33% of the younger adults who exhibited consistent use of the strategy on four recalls written prior to instruction.

Three groups of young and old adults were examined in this study to better understand the critical aspect of the training program as well as reasons for differences in prose learning between young and old adults. In order to better differentiate between the two versions of the experiential model for explaining aging effects (practice versus strategic practice), two instructional groups were studied as well as a control group that participated only in the testing sessions. Young and old adults were matched on vocabulary scores and then randomly assigned to the three groups. One group learned about five basic top-level structures or writing plans used by authors to organize their ideas. They learned to recognize these structures in everyday reading materials and use these structures as a framework for learning. Then, they learned to use these structures to systematically search their memory for what they learned from an article. Another group simply practiced reading and remembering information from their reading. They started with short materials and worked up to longer ones. They read the same materials as the people in the strategy group. Both the strategy and practice groups met for 1½ hours a day for 5 days spread over 2 weeks. The final group received no instruction.

All participants were tested a day prior to instruction, 2 days after the completion of the instruction, and 2 weeks after the instruction. During the testing sessions the subjects read and recalled four passages, recalled one of these passages again after a delay, took a standardized reading comprehension test, underlined the most important ideas in passages, answered main idea, detail, and problem solving questions about texts, and filled out questionnaires about reading strategies and attitudes.

Details about these materials and procedures for conducting the study are found in the third chapter of this book. The results of the study are presented in chapter four and they are discussed in the fifth chapter. The final chapter presents the actual training program used in the study; it includes both the teacher's manual and a copy of the materials used by the students.

The remainder of chapter 1 presents a rationale and brief history of our work uniting the two research areas of prose learning and aging. The literature in these research areas is reviewed in the next chapter.

RATIONALE AND HISTORY OF OUR RESEARCH UNITING TWO RESEARCH DOMAINS: PROSE LEARNING AND AGING

Over the last decade our research program has sought to unite two research domains: prose learning and aging. On the one hand, research on prose comprehension has shown the importance of utilizing organizational structures suggested by text in order to better remember it (e.g., Meyer, 1985a; van Dijk & Kintsch, 1983). On the other hand, aging research on verbal learning tasks (primarily with lists of words or word pairs) has indicated a deficit in the use of organization by older adults (Burke & Light, 1981). Our work has attempted to integrate prose learning and aging research to see if age deficits in learning and memory occurred with the more naturalistic prose materials and if deficits were related to failure to use organizational components of prose.

As shown in Fig. 1.1 reading comprehension can be viewed as an interaction among three types of variables: *Reader* variables, such as verbal ability and world knowledge, *text* variables, such as text structure, and *task* variables, such as telling all you remember from what you read or solving a problem with the information read. Meyer's work (e.g., Meyer, 1975. 1985a) has primarily

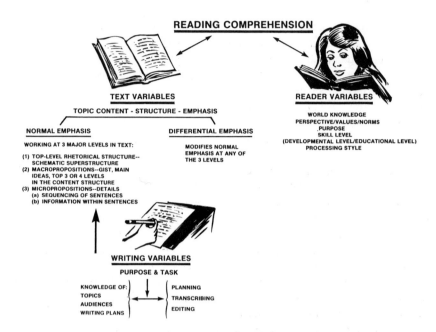

READING COMPREHENSION

TEXT VARIABLES

TOPIC CONTENT - STRUCTURE - EMPHASIS

NORMAL EMPHASIS

DIFFERENTIAL EMPHASIS

WORKING AT 3 MAJOR LEVELS IN TEXT:

(1) TOP-LEVEL RHETORICAL STRUCTURE--
    SCHEMATIC SUPERSTRUCTURE
(2) MACROPROPOSITIONS--GIST, MAIN
    IDEAS, TOP 3 OR 4 LEVELS
    IN THE CONTENT STRUCTURE
(3) MICROPROPOSITIONS--DETAILS
    (a) SEQUENCING OF SENTENCES
    (b) INFORMATION WITHIN SENTENCES

MODIFIES NORMAL
EMPHASIS AT ANY OF
THE 3 LEVELS

READER VARIABLES

WORLD KNOWLEDGE
PERSPECTIVE/VALUES/NORMS
PURPOSE
SKILL LEVEL
(DEVELOPMENTAL LEVEL/EDUCATIONAL LEVEL)
PROCESSING STYLE

WRITING VARIABLES

PURPOSE & TASK

KNOWLEDGE OF:
TOPICS
AUDIENCES
WRITING PLANS

PLANNING
TRANSCRIBING
EDITING

FIG. 1.1.   Reader, text, and writer variables that influence comprehension from text (from Meyer, 1981). Originally published in *COMPREHENSION AND THE COMPETENT READER Inter-Specialty Perspectives,* Dennis F. Fisher and Charles W. Peters, Eds. (Praeger Publishers, a division of Greenwood Press, Inc., New York, NY). Copyright © 1981 by Praeger Publishers. Reprinted with permission.

focused on specifying the effects of various text variables on the amount and type of information people can remember after they read a passage.

Text structure.   The structure of text from Meyer's theoretical orientation is hierarchical with main ideas located at the top of the structure and details located at the bottom of the structure. The structure of text is the organization that binds it together and gives it an overall organization. The structure shows how some ideas are of central importance to the author's message, which is bound by this overall organization, while other ideas are shown to be peripheral. For example, Fig. 1.2 shows the top-level structure and major logical relationships of a magazine article about supertankers; the overall or top-level structure for this passage is a problem and its solutions. Central ideas include the problem of environmental damage resulting from oil spilled by wrecked supertankers and three possible solutions involving the training of officers, the building of tankers, and the installation of ground control stations. Peripheral ideas include specific descriptions from examples of oil spills, such as the fact that 200,000 dead seabirds washed ashore off the coast of Cornwall. The entire passage contains 388 words

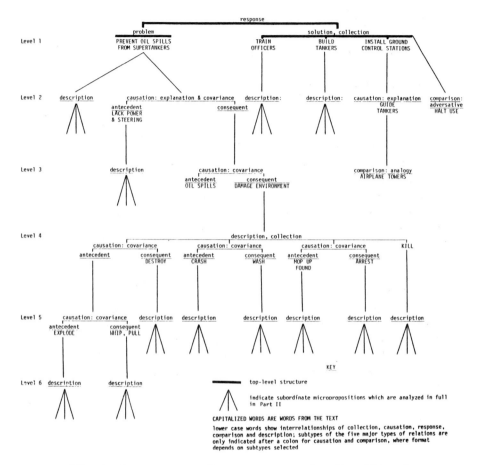

FIG. 1.2. Content structure for a text on supertankers. From Meyer, B. J. F. (1985a). Prose analysis: Purposes, procedures, and problems. In B. K. Britton & J. Black (Eds.), Understanding expository text (pp. 18–19). Hillsdale, NJ: Lawrence Erlbaum Associates, courtesy of the publisher).

and 244 scorable units in the complete analysis of the text; this structure arranges the ideas from the passages into nine levels of importance.

The text structure specifies the logical connections among ideas as well as subordination of some ideas to others. It is this structure of text that primarily differentiates text from simple lists of words or sentences.

Drawing upon linguistics and rhetoric, Meyer (e.g., Meyer, 1985a; Meyer & Freedle, 1984) gathered evidence for five basic ways to organize discourse: collection, description, causation, problem/solution, and comparison. The typology is not intended to be exhaustive or definitive, but there is good support that there are significant distinctions among these discourse types. Figure 1.3 points out differences in the amount and type of organization inherent in each of these structures. The collection and description structures have the least organization. If you read a passage that gives a collection of descriptions about whales, the best way to utilize the structure is to count and remember the group of attributes of whales that are described, such as their appearance, appetite, and family structure. The sequence type of collection structure gives you more organization in that the ideas presented are ordered in time. The causation structure has the organization of time with the cause preceding the effect as well as the added organization of the cause and effect relationship. The problem/solution structure has all the organizational components of causation with the addition of overlapping ideas between the problem and solution where the solution attempts to block a cause of the problem. Thus, the problem/solution structure provides the most inherent structure of these four structures and should provide the greatest aid to memory. In contrast, the comparison discourse type does not organize on the basis of time or causality, but on the basis of similarities and differences. Often when opposing views are compared they are compared on many of the same issues; for example, one political candidate's views are stated on abortion, taxes, government spending, and defense, and then the other candidate's views are posited on these same issues. Memory will be improved if we remember that a comparison structure was used along with the number and name of the issues compared; for our example we should remember that the candidates were compared on four issues: abortion, taxes, government spending, and defense. Re-

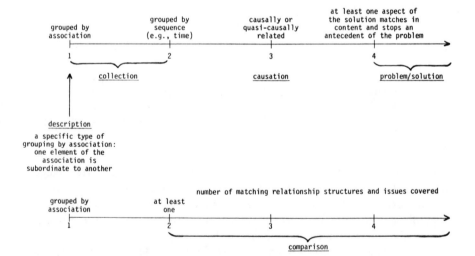

FIG. 1.3. Type and number of specified organizational components required for the different discourse types. From Meyer and Freedle, 1984, courtesy of American Educational Research Association.

membering that one candidate said something about taxes can help us to remember to search our memory for what the other candidate said about this same issue.

These basic discourse types are familiar in various contexts. Political speeches are often of the comparison type, and in particular, its unequally weighted subtype. Newspaper articles are often of the descriptive type, telling us who, where, how and when. Scientific treatises often adhere to the problem/solution type, first raising a question or problem and then seeking to give an answer or solution. History texts often exemplify the collection/sequence structure.

We have used expository texts to probe how these five top-level structures affect reading comprehension. In one study we found that 9th grade students who used the author's top-level structure to organize their recall remembered more, even a week later, than those who did not (Bartlett, 1978). Ninth grade students evaluated by reading comprehension tests and by their teachers as good readers used the text's top-level structure to organize their recalls, while those evaluated as poor readers did not (Meyer et al., 1980). In another study (Meyer & Freedle, 1984) we found that university students remembered more from discourse which was written in a comparison structure than from that written in as a collection of descriptions.

The earlier work looking at text structure involved high school and college students reading and recalling texts. Five basic research findings emerged from these investigations. First, ideas that are located at the top levels of an analysis of a text's structure are recalled and retained better than ideas located at the lower levels (e.g.. Meyer, 1971, 1975). These main ideas located high in the structure also are more likely to be integrated in memory than ideas located low in the structure (Walker & Meyer, 1980).

Second, the type and structure of relationships among concepts in text dramatically influence recall when they occur at the top third of the structure; however, when the same relationships occur low in the structure, they affect recall minimally (Meyer, 1975). This finding led Meyer to focus her research on the different types of overall text structures used in expository text since it is this overall plan and major logical relationships among paragraphs in texts that affects what people remember, rather than how the details are organized.

Third, different types of these overall plans or top-level structures differentially affect recall: comparison and causation top-level structures facilitate recall more than descriptive structures (Meyer & Freedle, 1984). Later research (Meyer, Rice, Knight, & Jessen, 1979; Meyer & Rice, 1983b; Vincent, Meyer, & Rice, 1985) showed this finding only to hold for adults listening to prose who scored at high average to high levels on vocabulary tests.

Fourth, students who are able to identify and use these top-level structures remember more from their reading than those who do not (e.g., Meyer et al., 1980).

Fifth, training in how to recognize and use these top-level structures improves recall for text materials (Bartlett, 1978).

The Use of Text Structure across the Adult Life Span.   From looking at what over 1000 adults write down after they read passages and asking adults to predict what will come next as they read each sentence in a text, we have identified a reading strategy for successful readers. We call this strategy the structure or plan strategy in that the readers follow the structure or writing plans of text. Successful readers search out and follow the text's superordinate relational structure and focus on the text's message and how it relates to supporting major details. They approach text with knowledge about how texts are conventionally organized and a strategy to seek and use the top-level structure in a particular text as an organizational framework to facilitate encoding and retrieval. Processing activities for the structure strategy focus on a search for major text-based relationships among propositions. That is, there is a search for relationships which can subsume all or large chunks of this information and tie it into a summarized comprehensible whole. Readers employing this strategy are hypothesized to approach text looking for patterns that will tie all the propositions together and the author's primary thesis, which will be the ideas organized by the text's top-level structure. Then, they search for relationships among this primary thesis and supporting details. Figure 1.4 depicts a model for the encoding aspects of this strategy.

The top-level structure and major interrelationships also are employed to guide retrieval and production of the recall protocol; it is hypothesized to be primarily a top-down retrieval search guided by the structure of relationships. When recalling the text, the reader begins the retrieval search with the top-level structure and systematically uses the particular discourse structure to search memory.

Readers process text line by line in a linear fashion; they do not wait until after they have read the entire text to find the top-level structure and other superordinate relations which organize large chunks of text. Signaling words in the text, such as "problem," "need to prevent," "in contrast," "others disagree," "others believe," "as a result," and other content words, help readers to make educated guesses about which top-level structure or schemata to assign to the text. This view is consistent with research indicating that readers automatically update their representations of text with important text content as they read (Cirilo & Foss, 1980; Dee-Lucas & Larkin, 1987; Goetz, Reynolds, Schallert, & Radin, 1983; Just & Carpenter, 1980; Lorch, Lorch, & Mathews, 1985).

Forty-eight percent of a sample of 9th grade students showed evidence of using the structure or plan strategy in their recall of a text. Use of the strategy is associated with recall protocols organized with the same top-level structure as the text, high recall of the logical relations from the text, and a strong levels effect; that is, information high in the text structure is remembered much better than information low in the structure.

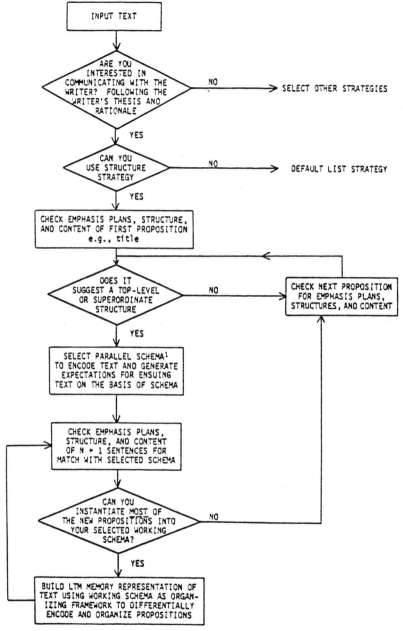

[1]Type of schema selected here influences processes of selection and buffer rehearsal.

FIG. 1.4. Model of encoding aspects of the plan strategy. From Meyer, B. J. F. (1984). Text dimensions and cognitive processing: In H. Mandl, A. Stein, & T. Trabasso (Eds.), Learning from texts (pp. 3–52). Hillsdale, NJ: Lawrence Erlbaum Associates, courtesy of the publisher.

More than half of the 9th graders that did not use this strategy did not employ some other type of organization as we have observed from graduate students who disagree with an author's viewpoint. Instead, the 9th grade students employed what we have called the default list strategy. At best their recall is characterized as a collection of descriptions about the topic. One idea is listed, then another, and another with no attempt to interrelate the ideas together. These recalls are organized as a list of things the person remembers from the passage with poor recall of the text's logical relationships and significant, but smaller level effects.

When we first started to look at aging and prose learning, we expected to see all older adults recalling much less information from their reading than young adults. In addition, we expected that all older adults would have difficulty utilizing the structure of text since age deficits in organization and memory were consistently found in the verbal learning literature. To our surprise in our first study with Arizona State University alumni from 18–32, 40–55, and 62 and older we found no age deficits. These adults were all college graduates with high average to high scores on the Vocabulary Test of the WAIS. In addition, the adults were given unlimited reading and recalling time. We now know that the magnitude of age deficits is affected by characteristics of the readers, the text, and the task.

Most recent studies of prose learning and aging point to age deficits in memory for prose for old adults, but not for middle-aged adults. Age deficits are greater under conditions of controlled presentation rather than self-paced reading. College educated old adults with extremely high vocabulary scores (99% on the Vocabulary Subtest of the WAIS) show little or minimal age deficits, while high school educated old adults with average vocabulary scores show large age deficits. Although high verbal old adults read more slowly and remember slightly less than comparable young adults, these older adults can effectively utilize the organization in text to aid their memory.

Meyer and Rice (1988) found that young and old adults with high verbal skills did not differ in their use of the plan strategy. In passages that clearly signaled the text's top-level structure with such words as "the problem is" or "in contrast," 90% of these young and old adults used the author's top-level structure to organize what they remember. In passages without explicit signaling 70% used the same top-level structure to organize their recall.

Older adults with average vocabulary performance can remember more main ideas than details, but recall substantially less of both types of information than comparable younger adults (Meyer & Rice, 1988). In addition, average verbal old adults show large age deficits in using the organizational structure of text. Meyer and Rice (1988) showed that 53% of a group of average verbal old adults who read problem/solution and comparison passages followed the plan strategy on one passage read, while 69% of young adults with comparable education and vocabulary scores followed the strategy. Also, average verbal old adults do not benefit from signals in text to cue readers to the text structure (e.g., Meyer & Rice, 1988).

Our research findings as well as most of the research from other laboratories have shown that age differences appear to be attenuated when subjects possess superior levels of semantic abilities. In an attempt to determine factors underlying verbal ability that affect reading comprehension, Rice and Meyer (1985) examined the reading behaviors of young and older adults of high and average verbal ability. Answers to questionnaires indicated that certain reading behaviors were related to success on prose learning tasks for both young and old adults, and old adults with average vocabulary scores reported the lowest incidence of these behaviors. High scorers on recall tasks were those who were highly practiced at reading and who took an analytical approach to reading of text. Specifically, older adults of high verbal ability reported more enjoyment of reading and spent more time reading than did older adults of average verbal ability. These data are compatible with a practice explanation; that is, older adults with high verbal skills perform as well as young adults on some prose recall tasks because they practice the necessary reading skills.

This practice explanation was further investigated in our laboratory with a diary study (Rice, 1986a, 1986b). Over the space of 5 weeks, 54 participants kept structured diaries in which they recorded how they spent their time, including what materials they read and the length of time spent reading each item. These data were used to determine if activities varied as a function of differences in the age and vocabulary skills of the participants. Of particular interest was whether older adults who were high in verbal ability did more reading than average ability ones, as would be predicted by the practice effect of the experiential model.

With respect to the effects of age and vocabulary level on the everyday activities of adults, the findings demonstrated that age and vocabulary were secondary to requirements of daily life (school, employment, retirement) in determining the patterning of daily activities. The daily requirements of schooling and career were of overriding importance in determining the types of activities engaged in by adults. Thus, it was not the case that older adults who were high in verbal ability showed markedly different patterns from average ability adults in their reading and other activities, as would be predicted by the practice effect. However, there were some significant differences between the older high vocabulary adults and the older average vocabulary adults in reading activities, but not other activities. Older average vocabulary adults read less, spent less time reading for interest, and spent less time reading materials other than the newspaper. Thus, the data provide some indirect support for the practice hypothesis of the experiential model in that older adults of high verbal ability did get more practice at reading than did older adults of average ability.

Although the questionnaire and diary data lent some support to the practice effect, an exploratory multivariate analysis (Rice & Meyer, 1986) did not give much support to the power of this practice effect in explaining prose recall performance. Four hundred twenty-two young, middle-aged, and old adults read and recalled two passages and answered questions about their background, reading habits, and recall strategies. Results indicated that a decrease in quantity of recall appeared with increasing age, though verbal ability was a better predictor of recall than was age. A recall strategy factor representing a paragraph-by-paragraph retrieval strategy produced the highest simple correlations with total recall. Reading habit factors appeared very seldom in the multiple regression analyses and produced only a few positive correlations in the simple regressions. This almost total absence of the reading habit factors from the multiple regression analyses would appear to provide little support for the practice effect explanation of age differences in recall performance.

Relating the diary data to recall data, Rice and Meyer (1986) showed that total time spent reading in everyday life correlated with recall performance in the laboratory ($.32, p < .05$). In a multiple regression analysis four reading categories together accounted for 40% of the variance. They included technical journals, science books, textbooks, and religious materials (primarily the Bible) for 12%, 10%, 6%, and 6%, respectively. These findings are in line with the questionnaire data reported in Rice and Meyer (1985) and the practice explanation for aging deficits.

However, the study (Rice & Meyer, 1986) indicated that it is not only quantity of practice, but quality as well. Completely opposite relations between newspaper reading and prose recall performance were found for average and high verbal older adults. For older adults of average ability, time spent reading newspapers correlated negatively ($r = -.91$) with recall, while older adults of high verbal ability showed a strong positive correlation ($r = .89$). Total time spent reading all materials showed a similar pattern for the average verbal old adults; the primary material read by the average verbal old adult was the newspaper. There does not appear to be a simple linear relation between practice in reading and recall, but instead, a certain skill level may be necessary before practice is effective.

Previous research indicates that one of these important reading skills is the ability to use the structure or plan strategy (Meyer et al., 1980) in which the reader identifies and uses the text's organizational plan for a passage to guide comprehension and recall. The study presented in this book gives adults instruction and practice with this reading strategy and compares this instruction with another that simply gives an opportunity to practice reading and recalling texts. The materials used in both instructional programs were of the same type read by adults in their daily lives as ascertained by the diary study and questionnaires. Thus, the study presented in this book further investigates the experiential model of aging differences by comparing the practice alone explanation versus the strategic practice explanation.

2 Background Literature in Aging and Reading

This chapter discusses research that applies to the study presented in this book. Since this research unites concerns from different research domains, each re-search area is considered. The literature on aging and reading comprehension is reviewed first. Much of the rationale for conducting the current study comes from this work. The current investigation appears to be the first systematic intervention study designed to teach older adults an effective reading comprehension strategy. The second area we review deals with cognitive skill training for the elderly. The final area concerns research focusing on teaching reading comprehension skills and strategies to younger people.

AGING AND READING COMPREHENSION

Reading comprehension is influenced by the individual differences variables listed under reader variables in Fig. 1.1 as well as by the task and text variables listed (Meyer, 1981). The study of reading comprehension has been an active area of research in psychology and education over the last 2 decades (e.g., Calfee & Drum, 1986; Pearson, 1984). The interaction of the reader and the structure of texts has been a particularly productive area of research on reading comprehension during this time. Contributions to our understanding of texts and reading comprehension have come from the areas of linguistics (e.g., Beaugrande, 1980; Grimes, 1975; Halliday & Hasan, 1976), rhetoric (e.g., Aristotle, 1960; Christensen, 1967; D'Angelo, 1979), folklore and story grammar (e.g., Mandler, 1987; Propp, 1958; Rumelhart, 1975; Stein & Glenn, 1979), artificial intelligence (e.g., Lehnert, 1981; Schank, 1975), education (e.g., Niles, 1965), educational psychology (e.g., Meyer, 1975, 1985a; Trabasso, & van den Broek, 1985) and psychology (e.g., Graesser, 1981; Kieras, 1985; Kintsch, 1974; Frederiksen, 1977).[1]

This basic research on prose learning stimulated gerontologists to examine age related changes in memory with more naturalistic materials (Hartley, Harker, & Walsh, 1980). Research dealing with reading comprehension and aging has increased substantially within the last decade and has primarily utilized the approaches of Kintsch (1974), Meyer (1975), and Mandler and Johnson (1977). Although age-related deficits are well-documented with verbatim recall of lists of words, numbers and such (Burke & Light, 1981), deficits are not always found with substantive recall of texts. Certain types of older adults under some task conditions with particular types of text can remember as much information as younger adults (Hultsch & Dixon, 1984; Meyer & Rice, 1983a, 1988). However, under the majority of reader, task, and text conditions tested so far in the laboratory age differences in prose processing have been found. A number of reviews have been written recently about this growing body of literature on prose processing and aging (Cohen, in press; Hartley, 1988, in press; Hartley et al., 1980; Hultsch & Dixon, 1984; Meyer, 1987; Meyer & Rice, 1983a, 1988; Zelinski & Gilewski, in press).

This review of the literature on prose learning and aging looks at some aspects of the readers, tasks, and texts involved in this research area. The issues discussed in this review were considered in designing the current study or in explaining some of the outcomes of the study.

Issues related to the reader.   Some of the differences among extant studies on reading comprehension and aging can be explained by differences in education and verbal ability of sample participants. Age differences in text recall have been reported to interact with level of verbal ability (Meyer & Rice, 1983a; Poon, Krauss, & Bowles, 1984; Taub, 1979; Zelinski & Gilewski, in press). Individual differences approaches in cognitive psychology have indicated compatible findings related to the advantage for individuals with good verbal skills (e.g., Hunt, 1978; Perfetti, 1985).

Meyer and Rice (1983a) presented an analysis of four subsamples selected from a group of 314 younger and older adults, all of whom had read and recalled two expository texts. The subsamples were formed on the basis of their vocabulary scores on the Quick Word Test. These data suggested rather clearly that there are age-related deficits in memory performance for adults with average or below average abilities and little post-high-school education. The situation is not as clear for individuals with above average verbal ability and college education. Old adults with high vocabulary scores performed as well as a random sample of

---

[1]See Meyer and Rice (1984) for a discussion of work from these domains and Meyer (1985a) for a comparisons of some of these approaches.

college educated young adults; these young adults had the same education level, but lower vocabulary scores. However, moderate age differences in recall were observed when the highest scorers on the vocabulary test from both the young and old groups were compared. Thus, age differences in memory performance may be present or absent depending on how the investigator equates the age groups on education and verbal ability.

Most of the extant studies on text comprehension and aging where aging deficits have not been found involved subjects with some college education (Harker, Hartley, & Walsh, 1982; Mandel & Johnson, 1984; Meyer & Rice, 1981; Simon, Dixon, Nowak, & Hultsch, 1982 (intentional learning condition); Smith, Rebok, Smith, Hall, & Alvin, 1983; Taub, 1979; Young, 1983); all but the Smith et al. study (1983), where vocabulary was not reported, indicate at least a slight superiority by the old adults for either years of education or vocabulary scores. The one exception is a study by Thompson and Diefenderfer (1986); the older adults in this study averaged 11 years of education, while young adults averaged 15 years. In this study a very long text (1600 words) was read by a group who also read an advanced organizer for the passage and a group allotted extra time to read the passage. The dependent measure was a recognition test. The effects of age and presence of the advanced organizer were nonsignificant. Divergence between the Thompson and Diefenderfer (1986) study and the many other studies of old adults with no more than high school education, where age deficits have consistently been found, may be due to the recognition test or the passage length. Several studies with nonsignificant age effects have used longer texts.

Rice and Meyer (1986) conducted an exploratory multivariate analysis designed to ascertain the relative contributions of age, verbal ability, education, reading habits, and recall strategies to the variation in performance on prose recall tasks among 422 adults from young, middle, and old age groups. Results showed a decrease in the amount of information remembered with increasing age ($r = -.24$), but verbal ability ($r = .37$) was a better predictor than age. Multiple regression analyses were performed to clarify the relative contributions of different reader variables for predicting prose recall. Vocabulary explained about 19% of the variance, followed by age (12%), a paragraph by paragraph recall strategy (5%), a detail encoding strategy (4%), a main idea encoding strategy (1%), and the text variable of signaling (1%). The reading habits factors made no significant contributions. These proportions of variance in total recall accounted for by age and vocabulary are very similar to those found by Glynn, Okun, Muth, and Britton (1983) with 108 adults ranging in age from 18 to 56. In contrast, a similar study by Hartley (1986) found vocabulary scores to be only weakly related to recall. The strongest predictor in this study was time spent reading (accounting for 18% of the variance); the young adults tended to spend more time reading short (246–286 word) texts. Age accounted for 9% of the variance in recall performance. The strength of the reading time predictor suggests that some of the disadvantage for the old adults may relate to faulty strategies and unfamiliarity with the task demands. The training study presented in this book aimed to familiarize older adults with an effective strategy and demands of the recall task.

Hultsch, Hertzog, and Dixon (1984) related text performance by young, middle-aged, and old adults to a set of intellectual ability factors (Ekstrom, French, Harman, & Derman, 1976). The ability with the largest overall relationship with text memory was general intelligence. Regression analyses indicated that age differences in text recall performance were reduced drastically, but not eliminated, when the contribution of intellectual ability was partialled out (a drop from between 20% and 30% to between 3% and 4%). An age by verbal comprehension interaction was not found, but an interaction was found between age and verbal productive thinking (as well as for associative memory).

Both sample selection and type of vocabulary test are considered in an attempt to reconcile the findings of the studies of Hultsch et al. (1984) and Meyer and Rice (1983a). The sample of 150 young, middle, and old adults in the Hultsch et al. study varied significantly on education (young, 14 years; middle-aged, 13 years; old, 11 years). Hultsch et al. pointed out that these differences match the average years of education for these age groups reported by the 1977 U.S. Census Bureau. The subjects in their study were white female adults from a small city in central Pennsylvania, while Meyer and Rice (1983a) have worked with volunteers from Phoenix, Arizona, an area that attracts healthy, mobile, and relatively wealthy older adults. Their high verbal old adults had an average of 16.1 years of education, while their lower verbal old adults had an average of 12.5 years of education.

Also, Meyer and Rice utilized the Quick Word Test (Borgatta & Corsini, 1964) to measure vocabulary. Adults that score at the 25 percentile on the Quick, score at the 75 percentile on the Vocabulary Subtest of the WAIS. The high verbal old adults scored at the 93rd percentile on the Quick and hit the ceiling of the WAIS. The Quick is a tricky 100 item multiple choice test (i.e., heart = beat, draw, core, or vein; shoot = bang, push, twig, or jump) that appears to require considerable associative memory and verbal productive thinking. Therefore, the results of Hultsch et al. (1984) showing that these factors relate to prose recall more than verbal comprehension may not be contrary to the findings of Meyer and Rice, but may only reflect differences in tests used. Differences in the construction of vocabulary tests may also explain the discrepancy in the contribution attributed to vocabulary for predicting recall performance found by Rice and Meyer (1986) and Glynn et al. (1983) who used the Quick versus Hartley (1986) who used the Shipley-Hartford Scale (Shipley, 1940). In the current investigation two vocabulary tests, the Quick and the WAIS, and a reading comprehension test were administered as specified in chapter 3.

In conclusion, some incompatibility among the findings from studies on prose learning and aging can be explained by differences in education and verbal ability of samples. Age deficits in prose recall are regularly found for average and low verbal adults with mainly high school education (Cohen, 1979; Dixon & von Eye, 1984; Dixon, Hultsch, Simon, & von Eye, 1984; Dixon, Simon, Nowak & Hultsch, 1982; Glynn et al., 1983; Meyer & Rice, 1983a, 1983b; Spilich, 1983; Spilich & Voss, 1982; Surber, Kowalski, & Pena-Paez, 1984; Taub, 1979; Zelinski, Light, & Gilewski, 1984). However, all of the discrepancy cannot be explained since some studies with highly educated, high ability old adults report aging deficits (Cohen, 1979; Gordon & Clark, 1974; Light & Anderson, 1985; Meyer & Rice, 1983b; Zelinski et al., 1984), while others do not (Harker et al., 1982; Mandel & Johnson, 1984; Meyer & Rice, 1981, 1983a; Young, 1983). In general, age differences appear to be attenuated when subjects possess superior levels of semantic abilities.

Prior knowledge of text content, rather than structure has been investigated. Hartley (1988) reported moderate, but significant correlations between the prior knowledge of adults and how well they recalled texts on those topics. Hartley, Cassidy, and Lee (1986) found that knowledge about a topic acquired from sources other than the text improved recall by young, middle-aged, old, and old-plus groups; this finding is compatible with research on novice and expert learning in the domain of baseball indicating the expertise facilitates learning from texts in that domain (Chiesi, Spilich, & Voss, 1979). Hartley et al. (1986) predicted that the benefits of prior knowledge would be greater for older adults who they assumed had reduced processing resources; however, the benefits of prior knowledge appeared to be the same for all four age groups.

Hultsch and Dixon (1983) systematically investigated prior knowledge and age effects on prose learning. Average verbal, high school educated adults from three age groups read short biographical sketches about famous entertainment figures of various eras. The findings suggested that age differences in recall performance may be present or absent depending on the level of preexperimental knowledge about the topic possessed by the various age groups.

Older adults appear to be especially likely to intrude bits of prior knowledge into their recall of new information (Hultsh & Dixon, 1983). Smith et al. (1983) found that the amount of distortions and additions from adults' prior knowledge was a function of an age by text organization interaction. Young adults added prior knowledge to make the unorganized stories more coherent, while old adults added prior knowledge to make well-organized stories more interesting. Also, Surber et al. (1984) found young adults to make more theme related intrusions in their recall of a long expository text than old adults. These findings suggest that differences between age groups in prose recall could result from differences in perspective or purpose related to the social and intellectual contexts of each age group.

A reader's prior knowledge has been shown to play a critical role in determining what is learned from text (Dee-Lucas & Larkin, 1987). Types of prior knowledge investigated with students range from domain-specific representations of a content area, such as the goal structure of baseball (Chiesi et al., 1979) and knowledge structures in physics (Dee-Lucas & Larkin, 1986), to structural features of text, such as the topic-comment structure of sentences (Danner, 1976; Kieras, 1980, 1985) and passage organization (Garner et al., 1986; Meyer et al., 1980; Williams, Taylor, & Ganger, 1981; Taylor & Samuels, 1983). All of these types of prior knowledge aid in comprehension by guiding attention to important content, facilitating encoding of that information into existing knowledge structures, and presenting readily available retrieval cues. The type of prior knowledge investigated in the research in this book deals with knowledge of text structures, signals in text to cue these structures, and a strategy to utilize this information to aid encoding and retrieval. One aspect of the investigation looks to see if teaching people this knowledge changes the types of information that they rate as important to remember and do in fact remember.

Issues related to the task.   Investigations of presentation by listening versus reading have found that performance is similar after both listening and reading when reading time is equal to listening time (Sticht & James, 1984). However, when reading is self-paced, then recall after reading is superior (Stine, Wingfield, & Poon, 1986; Taub & Kline, 1978).

Dixon et al. (1982) examined the effects of input modality on the immediate and delayed recall of short newspaper articles by average verbal, high school educated adults. Young and middle-aged adults were found to benefit more from the opportunity to read material than older adults. These findings were explained as a result of older adults taking less advantage of the opportunity to review material during reading than younger adults. Taub and Kline's study (1978) is compatible with this explanation that old adults benefit less from an opportunity for review.

In both the Dixon et al. study and the Taub and Kline study, the adults were average in verbal ability and were primarily high school educated. In comparing high verbal and average verbal old adults (Meyer, 1984; Rice & Meyer, 1985), average verbal old adults appear deficient in their use of text structure, recall of logical relationships in text, and ability to find and underline the important ideas in a text. Average verbal old adults may be unable to take advantage of opportunities to review because of ineffective strategies for finding and utilizing the organization in text. Studies sampling high verbal adults may not find these age deficits in utilization of review opportunities since these readers are more practiced and more analytical than their average vocabulary counterparts.

In a study with high verbal, college educated adults, Cohen (1981) reported that memory for spoken information was more impaired for old adults than memory for written information. She stated that old adults performed better when they read than when they listened, while young adults showed no differences between input modes. Also, Cohen (1979) found age deficits in free recall for old adults when listening to a short passage at 120 wpm. However, at this presentation rate and at 200 wpm for one paragraph descriptions, Cohen

(1979) did not find age effects on verbatim questions. Presentation rate had no effect for old adults for verbatim questions, but impaired their performance on inference questions. Rate had no effect on either type of question for young adults.

Stine et al. (1986) reported age-related deficits in recall of speech to be larger at a faster rate; time-compressed speech was used to vary rates of presentation from 200 to 400 wpm. These investigators also had learners stop speech input as often as necessary in order to recall it perfectly. Older adults stopped the speech after fewer words than young adults. These findings suggest a slowing in the ability to process verbal information.

Slowing in processing ability also is evident with discourse. Six of the extant prose learning studies controlled presentation time. Only one of these studies (Mandel & Johnson, 1984) did not report age deficits and this study had the slowest presentation time (102 wpm); the rates of the other studies were 120 wpm or faster. Four (Cohen, 1979; Mandel & Johnson, 1984; Meyer & Rice, 1983b; Petros, Tabor, Cooney, & Chabot, 1983) presented texts orally without visual exposure. Zelinski et al. (1984) had their subjects read the text while it was being read to them at a fast pace. Surber et al. allowed their subjects 11 min and 30 sec to read a 5½ page text. Petros et al. expected an age by rate (120 wpm vs 160 wpm) interaction, but did not find it. Rate impaired the recall performance to an equivalent degree for young and old subjects. The speed between 102 wpm and 120 wpm appears critical for exceeding an optimal level of processing by old adults. Meyer and Rice (1988) reported the reading time data from a study with 160 high and average verbal old and young adults; the average reading speed of old adults was 121 wpm, while it was 144 wpm for young adults. A pace of 120 wpm is too quick for about half of the old adults, while it is well within the optimal range for nearly all young adults. However, other researchers using shorter texts (Hartley, 1986; Light & Anderson, 1985) have reported nonsignificant differences in the reading times of young and old adults.

Hartley et al. (1986) reported slower reading times per proposition for older adults than younger adults. After determining each subject's normal reading rate they presented texts to them at a fast or slow rate. Working under a model of reduced processing resources with aging, they expected speed to hurt the older adults more than the younger adults. However, they found age deficits and speed deficits, but age and speed did not interact.

The extant studies with long texts and a self-paced presentation have reported no age-related deficits (Harker et al., 1982; Meyer & Rice, 1981; Thompson & Diefenderfer, 1986). Surber et al. (1984) and Zelinski et al. (1984) also used long texts and found aging deficits, but they limited reading time to 136 wpm for Surber et al. and 155 wpm for Zelinski et al. Longer articles may call for reading skills more frequently used in the lives of older adults.

One explanation for greater age deficits for faster paced presentations than for slower or self-paced presentations focuses on slowing with aging (Birren, 1974).

Older adults are thought to be disadvantaged primarily in terms of the speed with which they can carry out mental operations such as encoding, comparison, and response selection and execution (Birren, Woods, & Williams, 1980). Another explanation emphasizes a reduction in working memory capacity with increasing age (Cohen, 1979, in press; Petros et al., 1983; Spilich, 1983). Self-paced conditions should help to reinstate information lost from working memory and serve as a memory aid to compensate for any lost capacity. As discussed above, some sophistication in reading skills may be necessary before older adults can compensate through rereading and review.

On many of the other task variables, such as recall versus recognition and immediate recall versus delayed recall, conflicting results appear concerning the relative amount of age deficits (Hultsch & Dixon, 1984). Some studies have found equivalent age deficits for both recall and recognition (Gordon & Clark, 1974; Spilich, 1983); others have found age difference for recall, but not recognition (Spilich & Voss, 1982); while still others have found no age deficits for recall and questions or recognition (Labouvie-Vief, Schell, & Weaverdyke, 1981; Meyer & Rice, 1981; Thompson & Diefenderfer, 1986). In addition, in terms of delay interval some studies found greater aging deficits immediately (Dixon et al., 1982; Hultsch & Dixon, 1983), while others found greater deficits one or more weeks after presentation of texts (Gordon & Clark, 1974; Hultsch et al., 1984).

Issues related to the text.   In order to clarify the literature on reading comprehension and aging it is important to understand variables in texts that affect learning and memory. Some of the inconsistencies in the research can be clarified by specifying differences among texts employed in the research and methods used to measure memory from texts. This section discusses methods used to examine recall from texts, the top-level organization of texts and its use by readers, readers' evaluation of important text information, and the differential recall of main ideas and details in texts by readers.

Most experiments examining reading and aging have used the prose analysis systems of Kintsch (1974) or Meyer (1975). Two (Mandel & Johnson, 1984; Smith et al., 1983) have used systems based on the story grammar of Mandler and Johnson (1977); both studies found no age deficits for well-organized, multi-episode stories with similar subjects under similar task conditions. Two other studies (Petros et al., 1983; Surber et al., 1984) used a procedure developed by Johnson (1970) that empirically, rather than linguistically, determines structural importance by having groups of subjects delete different amounts of unimportant text. Both studies reported age deficits.

Although different methods correspond with different findings for the above studies, an examination of most of the prose learning studies points out that different analysis systems cannot explain the discrepant findings. More specifically, the Kintsch system was used by Dixon et al. (1982) and by Harker et al.

(1982). The study by Dixon et al. reported that old adults remembered considerably less from expository text than did young adults. However, the Harker et al. study with expository text found no age differences in the amount of information remembered by young and old adults. The Meyer system has been utilized by Meyer and Rice (1981), Zelinski, Gilewski, and Thompson (1980), and Zelinski et al. (1984). Meyer and Rice found no significant age differences, while Zelinski et al. reported age differences.

Age differences may reach statistical significance more easily using the Kintsch system where partial credit is not given. Smith et al. (1983) found age differences with strict scoring that required recall of every idea in a complex sentence for credit in recalling that sentence, but found no age differences with more lenient scoring. Differences in types of ideas recalled between old and younger adults can be more sensitively measured with the Meyer system where parts of a proposition can be scored separately. That is, instead of simply finding a deficiency in recall of propositions, the types of relationships and content present and absent in the recall can be specified. In addition, the underlying logic processed by learners from text can be examined.

Dixon, Hultsch, and Hertzog (1986) have recently developed 25 similar narratives. In addition, three sets of three structurally equivalent expository texts were used in the investigation presented in this book. These narrative and expository texts could provide a common pool of passages to use in future studies. Such pooling may reduce some of the confusion in the literature. However, text variables can interact with age effects. Therefore, a variety of texts will require systematic investigation.

As discussed in chapter 1 a number of studies from our research program have examined the use of a text's top-level structure by readers in their recalls. In a study (Meyer, 1983) with average verbal old adults (48th percentile) the best predictor of their recall from texts was whether or not they used the text's top-level structure to organize their recall protocols. These findings indicate that the ability to identify and utilize the author's top-level organization is a crucial skill in reading comprehension for older adults. Another interesting finding was an age and structure interaction when high school educated old adults were compared to 9th graders of average vocabulary performance. For both groups, use of the top-level structure greatly facilitated recall. However, ability to utilize the author's top-level structure was even more crucial to recall for the older group (34% recall when the structure was used and 13.5% when not used, versus 28% recall when the structure was used and 15% when it was not used for the 9th graders). For both the older subjects and the 9th graders when the text's structure was not used, the subjects tended to simply list sentences they remembered from the passage with no attempt to interrelate the sentences.

In contrast with the finding with average verbal adults, a study with higher verbal ASU alumni from young, middle, and old age groups found no age-related differences in use of top-level structure; nearly all of the adults from each age group used the same top-level structure as that used in the text to organize their recall (Meyer, Rice, Knight, & Jessen, 1979). Other studies (Meyer & Rice, 1988; Rice & Meyer, 1985) looked at age and verbal ability and found that high verbal adults from all age groups used the text's top-level structure more often that average verbal adults. More significantly, age interacted with verbal ability. Old and young high verbal adults did not differ in their use of the text's top-level structure, but average verbal young adults used the text's top-level structure more than average verbal old adults. The intervention program described in this book aimed to teach adults deficient in using text structure to utilize it in a strategic manner.

Another way to study text structure has been to see if one discourse type is more memorable than another. Meyer and Rice (1983b) looked to see if older adults perform better after listening to passages organized with a comparison top-level structure than with a collection of descriptions. Meyer and Freedle (1984) found that graduate students remember more facts about such topics as dehydration if two views about the topic are compared rather than simply describing three paragraphs of attributes about the topic. This finding has been replicated by Carrell (1984). In the Meyer and Rice (1983b) study young, middle-aged, and old adults with above average scores on the WAIS vocabulary test listened to passages on two topics organized either as a comparison or as a collection of descriptions. Main effects of discourse type and age were statistically significant. The comparative structure yielded superior performance on recall of the identical information for all three age groups. In contrast, adults with average scores on the Vocabulary Subtest of the WAIS do not show facilitation in recall from the comparative structure (Vincent, 1985). This lack of effect from discourse type held for young, middle-aged, and old adults with these lower scores on the WAIS. Thus, lack of facilitation by the comparison structure was related to verbal ability, but not to age.

In addition to looking at the top-level structure of the text and its recall as discussed above, another method for investigating age differences in sensitivity to the hierarchical structure of text has been to ask subjects to rate the information in text according to its importance. Using this method, Mandel and Johnson (1984) and Petros et al. (1983) had subjects judge the importance of ideas in stories. Both found that young and old adults did not vary in rating the importance of information. Petros et al. also examined their data in terms of the education level of the adults (high = mean of 18 years versus low = 12 years); no differences were found in rating the importance of ideas in a Japanese folk tale from the 5th grade level. These findings for the high and low education groups of old adults are contrary to findings reported by Meyer (1984). Adults higher in education (M = 17 years) judged information high in the structure of an expository text from the high school level as more important than did adults with less education (M = 12 years).

Most studies examining age differences in sensitivity to text structure have examined the levels effect. The levels effect, in which information high in the hierarchical structure of a passage is better recalled than information low in the structure, is taken as evidence that the reader is sensitive to the relative importance of the ideas in a passage as it is organized by the author. Research has consistently shown the levels effect (e.g., Mandler & Johnson, 1977; Meyer, 1975).

Several explanations have been proposed to explain the levels effect in memory (Meyer, 1975). One explanation states that the influence of level on recall is due to selective attention; that is, readers recognize high level content as important and therefore devote extra effort to learning it. Support for this position comes from studies finding longer reading times for high level information (Cirilo & Foss, 1980; Dee-Lucas & Larkin, 1987). Other explanations do not predict a correlation between reading time and level. The model of comprehension proposed by Kintsch and van Dijk (1978) attributes the levels effect to repeated processing received by high level information as readers integrate low level ideas with high level information. Also, Britton (Britton, Meyer, Simpson, Holdredge, & Curry, 1979; Britton, Meyer, Hodge, & Glynn, 1980) and Yekovich and Thorndyke (1981) have proposed accounts of the levels effect which rely on retrieval mechanisms. Probably all of these phenomena, selective attention, extra rehearsal, and retrieval, are related to the levels effect (Meyer, 1984).

The recent work by van Dijk and Kintsch (1983) explains that both global macroprocesses and local integrative processes can contribute to the levels effect in recall. The plan strategy taught in the current investigation is thought to influence attention, focusing the readers attention on an overall structure for a text and the main idea embodied in that structure. The readers are explicitly taught to find such a structure and main idea. In addition, when reading and recalling the text they are taught to keep this structure in mind, giving it extra rehearsal and using it as a retrieval device. This strategy can be thought of as a macrostrategy within the framework of the Kintsch and van Dijk (1978; van Dijk & Kintsch, 1983) model of comprehension.

Numerous recent studies have looked for age differences in sensitivity to prose structure by examining the levels effect for each age group. These studies do not present consistent findings with respect to older adults' use of text structure; they are reviewed in this section and an attempt is made to understand the reasons for these inconsistent results.

Mandel and Johnson (1984) presented clearly organized stories auditorially at a slow pace to adults who were above average in verbal ability and education and found no deficits in total recall nor in the levels effect for older adults. Meyer and Rice (1981) had the same type of subjects read a lengthy expository text without many explicit organizational cues; they also found no deficits in total recall. However, the age by level interaction narrowly missed significance. Post-hoc multiple comparison tests showed that the young group's recall of high level information was significantly greater than their recall of medium and low level information, but the levels effect, while in the usual pattern, did not reach significance for middle-aged and old subjects. With respect to answers to questions, the old and middle groups were able to correctly answer significantly more detail questions than did the young group. There were no differences in questions about main ideas. All age groups remembered the main ideas equally well, but young adults recalled more of the logic and major details that supported these main ideas, while the older groups recalled more of the minor details at the lowest levels of the content structure.

In a study with 300 young, middle, and old adults with high or average verbal ability, subjects assigned to different conditions read different versions of two expository texts (Meyer & Rice, 1983a, 1988). In some conditions the top-level structure, hierarchical structure, and major logical relations were emphasized, while in other conditions the structure was deemphasized and the details were emphasized. An interaction among the emphasis plans, level in the content structure, age, and verbal ability appeared over tasks and times. This interaction resulted from little or no levels effects for the average verbal young adults and the high verbal old adults under conditions that deemphasized the structure and emphasized the details in comparison to the other groups where larger levels effects were found. In addition, the group of high verbal old adults showed the greatest changes in the type of information remembered in response to different emphasis conditions. For this group of subjects a 19% difference was found in the recall of high and low level information with structure emphasized, while only a 1% difference was found between the two levels without emphasis of the structure. It is interesting to see in light of the results of Meyer and Rice (1981) that the only age comparison not showing age deficits for old adults was recall of details by high verbal adults under emphasis conditions focused on details and away from structure.

Evidently, high verbal old adults can be highly sensitive to the levels in the organization of prose. However, their display of the levels effect is dependent on how clearly the structure of the text is emphasized and signaled. When this structure is not explicitly signaled and emphasis is placed on specific details, the older adults focus on these details and are either drawn away from the main ideas and logical relationships or are unable to identify these logical relationships without explicit cues (Cohen, 1979).

Further analyses (Meyer & Rice, 1988) showed that the high verbal old adults were the only group that improved their recall of details (9%) when details were emphasized in the text (e.g., "notable" year of 1840). Young and old adults of high verbal ability were equivalent in their recall of details when they were emphasized, but when they were not emphasized the old adults recall of them fell while the emphasis manipulation did not affect the young adults. The passage used by Meyer and Rice (1981) contains little signaling, many dates, names, and numbers, and is not highly organized; it is similar to the manipulations in the

Meyer and Rice (1988) study involving no signaling of structure and specific details. Thus, the findings of Meyer and Rice (1981) appear to be limited to high verbal old adults with passages that contain historical dates, names, and other details where the structure is not explicitly signaled.

The issue remains whether the minimal levels effect exhibited by high verbal older adults on passages without signaling and with emphasized details results from processing the details at the expense of the main ideas or simply from an inability to comprehend the logical relationships among the main ideas when they are not explicitly signaled. Research exists on both sides of the latter issue; some studies show age-deficits in making inferences (Cohen, 1979, 1981), while others do not (Belmore, 1981). Light and Anderson (1985) found that old adults could make inferences to correctly match pronouns to their referent if they could remember the sentence with the referent. However, they had more trouble remembering these sentences than young adults as the distance between the pronoun and the referent sentence increased.

Meyer and Rice (1988) systematically manipulated signaling of logical structure, signaling of details, and the specificity of details in order to better understand this issue. The detail manipulation involved substituting general details, such as "early last century," for specific details, such as "1829." The magnitude of the levels effects was examined for high verbal old adults to see if they process details at the expense of logical relations and main ideas thereby reducing the levels effect, or if instead they cannot figure out logical relations without signaling thereby decreasing their recall of main ideas and the magnitude of the levels effect. The data supported the first explanation; the recall data for both free and particularly the cued conditions for logical relations indicated that high verbal older adults can identify and store these relationships when they are not explicitly signaled. When specific details are present and text structure is not emphasized, high verbal old adults appear to process details at the expense of logical relationships and main ideas. The greater effects of these emphasis conditions on high verbal old adults over high verbal young adults may result from reduced cognitive capacity with aging (Cohen, in press; Light, Zelinski, & Moore, 1982) where the effort processing details reduces that available for main ideas.

The research reviewed above (Mandel & Johnson, 1984; Meyer & Rice, 1981, 1988) indicate that when text is clearly organized with emphasis on structure and main ideas, young, middle-aged, and old adults are sensitive to text structure. Average verbal old adults do not show the facilitative effects of signaling for either free or cued recall of logical relations as do the other groups of adults (Meyer, 1983; Meyer & Rice, 1988). This taken with their deficient use of top-level structure suggests that although they show a levels effect they are deficient in some aspects of their utilization of text structure. In contrast to average verbal old adults, high verbal old adults are very sensitive to the emphasis plans of an author: When specific details in a passages are emphasized over the structure these older adults appear to use their resources to process the details at the expense of fully processing the main ideas and logical relations. Therefore, the disparate findings with respect to the levels effect for these three studies can be reconciled by examining the clarity of organization and emphasis of the prose and the verbal ability of the learners.

Hultsch and Dixon (1984) argue that their recent study (Dixon et al., 1984) as well as the literature support the claim that age differences in use of organization in text depends on the verbal ability of the subjects. Specifically, they state that high verbal, college graduates show greater age deficits for details (low level information), while lower verbal, high school graduates show greater deficits for main ideas. The Dixon et al. study asked 108 young (20–39), middle-aged (40–57), and old (60–84) adults to read six short (98 words) passages about health and nutrition at their own pace. Young and middle-aged adults recalled more information than old adults. They reported an age by verbal ability by level interaction. For high verbal adults, the three age groups did not differ in their recall of high level information, but the young recalled more than the middle-aged adults and they both recalled more than the old on the lower level ideas. In contrast, all three of lower verbal groups differed significantly on the high level ideas and showed clear age deficits; for the other levels the young and middle-aged subjects did not differ but were superior to the old adults.

Dixon et al. (1984) suggest that the literature also supports this pattern; Cohen (1979) and Dixon et al. (1982) found greater age deficits on main ideas and are said to have tested low verbal adults. This is the case for the Dixon et al. study. However, Cohen reports deficits in gist or main idea recall for high verbal adults; recall of details was not reported. Dixon et al. (1984) explain that Byrd (1981), Labouvie-Vief, Schell, and Weaverdyck (unpublished, cited in Dixon et al., 1984), Spilich (1983), and Zelinski et al. (1980) found greater deficits in recall of details and tested high verbal, college educated adults. However, information on the types of subjects in terms of verbal ability and education is not available for Zelinski et al.

The only study that Hultsch and Dixon (1984) could not incorporate into their interpretation was the Meyer and Rice (1981) study, because in this study with high verbal, college graduates older adults recalled details as well (free recall) or better (questions) than young adults. However, the data from Meyer and Rice (1988) show that this discrepancy can be clarified by examining the organization and emphasis of the texts. For the texts with emphasized structure, the pattern found by Dixon et al. (1984) holds. In contrast, on the versions with deemphasized structure and emphasized details, this pattern is reversed; for high verbal adults the results are consistent with Meyer and Rice (1981), while for the lower verbal adults there are greater age deficits on details than on main ideas.

Petros et al. (1983), Surber et al. (1984), and Zelinski et al. (1984) also have examined aging and the levels effect. Petros et al. asked adults with high and low education (no vocabulary data) to listen to two stories; they report no interaction between age, level, and education and the scores are not available to examine the education groups with respect to age and level. However, collapsed over education a pattern similar to that for high verbal adults on well-structured texts is found; greater aging deficits are found on the lowest level details (young = .49, old = .37) than on the most important ideas (young = .87, old = .81). The authors point out that both age groups are sensitive to text structure as a levels effect is found for both groups. Surber et al. asked above average verbal young and older adults to read and recall a 1563 word passage on commercial fishing. Young adults recalled more information overall and more information at the three most important levels than old adults, but the two groups did not differ at the lowest level details. These results fit the pattern for text whose structure and main ideas are not clearly emphasized; perhaps this is the case for this lengthy article. The study by Zelinski et al. (1984) does not appear to fit neatly into the age by verbal ability by organization interaction outlined earlier.

Many of the discrepancies in the literature with regard to the magnitude of age deficits in prose learning can be explained by examining reader, task, and text variables. A number of factors are associated with a reduction of age deficits in reading comprehension; greater prose recall in older adults is related to higher levels of education and higher scores on vocabulary, verbal productive thinking, and associative memory tests. Also, better memory from text by older adults is associated with more time spent reading in everyday life (particularly for adults with effective reading comprehension strategies), more prior knowledge on a topic, and greater familiarity with the reading and recall task. Better performance is found for slower or self-pace presentation; a pace of 120 wpm or faster appears to adversely affect the recall of old adults more than young adults.

The text variable of emphasis was shown to correlate with different findings reported by investigators. For texts with emphasis placed on well-organized structures, young and old adults with high vocabulary scores are sensitive to text structure; they exhibit large levels effects and greater age-related deficits are found in recall of details. On these same texts, old adults with average vocabulary scores show less sensitivity to text structure and exhibit greater deficits on main ideas. However, with text that deemphasizes organization and emphasizes details, the opposite pattern is found. For the highly verbal adults fewer age deficits are found for details than main ideas. For average verbal adults fewer age deficits are found for main ideas than details. High verbal old adults appear to utilize text structure as well as young adults. They show facilitation in recall after listening to text structured with the more organized comparative structure than the less organized descriptive structure. They are very sensitive to the emphasis plans of an author. When specific details are emphasized over structure, old adults appear to use their resources to process details at the expense of fully processing main ideas and logical relationships. These findings suggest that when writing for these older adults, care should be given to explicitly signaling the major logical relationships if examples with specific facts are given in the text. If dates, names, and numbers are not critical to the message, then they should be deleted.

The greater effects of emphasis conditions for high verbal old adults than for high verbal young adults may result from reduced cognitive capacity with aging where the effort required for processing details reduces that available for figuring out implicit logical relationships among major propositions in text. It has been shown moreover that text without signaling requires more cognitive capacity than the same text with signaling (Britton, Glynn, Meyer, & Penland, 1982). The performance of young adults with average vocabulary scores on these same texts mirrors the pattern for old high verbal adults. It could be argued that these manipulations have similar effects on these two groups and not on high verbal young adults because high verbal young adults have more cognitive capacity than average verbal young adults who were less endowed and high verbal old adults who have experienced declines in capacity with increasing age. Alternatively, the structure or plan strategy may be more automatic requiring less conscious capacity in the high verbal young adults. These text manipulations have no effect on average verbal older adults who perform quite poorly under all text conditions; this could reflect their initial limited capacity that was further reduced by aging. However, performance of old adults with average vocabulary scores also could result from changes in educational practice over the generations. Signaling words and text structures may have been taught to the young adults, but not to the old adults. The intervention study presented in this book examines whether or not this group of older adults with average to high average vocabulary scores can learn to use these aspects of text.

COGNITIVE SKILL TRAINING FOR THE ELDERLY

When considering the potential fruitfulness of a training program designed to improve any type of cognitive skill among elderly adults, it is important to question whether older adults have the plasticity to benefit from such a program. Although there is not an abundance of research speaking to that question, there is clear evidence from several studies that elderly persons can benefit from cognitive training.

Two studies by Sanders and Sanders and their colleagues (Sanders, Sterns, Smith, & Sanders, 1975; Sanders, Sanders, Mayes, & Sielski, 1976) trained elderly subjects (mean age of 71) to solve concept identification problems. In the first study, the test problems were 3-dimensional concepts which had to identified from a series of pictures illustrating them. Four groups of subjects were formed, two of which received training in how to solve this type of problem. The training was done by first teaching 1-dimensional, then 2-dimensional, and finally 3-dimensional problems similar to those on the tests. One of these trained groups received tokens for reinforcement as they progressed, and these tokens could later be traded for prizes. The third group received practice only on 3-dimensional problems between the pre and posttests and the fourth group, a control group, did nothing relevant between the tests. The results were clearcut: The two trained groups improved in concept identification significantly more than the practice and control groups. The two training groups did not differ from each other and the practice and control groups did not differ. The lack of any effect of reinforcement was attributed to the high internal motivation of the subjects.

The second study eliminated the reinforcement, and so had only three groups, training, practice, and control. The test problems were 4-dimensional concepts, but otherwise the training procedure was the same as in the previous experiment. Again a significant effect of training was observed on the posttest. The authors identify the elements of successful training as (1) breaking the whole task down into sequential component tasks, and (2) instruction in verbalization and problem-solving strategies.

About this time, another line of research was developing from the theory of fluid and crystallized intelligence proposed by Horn and Cattell (1966). This theory has been used to analyze the pattern of cognitive changes that occur with aging and to help identify the causes of the observed changes (Horn, 1982). It has been noted that several of the tasks comprising the fluid intelligence concept show declining performance with age. Several of these tasks have therefore become the focus of training programs designed to combat that decline.

One such study (Labouvie-Vief & Gonda, 1976) utilized 60 elderly women (mean age = 76) to determine the effectiveness of three training procedures for solving inductive problems. The cognitive training group received instruction involving verbalization of the rules and procedures for solving the inductive problems. The anxiety coping group learned these problem-solving verbalizations as well as ways to overcome anxiety by self-approval statements and self-encouragement. An unspecified training group was given time to practice induction problems, but received no guidance or feedback, and the no-training group did an irrelevant task while the others were receiving training. In an immediate and delayed (2 weeks later) posttest, subjects were tested on their ability to solve the type of problems they had received during training (letter sets) as well as problems from Raven's progressive matrices, which also require inductive thinking. The results showed that all three of the training groups had significant advantages over the no-training group on the letter set problems at at least one of the test times. On the transfer tasks (the matrices) the unspecified training group only performed significantly better than the no-training group.

These results were somewhat disappointing because there was no support for the contention that direct instruction in cognitive skill is much better than simple practice. However, the studies that followed were strengthened by administering a pretest as well as several posttests, and were thus able to distinguish training effects from practice. They also explored transfer of training more thoroughly.

One short-term longitudinal study focused on the figural relations component of fluid intelligence (Plemons, Willis, & Baltes, 1978). Training utilized figural relations items similar to those on the Horn-Cattell intelligence test, and involved instruction and modeling of the rules for solving them and practice with feedback. Thirty subjects between the ages of 59 and 85 (mean = 69.5) were pretested on the figural relations, then half of them received the training. The posttest examined transfer of the training to the Horn-Cattell figural relations test (near-near transfer) and to a slightly different figural relations test (near transfer), as well as to other components of fluid intelligence such as induction (far transfer), and to crystallized intelligence measured by a verbal comprehension task (far-far transfer). Three posttests were administered, the first within 1 week of the conclusion of training, the second 4 weeks later, and the third approximately 6 weeks after the second. On all three of these occasions, trained subjects significantly outperformed untrained subjects on the near-near transfer task, showing a large benefit from training that was maintained over a substantial period of time. On the near transfer task, advantage for the trained group was observed only on posttest 1, on the remaining posttests the groups did not differ. There was no transfer to the induction task nor the verbal comprehension task.

A later replication and refinement of this study (Willis, Blieszner, & Baltes, 1981) verified these training effects, and also observed some far transfer of training to the induction task. It is also important to note that in both of these studies significant practice effects were observed due to the repeated testing. The significance of training effects was determined in relation to this general improvement.

Several more studies followed, in which different cognitive skills were the focus of training assessment of transfer (Baltes & Willis, 1982). Induction was taught to 52 older persons (mean age of 70) in five 1-hour sessions. While there was a significant effect of training on the near transfer tasks on the first two posttests, the difference was not maintained to posttest 3, mostly due to the control group improving to the level of the training group. Practice effects on this task and on figural relations were very strong.

More recently, another large study utilizing 204 adults (mean age of 72) was conducted in which training on figural relations and on induction were combined (Baltes, Dittman-Kohli, Kliegl, 1986). Again there was significant transfer of training to other near measures of fluid intelligence, but none to crystallized intelligence or perceptual speed. An item analysis was included in this study, and showed that trained subjects were answering more items correctly in all three (easy, medium, hard) levels of item difficulty. This means that the training effect was not limited to easy items only. The authors concluded that many elderly individuals possess a sizeable reserve capacity that can be accessed and utilized with the proper training.

This line of research is complemented by a longitudinal study conducted by Schaie and Willis (1986). A group of 229 adults, with a mean age of 72.8, were tracked for 14 years and were classified according to whether or not their abilities of inductive reasoning and spatial orientation had declined. Those who had declined on both, or on neither, were randomly assigned to receive one of the training programs. Thus those who were trained on inductive reasoning served as controls for those who were trained on spatial orientation, and vice versa. Two results are of special importance to our understanding of cognitive training for the elderly. First, a pattern of cognitive decline in either of these abilities could be reversed with training, even to the extent of returning subjects to their pre-decline levels of performance. Second, subjects whose abilities had not declined often showed enhanced levels of performance after training.

Clearly, there is substantial evidence that cognitive training benefits elderly persons' performance on a variety of intellectual tasks. Unfortunately, none of these studies compared the elderly subjects to young adults, and so do not tell us whether the elderly after training are similar in performance level to younger persons.

When elderly people are trained to use mnemonic strategies, such as the method of loci or the pegword system, their memory ability for lists of items improves significantly. Several such studies are reviewed by Belsky (1984) and by Rybash, Hoyer, and Roodin (1986). However, when younger subjects are included in the training, they often benefit more, and for a longer period of time than do the elderly. This may not be consistently true, however, since there have been demonstrations that memory performance differences between young and old can be eliminated by inducing the elderly subjects to use mnemonic mediators, particulary imagery (Treat, Poon, Fozard, & Popkin, 1978). The fact that they do not use these strategies spontaneously, but can use them successfully, makes a good case for training the elderly to apply memory strategies as a natural reaction to a learning situation (Yesavage, 1985).

Gillund and Perlmutter (in press) present a cogent review of the use of learning strategies by older adults. Older adults appear to have at least some strategies available although do not use them as often as young adults (e.g., Hulicka & Grossman, 1967), nor use them as effectively as young adults (e.g., Sanders, Murphy, Schmitt, & Walsh, 1980). In everyday life older adults appear to use effective strategies, such as writing reminder notes (Moscovitch, 1982; Perlmutter, 1978). Gillund and Perlmutter (in press) state that a likely explanation why older adults use strategies less than younger adults in the laboratory is that the older adults are not aware of the structure available for their use in the materials presented to them. Hulicka, Sterns, and Grossman (1967) had young and older adults study pairs of words and classified the types of mediators used for each pair. Older adults used less mediators and reported that about 20% of the pairs were too odd to interrelate; in contrast, young adults only identified about 3% as too odd for mediators to be found.

For the reading strategy to be taught in the study reported in this book we find equivalent use by young and older adults with outstanding verbal skills, but differences in use by young and old adults with average verbal skills. These older adults with average verbal abilities and less reading experiences in everyday life may need to have the structure available in texts explicitly pointed out to them. The training program described in this book does this as well as showing them how to approach reading tasks with a strategy that will utilize such structures.

READING AND COMPREHENSION TRAINING

Studies with adults.   None of the research described earlier bears directly upon increasing the reading comprehension and text recall abilities of the elderly. In fact, actual training research in this area is severely limited. A review paper by Glynn and Muth (1979) summarizes documentation of the deficits of the elderly in text-learning capabilities, and attributes the deficits primarily to defective attentional and organizational processes. The authors advocate the use of instructional strategies to counteract these deficits, and they provide evidence that such strategies do benefit elderly learners. They describe priming strategies, such as instructional objectives, conceptual prequestions and advance organizers, and processing strategies, such as mediational devices (verbal and imaginal), typographical-cuing systems (underlining and boldface), and note-taking techniques. They recommend the use of these strategies because they help students to focus on key concepts, better organize ideas for storage and retrieval, or integrate new ideas with related prior knowledge. However, notice how all of these strategies fall to the instructor to implement them or to instruct learners to use them. None have been treated as a comprehension strategy that learners, especially the elderly, need to be trained to use.

To find training studies of comprehension and reading skills, we have to turn to research with younger adults, and we find that the bulk of the published literature describes college or university remedial reading programs. A typical program was described by Burgess, Cranney, and Larsen (1976), as a laboratory-type class. Practice materials were available and progress folders maintained under minimal supervision. All participants in the program were volunteers and, in the assessment of program effectiveness, those who chose not to participate served as controls. After conclusion of the program, those who had participated had a significantly higher grade point average than those who had not, but clearly there was a motivational factor involved that could not be ruled out as an explanation for the findings.

In a review of college reading programs (Heerman, 1983), it is evident that much of the evaluative research in this area suffers from lack of adequate control groups. Nonetheless, the research shows distinct advantages in reading skill (rate, vocabulary, and comprehension) for experimental groups that receive reading instruction. Furthermore. the gains appear to last a substantial amount of time: 60 weeks in one study, 3 and 6 months in another, and 5 semesters in another. Other studies show positive effects of reading instruction on grades, as well as other measures of academic success, such as course hours completed. The instructional methods used in these studies varied from straightforward reading instruction, to general study skills, to tutoring in reading specific types of course material.

Reading instruction that is geared toward a specific type of material has met with success in various areas. Pachtman (1977) designed a training program for 1st-year law students that contained three components: Comprehension, study skills, and analytical thinking. Those students who received training in these three areas subsequently scored higher than control subjects on a measure of critical thinking and reading ability, and on a measure of reading comprehension. Trained students also had higher 1st-term grades than control students.

Research with Air Force personnel has shown that specific training in how to extract the vital information from a passage of text resulted in personnel who were better able to locate and remember information pertinent to their particular jobs (Huff et al., 1977).

Pertaining to reading programs for older adults, some excellent reviews of Adult Basic Education (ABE) are published, as well as some individual studies. The highlights of these will be presented here.

Gold and Horn (1982) evaluated a tutorial program for adult illiterates in the Baltimore City area. Seventy-six adults aged 16 to 60 years, all reading below 5th grade level, were assigned to experimental and control groups, and were pre- and posttested on verbal language development, word recognition, locus of control, listening comprehension, and reading skills. Between the testing, the experimental group was tutored by trained volunteers for an average of 3 hours a week for 12 to 15 weeks. Analysis of gain scores showed that the tutored group made significantly more progress than the control group on word recognition and a variety of reading skills.

A computer-assisted literacy program for adults was offered at Pennsylvania State University (Golub, 1980). This particular program used as its reading materials passages pertaining to an assortment of careers, so that adults were acquiring specific job-related content while improving their general reading skills. Pre- and posttests showed that students made significant improvement on phonics, vocabulary, comprehension, reading level, and reading rate. Unfortunately, there was no control group for comparison purposes.

The Army has also had considerable success in teaching illiterate soldiers how to read (Otto, 1970). The materials were especially developed, the pupil-instructor ratio was 15 to 1, and regularly scheduled appraisals of the training were conducted. Sixty-two percent of the participants initially reading at the 1st grade level were taught to read at the 4th grade level after 12 to 16 weeks of instruction. The most progress was made by soldiers who initially tested at higher reading levels.

Otto (1970) has reviewed the early published reports on several ABE literacy programs throughout the United States. These programs had a wide age range of clientele, all of whom were at such a low reading level as to be classified as functionally illiterate. The progress of students in the programs was regularly evaluated by means of standardized reading tests. Among the conclusions he notes are:

1. several different methods of teaching reading are effective, but which is most effective is related to the initial reading level of the student;

2. age, IQ, and beginning reading level did not affect a student's rate of progress in the program;

3. highly trained teachers are not necessary for a successful program; even high school graduates can be effective reading teachers; and

4. despite efforts to compact the education into a short period of time, it is still a quite lengthy process to bring adults' reading skill up to an acceptable level, and the actual amount of time it may take is highly individual.

Cook (1977) has recorded the history of adult literacy education. She notes that, while programs were started as early as 1900, no serious attempts to evaluate their success were made until the '60s. Then research began to appear that compared the numerous teaching methods in use to try to identify the most effective ones. Although no one or two methods ever consistently outperformed the others, the surge of research served to launch a healthy phase of curriculum development and expansion. The decade of the '70s saw literacy research expand to include topics of motivation, materials. and measurement criteria.

Clearly, there is much to offer to adults with poor reading skills to help them gain competence and complete their basic education. But what of training for older adults who have good reading ability, but want to improve their more advanced skills? There is very little research available in this area.

Shearin (1976) evaluated a program for teaching critical reading skills to adults. He used volunteers aged 20 to 59 and trained them over a period of 8 weeks to develop a questioning attitude, determine reliability of information, and detect propaganda material. He then compared them to a control group on a measure of critical thinking and a measure of reading comprehension skills. On the measure of critical thinking trained subjects improved from pre- to posttest significantly more than did untrained subjects, but not on the measure of reading comprehension. Also, this improvement was not related to the age, education level, nor initial reading skill level of the individuals.

In this study, as well as several that were reviewed earlier in this chapter, it is evident that subjects can benefit from cognitive skill training; often improvement is confined to the skill trained and does not generalize to related skills. Thus, an intervention intended to improve comprehension and memory for text needs to be structured around exactly those skills.

Glover and his colleagues (Glover, Zimmer, Filbeck, & Plake, 1980) found that college students could be taught to identify the semantic base of a passage of text simply by having the students practice with feedback. Students were told to identify the minimum number of words that expressed the meaning of each 5-line unit of a text. Periods of feedback were alternated with baseline periods for three groups of subjects, with the clear result that while feedback was available, subjects improved markedly in their identification of key words and their incorrect identifications decreased accordingly. But also of interest is the finding that general reading comprehension (measured by the Nelson-Denny Reading Test) improved significantly from pre- to posttest. Apparently this process of semantic base identification is closely related to reading comprehension as measured by this test, so that training in one transfers to the second.

A number of studies involving young adults relate more closely to instruction with the plan strategy specified in this book. The first (Geva, 1983) provided community college students with extensive training (20 hours over 5 weeks) on searching out expository formats of causation and process. The students used a flowcharting procedure to draw out ideas from a text or their related prior knowledge as nodes with specified relationships among them. On a posttest the students showed significant improvement in representing text structure and content. They outperformed controls who had received training in speed reading, text skimming, and searching out keywords and conjunctions. Geva (1983) reported similar significant gains in reading scores on the Nelson-Denny Reading Test (Nelson & Denny, 1973) for both the experimental and control groups. When the same types of subjects were separated into less skilled and moderately skilled subgroups a significant ability effect was apparent. Less skilled readers seemed to have profitted more from the instruction as ascertained by gain scores on the standardized reading test. For this less skilled group particularly, learning to recognize and use these types of text structures resulted in more effective reading of expository text.

Closely related to Geva's (1983) work is that of Dansereau and his colleages (e.g., Dansereau, Brooks, Holley, & Collins, 1983; Diekhoff, Brown, & Dansereau, 1982; Holley, Dansereau, McDonald, Garland, & Collins, 1979). They have found networking or mapping strategies to facilitate learning from text by college students. For example, Holley et al. (1979) trained college students to convert prose into hierarchically organized node-link diagrams, called networks, using a set of six experimenter-provided links (part of link, type of link, leads to link, analogy link, characteristic link, and evidence link). After training the students used the networking strategy in studying a 3000-word passages taken from a geology textbook. Five days later they completed four types of tests about this passage: Multiple choice, short-answer, essay, and a summary-oriented concept cloze. Compared to a control that received no treatment, the trained group showed superior performance, primarily on the cloze and essay tests. Also, like Geva (1983) they reported greater improvement for lower ability students, measured by Holley et al. (1979) via grade point averages.

Three studies exposing college students to indirect instruction or minimal amounts of training point to some facilitation of memory from identifying the structure of text. Thorndyke (1977) had one group of subjects read a story organized in the same way as a target narrative passage with different content. A second group read a story with the same content as the target passage, but organized differently. A third group had different content and different organization. He observed greater adherence to the organization of the target passage and better recall from the first group. Meyer, Rice, Bartlett, and Woods (1979) conducted a similar study with expository text and added another group that simply received a description of the structure for the target passage prior to reading it. There was a trend for information about the structure given implicitly or explicitly to facilitate recall and speed of reading, but the differences narrowly missed statistical significance. However, Barnett (1984) gave college students a brief description of the appropriate text structure before reading a research report or a journal article and found facilitation of memory. Subjects recalled significantly more information after 2 days than either subjects who received the description about text structure after reading or who received no description of text structure.

A more extensive training program with adults (Carrell, 1985) modified Bartlett's (1978) program for 9th grade students in order to teach students who have English as a second language (ESL) about the structure or plan strategy. The results showed that the training significantly increased the amount of information that intermediate-level ESL students could recall. Similar types of training procedures were used by Cook (1982) to help college students identify the structures found in science textbooks. A 10 hour training program taught students to recognize the major prose structures (generalization, enumeration, sequence, classification, compare/contrast) and to outline passages from their own chemistry textbooks. Trained subjects showed substantial pretest to posttest gains in recall of main ideas and in problem solving as compared to a control group.

The plan strategy taught to young and old adults in the present investigation has some similarities to these studies that taught college students about text structure. However, the plan strategy focuses more on looking for a top-level structure for a text and using this top-level structure to lead readers to the main idea or gist of the text. This training program was adapted from training programs teaching structure to children. The following section describes these training programs and related programs designed to teach children about the structure of text.

Studies teaching text structure to children.   Several studies (Gordon, 1980; Short, 1982; Singer & Donlan, 1982) have taught narrative structure or story grammar to children. All have reported benefits from explicitly teaching story structure and strategies for utilizing it when reading.

Most of the training studies have involved expository text due to its greater use for transmitting information and difficulty for children (Spiro & Taylor, 1980). Sensitivity to text structure by children has been clearly shown to relate to their comprehension and memory of text (McGee, 1982; Meyer et al., 1980; Taylor, 1980, 1985). The research literature as well as recommendations in the reading literature (e.g., Aulls, 1982; Chall, 1983; Herber, 1978; Niles, 1965) point to the importance of teaching students to follow the organization of texts. Thus, several approaches have been attempted to teach children to use text structure (Armburster, Anderson, & Ostertag, 1987). One way has been to have readers generate a diagram representing basic ideas and relationships in text, like flowcharting (Geva, 1983) and networking (e.g., Dansereau et al., 1979) described above. These techniques with children called mapping (Armbruster & Anderson, 1980; Berkowitz, 1986; Mosenthal, 1984; Smith & Brown, 1987) have had moderate success. A limitation of this approach pointed out by Armbruster et al. (1987) is that mapping strategies do not help readers identify the top-level structure or macrostructure (van Dijk & Kintsch, 1983); although the reader extracts a structure, it may not embody the gist or main ideas of the text. The approach is also quite meticulous and time consuming in comparison to the plan strategy reported in this book. The payoff from mapping does not appear commensurate with the effort involved.

Another way to teach text structure is to instruct learners to use headings, subheadings, and paragraph cues in the text (e.g., Mosenthal, 1984; Taylor, 1982). Research on hierarchical summarization (Taylor, 1982; Taylor & Beach, 1984) focuses on these typographical cues in text. The hierarchical summarization task consisted of preparing a skeleton outline reflecting the structure of a text. A roman numeral was listed for every section designated by a heading and a capital letter was listed for every subsection designated by a subheading; an arabic number was listed for every paragraph within a subsection (Taylor, 1982). Main idea statements were given for every paragraph, subsection, and section of the text. In the studies with 5th grade students (Taylor, 1982) and 7th grade students (Taylor & Beach, 1984), trained students performed better than control subjects on some of the dependent measures, particularly recall of unfamiliar texts. This approach appears quite useful for students when using texts that are well organized and use appropriate headings. Everyday reading materials in magazines and newspapers may not effectively nor often employ subheadings. The plan strategy utilized in this book provides a strategy that can be used regardless of the typographical cues in texts.

The final approach for teaching children about text structure is providing instruction about common text structures. Recently, Armbruster et al. (1987) have followed this approach to teach 5th graders how to use problem/solution structures when reading social studies materials. In this study four classes with a total of 82 5th grade students participated either in the structure group or a traditional training group that read and discussed answers to questions about social studies passages. The instruction took place during 11 consecutive school days and lasted 45 min per day per class. The findings indicated that the training with the problem/solution structure enhanced student's ability to abstract the gist of problem/solution texts, as measured by answers to a main idea essay question and by written summaries of two texts. While the structure training improved performance on the essay questions, it did not improve performance on short-answer questions that focused primarily on details. Students trained to use problem/solution structure also learned to include more main ideas in their summaries. However, less success in writing good summaries was found for lower ability 5th graders.

Armbruster et al.'s (1987) training program is similar to instruction with the plan strategy that taught five different structures, including problem/solution, to young and old adults. Both programs taught text structure and followed the principles of direct instruction; instruction that involves modeling by the teacher of explicitly defined procedures, much guided practice on increasingly longer and more difficult texts, teacher monitoring with corrective feedback, and independent practice (e.g., Palincsar & Brown, 1984; Pearson & Gallagher, 1983; Rosenshine & Stevens, 1984).

The first systematic program training children to use text structure following principles of direct instruction was prepared by Bartlett (1978). Bartlett developed a program to systematically teach 9th grade students about four commonly used expository structures, identified and described by Meyer and Freedle (1978, 1984).

Bartlett's (1978) instructional program had five, successive 1-hour sessions each run during the students' regular English class. Materials focused on the four structures of description, problem/solution, causation, and comparison. Individual packages were distributed daily with a remedial loop at session three for those who had not reached a mastery criterion tested after session two.

No prior knowledge of top-level structure or writing plans was assumed; instruction began with simple discussion and explanation of organization as a global concept, fading into its application in text. The many purposes of reading were outlined and students discussed that for some purposes remembering content was relatively unimportant, while for others, such as class tests, it was vital. At this point they were told that the instruction would help them remember more information from text; their interest in this goal was monitored by a self-report scale at the beginning of each of the five sessions.

To authenticate the claims made for instruction with the strategy students were asked to compare their performance on a reading and recall task during session one to their performance on similar task during session two. A requirement that students seek out texts encountered in everyday life that illustrated these structures helped them to see the application of the strategy beyond the training sessions.

Text materials used to illustrate and practice structure strategy were graduated across the five sessions with simple, clearly structured passages at first to more complex ones later. Most texts were selected from textbooks written for 8th and 9th graders, but a few were specially constructed.

Each session began with an outline of instructional objectives. Each session concluded with a review of group and individual performance during the session in relation to these objectives. Corrective feedback was used through the program. Students were appraised in writing of the content and procedural steps mastered and those yet to be mastered. Additionally, self-check and rating lists were built into practice exercises and review steps of the individual packages provided at each session. These followed the format of teacher feedback, allowing the student to check steps already mastered and those yet to be mastered. Students also received peer review during sessions three and four as part of small group work.

At the beginning of the program, the teacher led most of the discussion, demonstrated procedures, and directed the action. As the session progressed, students became more self-supporting. Individual and peer tutelage systems were operating by session three so that the teacher adopted the role of facilitator and remedial director and the students worked at their own pace.

The student was seen as responsive to evidence for the usefulness of the reading strategy and as responsible for the cognitive and metacognitive action required when reading and retrieving information. The teacher's role was to provide the evidence and to follow it up with a knowledge base from which students could adopt the strategy and use it appropriately as a mnemonic for learning from text. The instructional materials were selected and ordered to facilitate this learning process.

This instructional design appeared successful. Students acquired the strategy and improved their memory performance. They demonstrated superiority in comparison with their own pretested levels and with controls who had received the same texts, same teacher, but only instruction on principles of punctuation. Both the strategy and recall advantages were maintained across a one week, delayed measure. Interestingly, while students in the control group had equivalent grades prior to instruction, school authorities reported performance advantages across the curriculum for those students who had received training with the strategy (Bartlett, 1978).

The training materials used in the study presented in this book followed Bartlett's (1978) basic procedures for instruction and utilized his format for feedback to learners. Bartlett and Meyer (1981) and Bartlett, Turner, and Mathams (1981) modified Bartlett's original program to gear it to 5th graders. Bartlett and Meyer (1981) added an important aspect to the program that involved explicitly teaching students to use the top-level structure in text to identify the main idea of the text. The original program asked readers to find main ideas and also top-level structures, but did not show them how to use the top-level structure to find the main idea. The plan strategy described in this book includes this component from the Bartlett and Meyer (1981) materials. In addition, the first session of Bartlett's original program was changed quite drastically for the current training program. Important changes focus on the use of advertisements to define and describe the five structural plans taught and the addition of a table clearly specifying definitions, examples, and signaling words used with each plan.

The entire training program taken from Meyer and Bartlett (1985) is found in chapter 6 of this book. The training materials resulted from a number of sources.

1. Research over the last 10 years that has focused on differentiating different discourse types and examining their effects on memory (Meyer, 1985a; Meyer & Freedle, 1984).

2. Research which has shown that successful readers from high school to old age employ this strategy (Meyer, 1983; Meyer et al., 1980). They identify and utilize the writing plan used in their reading materials; they use this plan to help them remember what they have read when they discuss the information with others or write down what they remember about their reading;

3. Bartlett's (1978) training program to teach this strategy to 9th grade students;

4. Bartlett and Meyer's (1981) training program designed for 5th grade students;

5. Diary studies (Rice, 1986a, 1986b; Rice & Meyer, 1986) indicating the types of materials read by young and old adults; most of the reading materials used in the program were representative of the everyday reading of young and old adults; that is, selections from newspaper and magazine articles;

6. Feedback from two pilot studies with young, middle-aged, and old adults conducted to improve the materials.

Bartlett and his colleagues have continued to modify and teach the original 1978 program. Major changes to the original training materials were made by Bartlett and Briese (1979) in an attempt to teach the strategy to mildly intellectually handicapped adolescents. They introduced each of the four structures separately rather than jointly as in the original program. Materials were kept simple across the program; single sentence and short paragraph passages were used along with a heavy component of pictorial material and the students' own reading material. Sessions were about 20 min daily and were spread across 3 weeks. Instruction was more consistently directed by the teacher than in the original program. Bartlett and Briese (1979) reported some shift towards use of the strategy, but none of the students acquired lasting, deliberate use of it.

Bartlett, Turner, and Barton (1987) developed a program after a series of studies with children in the elementary school. This program has three levels each covering 2 school years. Level one for grades 1 and 2 concentrates heavily on organizational patterns in children's talk and play. Level two for grades 3 and

CRITERIA FOR MONITORING EFFECTIVENESS OF INSTRUCTION

1. Teacher models the metacognitive processes underlying the strategy and established a communicative vocabulary to enable meaningful discussion of the process.

2. Teacher talk focuses on the components of the metacognition involved in the strategy, rahter than on global and nonspecific references to the strategy. These include:

    (a) What do I the teacher need to know about text as communication?
    (b) What do I remember of what I know?
    (c) What are the common types of top-level structures or writing plans?
    (d) How do I know which is which?
    (e) When do I need to think about these things (a) to (d)?
    (f) How do I make a guess about the top-level structure?
    (g) How do I check (and change my guesswork)?
    (h) Who do I ask if I am confused or uncertain?

3. Teacher talk focuses on why (and conditions under which the strategy is useful.

4. Task-orientation involves highlighting key figures of the task. Also it shows how these are incorporated into metacognitive processing as part of the TO DO's in planning, doing, and checking the task.

5. Teacher talk involves useful ways for individual students to check the efficiency of their metacognitive processing.

6. Appropriate, individually paced practice is provided for the students in applying the top-level structure strategy.

7. Review is extensive on the process being taught, its use with text, and students' attempts at application.

8. Feedback is given to students, and by them to the teacher. This usually concerns success of the modeling, interaction during the sessions, and practice phases of the instruction.

FIG. 2.1. Criteria for monitoring the effectiveness of instruction.

4 focuses on organizational patterns in reading and writing. Children generate their own nonfictional books and learn to use the patterns to interpret information from pictures, graphs, instructions. and literary texts. Level three for grades 5 and 6 emphasizes metacognitive awareness of the strategy. Its intended outcomes are a range of deliberate study skills and classificatory systems for texts, and general preparation for the learning demands which will continue across the high school years.

Bartlett and Turner (1985) examined children who had been taught to use the top-level structure in text as 5th grade students 3 years later when these students were in the 8th grade. The students were still using the top-level structure of texts and could freely describe structure and its uses.

Bartlett and his colleages (Bartlett, Turner, & Barton, 1987; Turner, 1984; Usher, 1981) examined their past instructional procedures that taught children about top-level structure and arrived a criteria for monitoring effective instruction. This criteria is listed in Fig. 2.1.

Other studies that have shown improved recall after teaching specific text structures include a study by Slater (1985) with 9th grade students and passages from history textbooks. A second study was conducted by Rattanavich (1987) with 10th grade students in Bangkok, Thailand. She measured a significant shift in use of the structure or plan strategy with a related improvement in students' recall and identification of main ideas.

Thus, there is considerable evidence that teaching readers about text structure and a strategy to use this structure will provide them with an effective prose learning strategy and improve their memory. The current investigation adds to this growing body of literature in a number of ways. First, it investigates the efficacy of this strategy with older adults. Second, it provides an unusually well designed study in this research domain for investigating the effects of the structural training program. The three groups of randomly assigned subjects provide better experimental control than many of the past studies. Also, the comparison between the practice group and the strategy group enables us to separate out strategy effects from effects due to practice reading and recalling the texts. Third, the investigation utilizes more dependent measures than previous studies to assess a variety of possible effects of the training. Fourth, the training program teaches five common structures used to organize text rather than four taught in other programs (e.g., Bartlett, 1978; Carrell, 1985).

3 Method for the Evaluation Study

This chapter describes the procedures used to conduct an evaluation of training with the plan strategy. The training program also is described in this chapter, but the entire training program with the teacher and student manuals is found in chapter 6.

DESCRIPTION OF THE 107 SUBJECTS

Young and old adults were screened on the *Quick* vocabulary test (Borgatta & Corsini, 1964); they were stratified on age and matched on their vocabulary test scores and then assigned randomly to one of three groups. These groups did not differ significantly on the *Quick* ($F_{2,99} = .08$), the Vocabulary Subtest of the *Wechsler Adult Intelligence Scale* ($F_{2,99} = .96$ for raw scores; $F_{2,99} = .55$ for scales scores) (Wechsler, 1955), nor years of education ($F_{2,99} = 2.17$).

A total of 107 subjects participated in the study. However, six unusual subjects spread over the three groups were deleted from the experiment; they included one dyslexic, two with under 10 years of education, two with over 19 years of education, and one with English as a second language. Use of the plan strategy on the two major text structures studied was examined for all subjects on the pretest. Those subjects that consistently showed mastery of the plan strategy on the four opportunities to use text structure on the pretest were eliminated from subsequent analyses since they could effectively use the plan strategy prior to instruction. Table 3.1 shows the distribution of these subjects for young and old adults in the three groups. Mastery on the pretest was exhibited by 12% of the old adults and 33% of the young adults (chi-square = 5.63, $p < .02$). These findings

TABLE 3.1
Number of Young and Old Adults in All Three
Groups Who Did and Did Not Exhibit Mastery on the Plan Strategy
Prior to Instruction on the Pretest

Age	Group	Mastery on Pretest	No Mastery
Old	strategy	2	21
	practice	3	13
	control	2	18
Young	strategy	6	10
	practice	5	6
	control	3	12

Note: Mastery = use to the text's top-level structure to organize
a subject's recall on the problem/solution text, immediate and 30
minute delayed recall of the comparison text, and the comparison
text with the culturally salient comparison structure.

are similar to those of Meyer and Rice (1983a) for adults with average vocabulary test scores on the *Quick;* older adults with average vocabulary scores use the plan strategy less frequently than comparable young adults, while no age differences were found for adults with high vocabulary scores. None of the three groups receiving different training had proportionally more subjects exhibiting mastery on the pretest than the other groups (chi-square = 1.01, d.f. = 2).

Subsequent analyses used only those 80 remaining subjects who did not exhibit mastery of the strategy on the pretest. They are the subjects listed in the right column of Table 3.1. After completion of the study the subjects in the control group were provided with the opportunity to receive instruction with the plan strategy. This gave us the opportunity to increase the size of the Plan group with subjects who had failed to show up for the pretest usually due to unexpected commitments. Six of the 21 old adults from the Plan group and two of the 10 young adults in this group received the instruction after the others; however, the added subjects did not vary significantly from the original subjects on vocabulary, education, nor performance (posttest performance was slightly, but not significantly poorer for the eight subjects run a couple of weeks after completion of the main experiment). As seen in Table 3.1 the Practice group of young adults only has 6 subjects; unfortunately, most of the young adults with the lower vocabulary scores that were randomly assigned to this group failed to appear for the pretest after agreeing to participate during the screening session; nearly half the subjects from this group that did appear showed mastery of the strategy prior to instruction.

Characteristics of the subjects used in subsequent analyses are depicted in Table 3.2. The Strategy, Practice and Control groups did not differ significantly on age ($F_{2,74} = .10$), raw ($F_{2,74} = 1.38$) or scaled ($F_{2,74} = 1.11$) scores on the Vocabulary Subtest of the Weschler Adult Intelligence Scale (WAIS), Quick Vocabulary Test ($F_{2,74} = .66$), raw ($F_{2,74} = .69$) nor standardized ($F_{2,74} = .84$) scores on the Metropolitan Reading Test. Differences among the groups

TABLE 3.2
Traits (Averages) of Old and Young Adults Who Did Not Show
Mastery of the Plan Strategy on the Pretest

	Groups					
	Strategy		Practice		Control	
Traits	Old	Young	Old	Young	Old	Young
Age	69.00	24.80	67.69	24.83	69.39	24.58
WAIS						
raw	59.48	56.40	55.31	54.17	62.28	58.50
scaled	13.57	12.50	12.77	12.50	14.06	13.00
Quick	60.62	46.10	51.08	43.83	55.06	46.58
Reading Pretest						
raw	40.05	45.70	36.38	43.83	38.72	46.08
standard	839.81	888.80	801.92	874.00	827.83	901.58
Education	12.60	14.10	13.08	13.50	14.50	14.50

in education nearly reached significance ($F2,73 = 2.84$, $p < .07$); the Control group tended to have more years of education than the other two groups. Old and young adults did not differ on vocabulary performance on the WAIS (raw scores: $F1,74 = .99$; scaled scores: $F1,74 = 2.72$, $p < .11$) nor years of education ($F1,73 = 1.66$). However. the age groups did differ on the Quick Vocabulary Test ($F1,74 = 6.39$, $p < .02$) and the Metropolitan Reading Test (raw: $F1,74 = 13.06$, $p < .0006$; standardized: $F1,74 = 13.49$, $p < .0005$). The old adults performed better than the young adults on the Quick Vocabulary Test, while the young adults performed better than the old adults on the reading comprehension test. Similar patterns of results have been reported by Meyer and Rice (1983a) and Hartley (1986). None of the group by age interactions for any of the traits reached statistical significance.

DESCRIPTION OF THE INSTRUCTIONAL MATERIALS

The plan strategy.   Instruction with the plan strategy taught learners to employ a deliberate plan or strategy for remembering what they read; this strategy is depicted graphically in Fig. 3.1. In reading, they were taught to choose the organizational plan used by the writer to organize his or her ideas. In remembering, they were taught to use the same organizational plan. They learned that this strategy is a good one to use under certain conditions, but not others. They were told to use it when they want to know what a writer is trying to tell them; to use it when they want to tell someone or write them a letter about what they read in an article. It was not recommended when they were just reading to find out a particular detail and had no interest in the point the writer was trying to make.

The training materials are entitled *A Plan for Reading: A Strategy to Improve Reading Comprehension and Memory for Adults* (Meyer & Bartlett, 1985). The

A Plan
for
READING

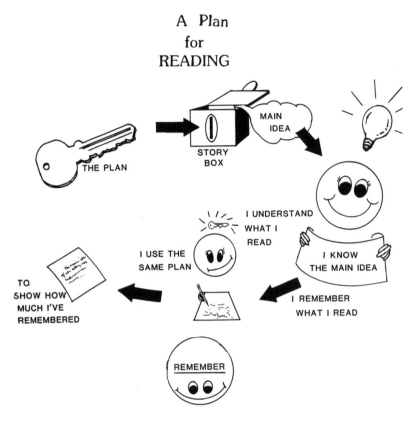

Do these things –

(1) Find the plan when you read

(2) Use the same plan to tell what you can remember

FIG. 3.1. A plan for reading.

antecedents of these materials in terms of research, prior training programs, and pilot studies were described in chapter 2.

On the first day the rationale, power, and limitations of the strategy were discussed. They learned about five basic plans for organizing expository text. These plans were description, sequence, causation, problem/solution, and comparison and are summarized in Table 3.3. During this first session only several of the most common signals listed in the table were presented with each plan.

In the training program each plan was discussed in detail and examples were given using the main captions of advertisements found in magazines. Advertisements were used the first day because they are familiar, fun to use, and often

TABLE 3.3

Five Basic Writing Plans and Signals that Cue Readers to These Plans

Writing Plan and Definition	Signals
Description Descriptive ideas that give attributes, specifics, or setting information about a topic. The main idea is that attributes of a topic are discussed. E.g., newspaper article describing who, where, when and how.	for example, which was one, this particular, for instance, specifically, such as, attributes of, that is, namely, properties of, characteristics are, qualities are, marks of, in describing,___
Sequence Ideas grouped on the basis of order or time. The main idea is the procedure or history related. E.g., recipe procedures, history of Civil War battles, growth from birth to 12 months.	afterwards, later, finally, last, early, following, to begin with, as time passed, continuing on, to end, years ago, in the first place, before, after, soon, more recently,___
Causation Presents causal or cause and effect-like relations between ideas. The main idea is organized into cause and effect parts. E.g., directions: if you want to take good pictures, then you must ....; explanations: the idea explained is the effect and the explanation is its cause.	as a result, because, since, for the purpose of, caused, led to, consequence, thus, in order to, this is why, if/then, the reason, so, in explanation, therefore,___
Problem/Solution The main ideas are organized into two parts: a problem part and a solution part that responds to the problem by trying to eliminate it, or a question part and an answer part that responds to the question by trying to answer it. E.g., scientific articles often first raise a question or problem and then seek to give an answer or solution.	problem: problem, question, puzzle, perplexity, enigma, riddle, issue, query, need to prevent, the trouble,___ solution: solution, answer, response, reply, rejoinder, return, comeback, to satisfy the problem, to set the issue at rest, to solve these problems,___

continued

47

(table 3.3 continued)

Writing Plan and Definition	Signals
Comparison Relates ideas on the basis of differences and similarities. The main idea is organized in parts that provide a comparison, contrast, or alternative perspective on a topic. E.g., political speeches, particularly where one view is clearly favored over the other.	not everyone, but, in contrast, all but, instead, act like, however, in comparison, on the other hand, whereas, in opposition, unlike, alike, have in common, share, resemble, the same as, different, difference, differentiate, compare to, while, although,
Listing can occur with any of the five writing plans. Listing simply groups ideas together. Passages are often organized as a listing of descriptions about a topic. A sequence always contains a listing of ideas, but the ideas are ordered sequentially. A listing can occur when groups of causes are presented, groups of effects are listed, groups of solutions are posited, groups of ideas are contrasted to another idea, and so forth.	common signals include: and, in addition, also, include, moreover, besides, first, second, third, etc., subsequent, furthermore, at the same time, another, and so forth,

48

clearly depict these writing plans. We started with the plan with the least organization available to aid memory, Description, and worked up the plans that can contain the most organization to aid memory, Problem/Solution and Comparison.

The participants were told that many texts will reflect more than one of these basic five plans. Examples from television programs, newspapers, and stories were used to point out to the students that the strategy involves finding the overall plan used in the text rather than plans used to organize details in a text. The concept of signaling words was introduced and then the students worked in pairs of partners for the remainder of the session. First, they examined five advertisements to determine the overall plans. Next the partners wrote advertisements in two specified plans to sell their new invention, the safety pin. Finally, they wrote about a dramatic cartoon of a tiger eating his trainer with the two other plans. Feedback was given for their performance on these tasks.

The second session focused on teaching other signaling words for each plan and the idea that listing can occur with any of the five plans. The students carefully read and quizzed their partner about Table 3.3. This table was used at all subsequent training sessions and in their home reading; additional signaling words discovered were added to the table. In this session they identified the plan and signaling for short magazine entries. After discussing their answers with their partners, the class discussed them with diagrams of the overall plan (see Fig. 3.2 for an example taken from the most difficult selection).

The remainder of the session was spent reading and sorting 17 passages into the five plans and reading and recalling two passages. In sessions 1 and 2 the five plans were taught, but no instruction was given in how to use the structure of these plans to facilitate encoding and retrieval of information in texts. In session 1 most of the young people caught on quite quickly to the five plans, but most of the older people appeared strained and a bit confused. In the second session many of the older people began to understand and enjoy this new way of thinking about reading. During session 3 nearly all the older people were understanding and attempting to use the strategy. Evaluation materials collected after session 2 showed that just teaching people the definitions and signals for the plans was not sufficient for their use of these plans to organize their recall of the text. The third session where using the strategy to aid recall was modeled was critical for the subjects' to master the strategy.

In the third session the rationale for using the plans in text to increase memory was emphasized. They were told to ask two questions before reading a passage: What is the plan for this passage? What is the main idea that fits this plan? In addition they were told that for best recall of what they read six steps should be taken

1. We find the plan in what we read;
2. We write its name at the top of the page, just before we recall;

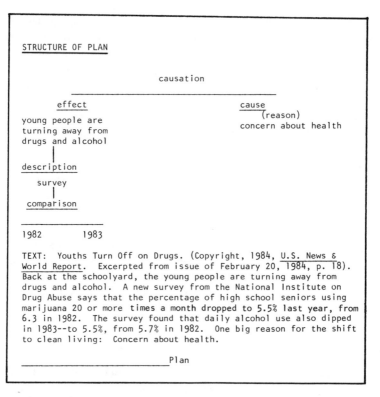

FIG. 3.2. Sample of materials used in session 2 to teach students in the strategy group how to find the overall plan for an article.

3. We write the main idea sentence;
4. We use the plan to organize what we recall;
5. We check to see that we have used it; and
6. We add anything else that we have just remembered.

A young adult modeled the reading and recalling of description, sequence, and causation passages. An old adult modeled the reading and recalling of problem/solution and comparison passages. Next, the students read and recalled two passages getting feedback on their progress in using the strategy after each passage was recalled.

In session 4 students received a detailed report of their strengths and areas to work on to master the strategy. For this session and the final session partners were assigned by pairing a proficient student with a less proficient student. In addition, instruction and practice were given in applying the strategy to longer passages and muddled passages.

In the fifth session another detailed report of their progress was given to each student. The session was spent eliminating any difficulties and giving the students practice in using the strategy. In sessions 3, 4, and 5 the mnemonic aspects of each particular plan was stressed. For example, for the comparison plan it was repeatedly pointed out that opposing 'views often are compared on many of the same issues; such as, one political candidates views on abortion, taxes, government spending, and defense, and then the other candidiates views on these same issues. They discovered that their memory will be improved if they remember that a comparison plan was used and the number and name of the issues compared; for the example one should remember that the candidates were compared on four issues: abortion, taxes, government spending, and defense. In recalling a passage they were instructed to check to see if they had mentioned each issue from the two perspectives. Remembering one issue often jogged their memory for the opposing view of the issue. During the session the partners filled out easy and enjoyable to use feedback forms for each other in evaluating their partner's use of the strategy on each passage read. To vary the tasks recalls from texts read were sometimes written and sometimes oral.

The practice program.   Instruction for the practice group followed a program of instruction entitled *Practice Makes Perfect* (Meyer, 1985b). This instruction focused on practicing reading and remembering texts. Subjects were told that research indicated that with practice people can learn to increase the amount of information they can remember and that while a man may never be too old to learn, it's a lot easier for him if he is in practice. In other words, when it comes to reading comprehension skill, use it or lose it. The subjects read the same passages as those read in the plan instruction and spent the same amount of instructional time.

Subjects were told that they were expected to practice recalling the information learned in reading both in class and after they left each day at home in their own reading. They began reading and remembering information from very short selections and worked up to longer selections. In the first of the five sessions they worked with a partner reading and recalling information from advertisements. Before beginning the task the same old and young adult models used in the strategy program modeled the reading and recalling procedure on two advertisements. While the old adults in the Strategy group were quite strained on the first session, the old adults in the Practice group exhibited joviality and appeared to relax and enjoy the task. Future use of the plan program with older adults might be less stressful by starting out the instruction with session 1 from the practice program.

The second session involved reading and remembering short articles from magazines followed by sorting the 17 texts sorted by the strategy group into five categories based on ease of remembering them and reading and recalling two texts. In these first two sessions the subjects appeared relaxed and to be trying very hard to remember what they read. After the third session an older married couple in this group asked for hints or tactics to improve memory; these were the only subjects that asked for such information throughout the practice program. In the third session subjects read and recalled the two texts read and recalled during that session by the strategy group. In addition, they were given lists of simple sentences adapted from the original texts to check the number of these items they recalled. For the texts where the plan strategy had been modeled for the Strategy group, the subjects in the Practice group scored a hypothetical student's recall of the passages and checked the reliability of their scoring with their partner. For the fourth and fifth sessions a proficient performer was assigned as the partner of a less proficient reader. For these sessions the subjects read and recalled (varying oral and written recall) articles switching booklets after recall so that their partner could score on provided checklists the number of items recalled; agreement and disagreement in this scoring was noted by the partners.

Thus, the Strategy and Practice instructional programs allotted the same amount of time for practice reading and recalling texts, involved the same texts and instructors, and utilized the same types of cooperative learning experiences between pairs of students (e.g., Larson & Dansereau, 1986) for similar durations of time. The instructional programs varied on whether or not the plan strategy was taught and types of feedback sheets used by the partners to score their progress; the feedback forms for the Strategy group gave students points on the basis of identifying the plan of the text and the main idea organized by that plan, while the feedback forms for the Practice group attributed points on the basis of the number of ideas remembered from the text regardless of the types of ideas recalled.

DESCRIPTION OF THE EVALUATION MATERIALS

Various evaluation materials were utilized to test the effectiveness of the plan strategy on recall and other skills and attitudes that might possibly be affected by the training. During the testing sessions the subjects read and recalled fifteen passages, recalled three of these passages again after a half hour delay and another after a 2 week delay, took forms JS and KS of the Metropolitan Achievement Test Advanced 2: Survey Battery in Reading (Prescott, Balow, Hogan, & Farr, 1978), answered three sets of six questions taken from the Davis Reading Test (Davis & Davis, 1956) that appeared to tap structure, sorted passages according to their organization, underlined the most important ideas in passages, answered main idea, detail, and problem solving questions about texts, and filled out questionnaires about reading strategies and attitudes. Three of the fifteen passages read came from materials used in the training program for the Strategy group (as well as the Practice group) in order to see if the subjects actually learned what they had been taught; recall from these texts were collected in case no improvement was found on the texts not used in the instruction. However, since improvement was evident for the new texts requiring some generalization of the skill, further discussion will not be given to these three texts used in instruction other than to say that subjects in the Strategy group showed mastery of the strategy on these materials.

Sets of three passages for the three testing times were written with identical content structures (Meyer, 1975), but different content; the passages within each set were counterbalanced over the three testing times. These evaluation texts were organized with the two plans that provided the most organization and previous subjects reported the most difficulty learning; the plans were problem/solution and comparison. Two primary sets of passages were used. The first set with a problem/solution structure contained 506 words and 193 scorable idea units. They were on the topics of reactors (taken from *Scientific American* [Seaborg & Bloom, 1970]), schizophrenia, and trusts; the first two came from Meyer (1975) with some slight modifications to lower the difficulty level of the schizophrenia text; the trust text was written for the evaluation to make a set of three texts with identical logical relations, case relations, idea units, and number of words. Copies of these passages and their content structures can be found in the appendix. The passage from this set that a subject read on the first posttest was recalled also 2 weeks later on the second posttest in order to look at memory for text over an extended period of time; Meyer and Rice (1988) reported greater age deficits in use of structure after such a delay than initially.

Also associated with this set of problem/solution texts were two other tasks, an underlining task and questions. The underlining task asked the subjects to go through the passage and as they read to underline the things felt to be the most important to remember. They were instructed to underline no more than ten things. The questions included (1) What are the three related problems discussed in the article? (3 points); (2) What does the author say is the solution to these problems? (1 point); (3) Give three reasons given by the author to explain why the proposed solution will solve some of the problems (3 points); and (4) What action was to be taken as a result of the strengths of the proposed solution? (1 point).

The second major set of texts had a comparison structure, 235 words, and 167 idea units; this set came from Bartlett (1978) and used a text on railroads from a 9th grade history text; topics of the other passages from this set were on fossils in Africa and a cultural revolution in China. These texts were recalled immediately after reading and again about 30 min later in the testing session.

The third set of texts were designed to examine the use of the plan strategy on passages with a culturally salient comparison structure; subjects were expected to have less difficulty finding and using this structure. The comparison involved contrasting views held by creationists and evolutionists and how these view led them to interpret data differently; the three passages in this set varied on the data: Fossilized tracks in Texas, a coal mine in Australia, and the Archaeopteryx fossil of Europe. These texts contained 230 words and 129 idea units.

The remaining texts read were primarily used for practice passages and to vary the structure of the texts (added the structure of description to the testing packet); they contained 184 words and 94 idea units on the topics of elephants, whales, and dehydration; although identical in number of words and idea units the rhetorical and case relations were not identical as in the other sets of passages.

EXPERIMENTAL PROCEDURE

Subjects were recruited for the study through newspaper articles, radio spots, and fliers distributed at churches, community centers, and on campus. The first contact with the subjects involved administration of the Quick Vocabulary Test and health and background questionnaires. Within each age group subjects were matched on their vocabulary test scores and randomly assigned to the Strategy, Practice or Control groups.

On the pretest subjects were first orientated to the reading and recall task and how to use digital times to record their reading and recall times. They were instructed to work through their booklets at their own pace and to record the time spent on each task. Standard prose recall instructions were given. Subjects were told to "Read each article as you would a magazine article of interest to you. After reading each article, fold it to the back of the booklet; then, write down what you remember on the provided paper. We want to see how many ideas you remember and if you remember how the ideas were interrelated so please write in sentences or paragraphs, rather than listing words. If you can recall an isolated idea, such as 'octopus,' but cannot remember how it was related to anything else in the passage, please write I remember reading 'octopus,' but can't remember its connection. Write down *everything* you can remember." First, subjects read and recalled the practice passage (elephants, whales, or dehydration). Next, they read and recalled the problem/solution passage (reactors, schizophrenia, or trusts); afterward, they underlined the most important things in that text and answered the questions about it. The next text read and recalled was the comparison text (railroads, African fossils, or China's cultural revolution). Then, a text from the set comparing creationists and evolutionists was read and recalled. Next they answered six multiple choice questions from the Davis Reading Test. Then, they again recalled the comparison text from the railroad/Africa/China set. At this point, they took a cookie and punch break followed by a form of the Metropolitan Survey Battery in Reading. The testing session lasted about 2 hours. The particular passage topic from each set of materials or form of a test was counterbalanced.

A day after the pretest the subjects assigned to the Strategy and Practice Groups met for their first sessions. The same instructor and assistants (comprised of young and old adults) taught the two programs in the same facility. Each session lasted 1½ hours; refreshments were provided. Sessions 2 and 3 were held on the following days; the final two training sessions were held the next week.

The first posttest occurred 2 days after completion of instruction and involved all subjects. The sets of materials in this posttest and their sequence was identical to that of the pretest. In addition, after the Metropolitan Survey of Reading two short passages that had been actually studied by the Strategy and Practice Groups were read and recalled.

The second posttest occurred 2 weeks after instruction and also included the same set of materials and sequence of materials as the pretest with some exceptions at the end of the packet. On this posttest the Metropolitan Survey of Reading was not given and instead a packet of questions and other tasks followed in its place at the end of the packet. First came questions about their memory, reading strategies, and any changes they had noted over the testing sessions. Then, came a recognition test for the topics read in the three testing sessions. Subjects were then asked to recall the problem/solution text read 2 weeks earlier (title was provided). Then, some thought questions followed which required them to solve novel problems based on what they had learned from the problem/solution texts read. Next they read a problem/solution text on supertankers used in previous research (Meyer, 1984) and underlined the most important ideas. Then, they read a descriptive text on parakeets (Meyer, 1975; Meyer & Rice, 1981) answered main idea and details questions about it, and described its structure. Next, they read a comparison text actually studied by the treatment groups, recalled it, and described its structure. Finally, they sorted 17 passages taken from magazine articles or the Bible into five piles based on their overall writing plans: description, sequence, causation, problem/solution, or comparison. After completion of this posttest each subject was paid $40, given a written description of the study, and booklets with tips to improve memory. Also, subjects who did not participate in the Strategy group could check out copies of the entire program or sign up to participate in the instruction. The final testing took about 2 hours; the session was self-paced and some subjects took more time to complete the packet. The Vocabulary Subtest of the WAIS was individually administered to each subject before or after the posttests for the Control group and before or after the training sessions for the Plan and Practice groups.

DESCRIPTION OF SCORING PROCEDURES

The Meyer (1975, 1985a) prose analysis procedure was used to score memory from text and organization of recall. Examples of the content structures used in scoring can be found in the appendix. Interscorer agreement was 94%. In addition, intrascorer reliability was calculated for all protocols written by subjects for the problem/solution set of passages in the two week delayed recall condition. First, they were scored for use of top-level structure (see Meyer, 1985a) without scoring the idea units recalled per passage. Three weeks to 2 months later the idea units recalled were scored along with the organization of the protocol to check reliability. Intrascorer agreement was 94%.

One point was given for each aspect of the questions correctly answered, passage correctly sorted, or topics correctly recognized. The underlining task was scored by counting the number of high and low ideas from the content structures of the texts that were underlined as important by a subject.

4
Findings from the Study

This chapter examines the effects of the training program. First investigated are changes in use of the plan strategy. Next, changes are examined in the amount of information remembered by the adults. After, data are presented focusing on changes in the type of information remembered or valued. Also investigated is far transfer of the training to measures of reading enjoyment and reading competency that do not require recall. Finally, descriptions are given of progress through instruction with the plan strategy of one young adult and one older adult.

DID TRAINING INCREASE USE OF THE PLAN STRATEGY?

Strategy use on the problem/solution passages. Data are shown in Table 4.1 for use of top-level structure to organize recall on the problem/solution texts. The only group that made significant and consistent gains in use of the top-level structure from pretest to posttests on the problem/solution passages was the Strategy group, both old (chi-square = 44.05. d.f. = 2, $p >$ .001) and young adults (chi-square = 25.22, d.f. = 2, $p <$ .001). The young adults in the Control group increased from no adults using the top-level structure on the pretest to half of the adults using the structure on posttest 1, but dropped to one using the structure on posttest 2 (chi-square = 11, d.f. = 2, $p <$ .01). On the pretest there was no significant difference among the Strategy, Practice, and Control groups (chi-square = 7.94, d.f. = 5). On the first posttest after instruction most (93%) old and young adults in the Plan group used the problem/solution structure to organize their recalls, while the old and young adults in the Practice and Control

57

TABLE 4.1
Use of the Problem/Solution Top-Level Structure in the
Reactor/Schizophrenia/Trusts Passages by Old and Young Adults
in the Strategy, Practice, and Control Groups on the Pretest,
Posttest, and Delayed Posttests

	PRETEST					
Use Top-Level	Strategy		Practice		Control	
Structure	old	young	old	young	old	young
yes	0	0	1	0	3	0
no	21	10	12	6	15	12

	POSTTEST 1					
Use Top-Level	Strategy		Practice		Control	
Structure	old	young	old	young	old	young
yes	18	10	1	2	4	6
no	2	0	12	4	14	6

TWO WEEK DELAYED RECALL OF TEXTS READ ON POSTTEST 1

Use Top-Level	Strategy		Practice		Control	
Structure	old	young	old	young	old	young
yes	10	7	0	1	5	4
no	10	2	10	5	8	7

	POSTTEST 2					
Use Top-Level	Strategy		Practice		Control	
Structure	old	young	old	young	old	young
yes	18	8	3	1	3	1
no	3	1	9	4	15	11

groups did not (chi-square $= 38.27$, d.f. $= 5, p < .001$). This superiority in use of top-level structure was maintained by both the old and young adults in the Strategy group over the other groups when these passages were recalled 2 weeks later (chi-square $= 14.37$, d.f. $= 5, p < .02$). Also, on the passages read 2 weeks after instruction 87% of the adults in the Strategy group used the problem/solution structure, while 83% of the adults in the other two groups did not (chi-square $= 36.74$, d.f. $= 5, p < .001$). There were no significant age differences in use of top-level structure at any of the test times when old and young adults within each of the three instructional groups were examined separately. Thus, it appears that instruction in using the text's top-level structure to organize learning and recall dramatically increases the use of top-level structure to organize recall protocols for both old and young adults on these problem/solution texts.

Strategy use on the comparison texts. The only group that made significant gains in the use of the top-level structure over pretest to posttests was the Strategy group. The old adults in the Strategy group made large gains in their use of the text's top-level structure from texts they had read 30 minutes earlier (chi-square = 22.35. d.f. = 2, $p < .001$). Young adults in the Strategy group also made these gains on this delayed recall task (chi-square = 11.96, d.f. = 2, $p < .01$) and nearly showed significant gains on the immediate task as well (chi-square = 5.95, d.f. = 2, $p < .06$).

As seen in Table 4.2 there were no significant age or group differences for the immediate recall task on the pretest (chi-square = 6.17, d.f. = 5). However, there were group differences on the delayed task (chi-square = 17.52, d.f. = 5, $p < .01$). The Strategy group was less likely to use the text's top-level structure on the delayed pretest than either the Practice (chi-square = 10.14, d.f. = 3, $p < .02$) or Control (chi-square = 11.72, d.f. = 3, $p < .01$) groups; the latter two groups were not significantly different from each other (chi-square = 7.72, d.f. = 3, $p < .10$). There were no significant age differences within the groups. On the first posttest immediately after reading the texts there were significant group differences (chi-square = 11.98, d.f. = 5, $p < .01$); the Strategy group used the text's top-level structure more than the Control group (chi-square = 10.44, d.f. = 3, $p < .02$). There were no significant differences for any of the other posttests (posttest 1 delay: chi-square = 7.71, d.f. = 5, $p < .10$; posttest 2 immediate: chi-square = 1.67, d.f. = 5; posttest 2 delay: chi-square = .53, d.f. = 5).

Strategy use on the culturally salient comparison texts.   Again, the only group that made significant gains in use of top-level structure from pretest to posttests was the Strategy group, both old (chi-square = 14.1, d.f. = 2, $p < .001$) and young adults (chi-square = 6.36, d.f. = 2, $p < .05$). As seen in Table 4.3 for the pretest there was a difference among the Strategy, Practice and Control groups (chi-square = 14.78, d.f. = 5, $p < .02$). The young and old adults within each of the three groups performed similarly, but the Control group used the top-level structure prior to instruction more frequently than the Strategy group (chi-square = 8.46, d.f. = 3, $p < .05$) and the Practice group (chi-square = 14.37, d.f. = 3, $p < .01$); the latter two groups did not vary significantly (chi-square = 2.47, d.f.=3). On the posttest there were no significant differences among the groups (chi-square = 9.33, d.f. = 5, $p < .1$). This finding held overall for the second posttest (chi-square = 9.689, d.f. = 5, $p < .1$), but the comparison between old adults in the Plan and Practice groups was significant (chi-square = 4.17, d.f. = 1, $p < .05$). In summary, the most improvement in use of top-level structure occurred for the young and old adults in the Strategy group. By the posttests nearly all of the adults (86%) were able to use the comparison structure in their recall of the texts organized with the cuturally salient comparison. This was the only set of passages in the study that repeated the same general topic; repetition of topic and structure itself may have had a facilitating effect. The superiority of the Control group prior to instruction disappeared after instruction for both the Strategy and Practice groups. The only

TABLE 4.2
Use of the Comparison Top-Level Structure in the
Railroad/China/Africa Passages by Old and Young Adults in the
Strategy, Practice, and Control Groups on the Immediate and
30 Minute Delayed Pretests and Posttests

PRETEST

Immediate Recall Task

Use Top-Level Structure	Strategy		Practice		Control	
	old	young	old	young	old	young
yes	17	6	8	6	12	11
no	4	4	4	0	5	1

Delayed Recall Task

Use Top-Level Structure	Strategy		Practice		Control	
	old	young	old	young	old	young
yes	7	3	7	6	8	11
no	14	6	4	0	7	1

POSTTEST 1

Immediate Recall Task

Use Top-Level Structure	Strategy		Practice		Control	
	old	young	old	young	old	young
yes	21	10	10	6	12	12
no	1	0	3	0	5	0

Delayed Recall Task

Use Top-Level Structure	Strategy		Practice		Control	
	old	young	old	young	old	young
yes	20	9	9	5	11	11
no	1	0	2	1	5	1

POSTTEST 2

Immediate Recall Task

Use Top-Level Structure	Strategy		Practice		Control	
	old	young	old	young	old	young
yes	18	8	12	6	15	10
no	3	1	1	0	3	2

Delayed Recall Task

Use Top-Level Structure	Strategy		Practice		Control	
	old	young	old	young	old	young
yes	17	8	10	5	14	11
no	3	1	2	1	2	1

significant difference among any of the groups on the posttests was the greater frequency of use of the top-level structure by the old adults in the Strategy group than that of the old adults in the Practice Group.

Other evidence for acquisition of the plan strategy. On the second posttest a number of other indices were collected to ascertain the subjects' ability to use the

TABLE 4.3
Use of the Culturally Salient Comparison Top-Level Structure in
the Creation Versus Evolution Passages by Old and Young Adults
in the Strategy, Practice, and Control Groups on the
Pretest, Posttest, and Delayed Posttest

	PRETEST					
Use Top-Level	Strategy		Practice		Control	
Structure	old	young	old	young	old	young
yes	12	7	6	2	15	12
no	9	3	7	4	3	0
	POSTTEST 1					
Use Top-Level	Strategy		Practice		Control	
Structure	old	young	old	young	old	young
yes	20	10	10	5	12	11
no	1	0	3	1	6	1
	POSTTEST 2					
Use Top-Level	Strategy		Practice		Control	
Structure	old	young	old	young	old	young
yes	20	9	8	5	16	10
no	1	0	5	1	2	2

plan strategy. For two passages subjects were asked how the passage they read was organized; one passage compared the eastern and western steamboats; it had been read during instruction by the Strategy and Practice groups; the other described qualities that make parakeets ideal pets (Meyer, 1975). In order to correctly identify how the passages were organized subjects did not need to give the label taught during the instruction, but simply some indication that the steamboat passage compared qualities of different types of steamboats, while the parakeet passage described aspects of these birds. Table 4.4 displays these data. Both the old and young adults in the Strategy group tended to correctly identify the comparison structure for the steamboat text, while the adults in the other groups did not (chi-square = 20.93, d.f. = 5, $p < .001$). The same pattern of results was found for the parakeet text (chi-square = 39.91, d.f. = 5, $p < .001$). These data provide clear evidence that the Strategy group acquired the plan strategy.

Data from the sorting task also support the superiority of the Strategy group in using the plan strategy after instruction. Subjects sorted 17 articles into the five plans based on their organization. These data are shown in Table 4.5. The Strategy group sorted more passages correctly than the other groups ($F2,73 = 3.46, p < .04$). There were significant age effects ($F1,73 = 4.77, p < .04$). It is interesting to note that the old adults in the Strategy group perform slightly better than the young adults in the Practice and Control groups. However, the group by age interaction was not significant ($F2,73 = .45$).

Five questions from the questionnaire about reading relate to the plan strategy;

TABLE 4.4
Ability to State the Type of Structure Used to Organize Passages
Read in Posttest 2 by the Old and Young Adults in the Strategy,
Practice, and Control Groups

Group	Age	Steamboat/Comparison Text		Parakeet/Description Text	
		Correct	Incorrect	Correct	Incorrect
Strategy	old	13	8	14	7
	young	8	1	9	0
Practice	old	1	12	0	13
	young	2	4	1	5
Control	old	4	14	2	16
	young	5	7	2	10

these data are shown in Table 4.6. The first four questions were open-ended; the responses were categorized during scoring. The fifth question asked subjects to circle *not really, sometimes,* or *consistently,* a procedure used previously by Rice and Meyer (1985). As seen in Table 4.6 the Strategy group stated that they tried to find the overall structure relating ideas in text during the testing sessions, while the other groups listed main idea, detail, or other strategies. The groups did not vary on mentioning rereading as a strategy. The Practice and Control groups did not vary significantly on stating a main idea or detail strategy. For the second question dealing with reading in everyday life, the Strategy group said that they use the plan strategy, while the other groups said they used the main idea strategy (chi-square = 28.78, d.f. = 5, $p < .001$). The third question dealt with observed changes in reading and remembering over the three testing sessions. The Strategy group reported that they learned to use the plan or structure strategy, while other changes or no changes were reported by the other groups. The old subjects in the Practice group tended to reread, while the old subjects in the Control group claimed to concentrate more (chi-square = 6.29, d.f. = 1, $p < .02$). The fourth question related to changes observed in everyday life. The Strategy group explained that they remembered more or tried to find the overall structure and author's purpose, while the other groups expressed other changes or no change at

TABLE 4.5
Means and Standard Deviations for the Number of 17 Passages
Correctly Sorted into the Five Structures for Expository Text
by Old and Young Adults in the Strategy, Practice, and
Control Groups on the Second Posttest

Group	Age	Mean	Standard Deviation
Strategy	old	12.14	3.05
	young	14.00	1.94
Practice	old	10.85	2.85
	young	11.67	2.16
Control	old	9.28	4.32
	young	12.08	4.21

TABLE 4.6
Questions About Reading and Remembering Strategies Administered
on the Second Posttest to Old and Young Adults in the
Strategy, Practice, and Control Groups

	Strategy		Practice		Control	
	Old	Young	Old	Young	Old	Young
When you read an article and try to remember it in these testing sessions, what do you try to do?						
Plan strategy	17	8	0	0	3	1
Main ideas	3	1	8	2	6	5
Facts/dates	0	0	2	1	4	3
Reread	0	0	0	1	2	1
Other	1	0	3	2	2	2

Chi-square = 53.78, d.f. = 20, $p < .001$.

	Strategy		Practice		Control	
When you read an article and try to remember it in your everyday life, what do you try to do? Anything different from what you stated above?						
Structure strategy	12	6	0	0	0	0
Main ideas	2	0	6	2	4	1
Facts	0	0	1	0	2	1
Things that interest me	1	0	3	0	4	3
Relate it to other things I know	1	1	1	0	2	3
Other	5	2	1	4	5	4

Chi-square = 57.84, d.f. = 25, $p < .001$.

	Strategy		Practice		Control	
Since we first met together what changes have you observed in how you read and remember information in these testing sessions?						
Structure strategy	17	9	0	2	0	0
Concentrate	2	0	1	3	7	1
Slow/reread	0	0	5	0	0	0
No change	0	0	0	0	4	5

Chi-square = 102.86, d.f. = 15, $p < .001$.

	Strategy		Practice		Control	
Since we first met together what changes have you observed in everyday life?						
Remember more	9	3	2	2	1	1
Find structure/ author's purpose	7	3	0	1	0	0
Concentration	0	1	1	2	4	0
Slower/reread	0	0	2	2	0	0
Other	2	2	2	0	1	0
No change	3	0	5	0	8	11

$X = 67.04$, d.f. = 25, $p < .001$.

	Strategy		Practice		Control	
Do you try to outline the passage or figure out its organization?						
Not really	4	1	9	1	12	5
Sometimes	7	1	3	2	3	4
Consistently	9	7	1	3	3	3

Chi-square = 23.8, d.f. = 10, $p < .01$.

all. In examining the two categories of "remember more" versus "observe no change," we see that the old adults in the Strategy group claimed to remember more, while the old adults in the other two groups more frequently stated that they observed no change in everyday life (chi-square = 9.35, d.f. = 2, $p < .01$). Young adults in the control group claimed no changes, while the other two groups saw improvement (chi-square = 12.99, d.f. = 2, $p < .001$). For the fifth question adults in the Strategy group consistently or sometimes tried to outline a passage or figure out its organization, while adults in the other groups tended not to employ this strategy in their reading during the testing sessions.

In summary, instruction with the plan strategy did significantly and dramatically increase the use of this strategy by both young and old adults deficient in the use of the strategy prior to instruction. Old adults appeared to be able to acquire this skill after five lessons as well as the young adults on all tasks but the sorting task, where young adults in the Strategy condition could correctly sort more passage (82%) than the old adults in the Strategy group (71%).

DID TRAINING INCREASE THE AMOUNT OF INFORMATION REMEMBERED?

Number of Idea Units Recalled.   Table 4.7 presents the recall data averaged over the three sets of passages (problem/solution, comparison, and culturally salient comparison). The primary findings of interest held over the three sets of passages. In Table 4.7 three scores are given; the centered scores are presented to deal with the fact that some passages in a set yielded less recall than others; however the passages within a set were counterbalanced over the testing times. Proportion of idea units recalled and gain scores (posttest 1—pretest performance or, posttest 2—pretest performance) also are presented in the Table 4.7 to facilitate understanding of the findings. The main effects and interactions were the same in terms of level of significance regardless of whether centered scores or proportions were used in the analyses; the F values for the centered scores will be presented.

A four factor analysis of variance was calculated; the factors were group (Strategy, Practice, and Control), age (old and young), passage set (problem/solution, comparison, and culturally salient comparison), and time (pretest, posttest 1, and posttest 2) with repeated measures on the last two factors. The only statistically significant main effect was testing time ($F2,69 = 62.36$, $p < .00001$); as seen in Table 4.7 performance was much better on the posttests than the pretest. Thus, merely practicing reading and recalling text on the pretest appeared to improve performance on subsequent reading and recall tests. However, the expected time by group interaction was statistically significant ($F4,138 = 6.81$, $p < .00001$); this interaction is displayed graphically in Fig. 4.1. Thus, all groups of subjects improved in recall performance from the pretest to posttest,

TABLE 4.7

Means and Standard Deviations for Centered Scores, Proportions of Idea Units Recalled, and Gain Scores Achieved by Old and Young Adults in the Strategy, Practice, and Control Groups on the Pretest, Posttest 1, and Posttest 2 Summed Over the Problem Solution, Comparison, and Culturally Salient Comparison Sets of Passages

Age	Group	Scores		Pretest	Posttest 1	Posttest 2
Old	Strategy	centered	M	−7.48	9.29	9.17
			S.D.	(14.83)	(16.11)	(18.18)
		proportions	M	.21	.32	.32
			S.D.	(.12)	(.14)	(.15)
		gain (post-pretest)	M		17.27	17.38
			S.D.		(20.87)	(21.15)
	Practice	centered	M	−10.43	−.22	−.99
			S.D.	(11.84)	(14.91)	(15.01
		proportions	M	.18	.25	.27
			S.D.	(.09)	(.14)	(.14)
		gain (post-pretest)	M		11.11	13.58
			S.D.		(25.44)	(20.40)
	Control	centered	M	−9.91	−3.96	−3.28
			S.D.	(17.63)	(17.13)	(20.21)
		proportions	M	.20	.23	.24
			S.D.	(.13)	(.14)	(.14)
		gain (post-pretest)	M		4.57	5.56
			S.D.		(19.30)	(17.32)
Young	Strategy	centered	M	−7.18	11.92	10.00
			S.D	(13.66)	(20.34)	(12.67)
		proportions	M	.20	.35	.33
			S.D.	(.12)	(.15)	(.15)
		gain (post-pretest)	M		23.46	21.46
			S.D.		(18.39)	(18.79)
	Practice	centered	M	−7.02	11.64	5.11
			S.D.	(17.09)	(20.83)	(22.55)
		proportions	M	.23	.30	.29
			S.D	(.15)	(.15)	(.17)
		gain (post-pretest)	M		11.28	9.78
			S.D.		(17.79)	(20.66)
	Control	centered	M	1.31	8.92	1.44
			S.D.	(16.8)	(21.95)	(15.47)
		proportions	M	.27	.31	.27
			S.D.	(.15)	(.16)	(.14)
		gain (post-pretest)	M		7.61	.14
			S.D.		(20.52)	(19.59)

but not all the same amount. The age by time by group interaction was not statistically significant ($F_{4,138} = .9$); the instruction had similar effects on old and young adults.

Analysis of the gain scores (Overall & Woodward, 1975, 1976; Rogosa, Brandt, & Zimowski, 1982; Schaie & Hertzog, 1985; Willis, 1985) utilized the same four factors, with the minor change of two levels of time (gain on posttest 1 and gain on posttest 2) rather than three. The only significant finding for this

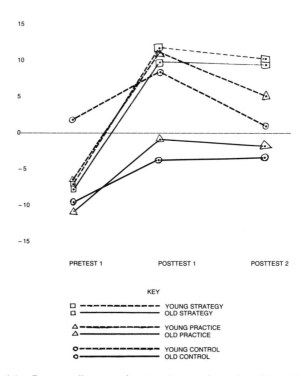

FIG. 4.1. Free recall scores (centered scores) produced by old and young adults in the strategy, practice, and control groups summed over three sets of passages on the pretest, posttest 1 (2 days after instruction) and posttest 2 (2 weeks after instruction).

analysis was a group effect ($F_{2,70} = 9.00$, $p < .0004$). The absence of a time effect in this analysis indicated that subjects' radical improvement was taking place between the pretest and the first posttest and then was being maintained 2 weeks later on the delayed posttest. The main effect of group verified the earlier finding that some groups made larger gains than others. Figure 4.2 depicts these gains (average posttest performance—pretest performance). Multiple comparisons of the three groups using Tukey's critical range statistic revealed that the largest gains made by the Strategy group were significantly greater than the gains made by the Control groups. The Practice group, whose gain was approximately halfway between the other two groups' gain scores as seen in Table 4.7, did not differ significantly from either of the other groups. Tukey tests comparing the three groups on centered scores also only showed reliable differences between

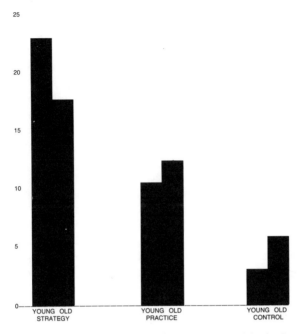

FIG. 4.2. Gain scores achieved by old and young adults in the strategy, practice, and control groups summed over the three sets of passages.

the Strategy and Control groups after instruction. Clearly, the effect of simple practice in recall is not negligible, but alone does not produce the striking improvement shown by the group that received training in the plan strategy.

The other significant interactions in the analysis of centered scores involved the sets of passages. There was a passage set by age interaction ($F2,69 = 9.3, p < .0003$); this interaction resulted from age deficits on the comparison passages ($F1,70 = 9.38, p < .003$), but no age deficits on the problem/solution passages ($F1,70 = .04, p < .86$) nor on the culturally salient comparison passages ($F1,70 = 2.29, p < .14$). There was also a statistically significant interaction between set of passages and group ($F4,138 = 3.2, p < .02$); although the Strategy group showed superiority on all sets of passages the group effect was particularly strong for the culturally salient comparison passages. There was a significant interaction among passage set, group, and age ($F4,138 = 2.9, p < .03$). This interaction resulted from the old and young adults in the Strategy group performing at the same level on the problem/solution and comparison sets of passages and the young adults in this group showing superior recall over the old adults on the culturally salient comparison set; in contrast, for the Practice and Control groups the biggest age differences were found on the comparison (railroad/ China/Africa) set. Although the sets of passages interacted with age and condition, consistency was found for the basic findings of time (problem/solution: $F2,69 = 36.14$, $p < .00001$; comparison: $F2,69 = 20.65$, $p < .00001$; culturally salient comparison: $F2,69 = 28.59$. $p < .00001$) and the group by time interaction (problem/solution: $F4,138 = 3.61$, $p < .008$; comparison: $F4,138 = 2.78$, $p < .032$; culturally salient comparison: $F4,138 = 4.98$, $p < .0009$). When the sets of passages were analyzed separately these were the only statistically significant main effects of interactions other than the age effect for the comparison set. Thus, for all passages examined practice with the reading and recall task increased recall, but instruction with the plan strategy was even more beneficial.

In order to see if improvement in recall from the pretests to the posttests was only a function of subjects realizing the difficulty of the recall task and slowing down their reading speed, a four factor analysis of variance (group, age, passage set, and time) was conducted on the number of words in each passage divided by the time subjects took to read the passage. Significant main effects were age ($F1,66 = 1070.55$, $p < .00001$—reduction in N due to missing reading time data for some subjects) and set of passages ($F2,65 = 5.33$, $p < .0072$). Young adults read the passages at an average rate of 136 wpm, while old adults read at 98 wpm. These findings are of interest in terms of the view that there is a general slowing with aging (Birren, 1974; Salthouse, 1982). Also, the results are consistent with a review by Meyer and Rice (1988) that showed age deficits in prose recall at presentation rates of 120 wpm or faster, but not at slower rates. The problem/solution (117 wpm) and comparison (118 wpm) texts were read at similar rates, but the culturally salient comparison text was read slower (103 wpm).

There was a trend for the subjects in the Practice group to read at a slower pace than those in the Strategy and Control groups ($F2,66 = 2.40$, $p < .0982$). Statistical significance was not found for time ($F2,65 = 1.20$) nor time by group ($F4,130 = .11$). Thus, the improved recall with instruction of the Strategy group appears to be due to a more efficient reading strategy not simply to slowing down their reading speed from the pretest to posttests.

As stated above the age by time by group interaction was not statistically significant. Contrary to predictions, the young adults in the Strategy group benefited as much from the training as the old group. In fact, as seen in Table 4.7 and Fig. 4.1 the pretest performance of the young adults in the Strategy group was at approximately the same low level as the old group prior to instruction; then both groups made equivalent and substantial gains with instruction. Thus, the initial age deficits expected on the pretest between the old and young adults in the Strategy group were not found. This could have resulted from removing subjects who exhibited mastery of the strategy on the pretest from the analyses since more young adults exhibited mastery than old adults.

To investigate this issue a three factor analysis of variance on centered scores was conducted for all subjects participating in the study (mastery and nonmastery on the pretest) who were young or old adults in the Strategy group or young adults in the Control group. Only the data from the problem/solution and comparison passages were analyzed. Significant findings were time (F2,47 = 37.15, $p < .00001$), passage by group (F2,48 = 7.24, $p < .0018$), and time by group (F4,96 = 3.51, $p < .0103$). These same findings held up when all (mastery and unmastered) of the young adults in the Strategy and Control groups were compared to the unmastered old adults in the Strategy group. As seen in the previous analyses concerning the time factor, recall was superior on the posttests. The passage by group interaction resulted from the superior performance of the old and young adults in the Strategy group on the problem/solution passages over the young adults in the Control group, while the young adults in the Control group were much superior to the other groups on the comparison passages. However, the finding of interest in this analysis is the interaction between time and group. As seen in Table 4.8 both the young and old adults in the Strategy group were inferior to the young adults in the Control group on the pretest. Tukey multiple comparison tests showed the young adults in the Control group to differ significantly from the other two groups at the .005 level with no significant difference between the two age groups in the Strategy group. On the first posttest differences among the three groups were eliminated. However, on the second posttest the old adults in the Strategy group surpassed the young adults in the Control group ($p < .05$); young adults in the Strategy group nearly surpassed young adults in the Control group ($p < .10$) and were equivalent to old adults who received the same instruction. Thus, the young adults in the Strategy group were as deficient in recall when compared to the young adults in the Control group as the old adults. Instruction with the strategy eliminated the deficiency

TABLE 4.8
Means and Standard Deviations on Centered Scores for
Problem/Solution and Comparison Texts Acquired
by Old and Young Adults in the Strategy Group and
Young Adults in the Control Group on Pretest, Post-
test 1, and Posttest 2

Time	Strategy Old	Strategy Young	Control Young
Pretest			
M	−7.43	−5.82	4.80
S.D.	(14.4)	(15.87)	(18.01)
Posttest 1			
M	10.28	11.38	12.35
S.D.	(14.74	(19.60)	(22.75)
Posttest 2			
M	11.29	7.18	6.64
S.D.	(19.50)	(17.15)	(20.36)

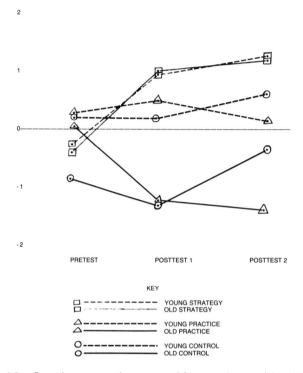

FIG. 4.3. Questions correctly answered (centered scores) by old and young adults in the strategy, practice, and control groups after reading the problem/solution passages at the three testing times.

from both age groups and even enabled the old adults to surpass the young adults in the Control group on the delayed test. Thus, the age by group by time interaction that was expected did not occur since initially the young adults in the Strategy group were as deficient in recall as the old adults. If the young adults in the Strategy group had been more like those in the Control group the expected interaction may have been found. In any event, instruction with the strategy brought the performance of the old adults at least up to the level of young adults in the Control group. Additionally, older adults were shown to learn as readily from the instruction as young adults. In fact, multiple regressions aimed at determining what subject characteristics (e.g., age, vocabulary, education, etc.) predicted the largest improvements after instruction with the plan strategy attributed no significant predictors. Thus, the instruction with the strategy appeared to be equally helpful for all ages and ability levels of subjects.

Number of Questions Correctly Answered.   After reading the problem/solution texts the subjects answered the same four questions worth a total of eight points. These questions were more easily answered from the passage about trusts (4.60) than from the passages on reactors (3.85) or schizophrenia (3.84); as a result, centered scores were used in a three factor (group, age, time—pretest, posttest 1, posttest 2) analysis of variance with repeated measures on time. A significant effect of age was revealed (F1,73 = 4.47, *p* < .04) because young subjects scored higher than the old. More importantly, a significant interaction of group with test time was present (F4,146 = 5.30, *p* = .005). This interaction is shown in Fig. 4.3. Analyses of the simple effects of group at each test time separately showed that the groups did not differ at the pretest (F2,73 = .53), but did differ at posttest 1 (F2,73 = 4.39, *p* < .02) and at posttest 2 (F2,73 = 5.79, *p* < .005). At each of the posttests, Tukey multiple comparisons of the three group means showed that the Strategy group scored significantly higher than the Control and Practice groups, whose scores did not differ. Again the expected age by group by time interaction was not found because the young adults in the Strategy group performed more like the old adults on the pretest and made equivalent and substantial gains with the training to those of the old adults. Although there were age deficits an examination of Fig. 4.3 shows that the old adults in the Strategy group performed better than the young adults in the Practice and Control groups on the two posttests.

DID TRAINING CHANGE THE TYPE OF INFORMATION REMEMBERED OR THOUGHT TO BE IMPORTANT?

In this section we examine the effects of training on the type of information remembered or appraised as important. We wanted to know if learning the plan strategy changed not only how much information people could remember, but also whether or not it changed the type of information people thought was important to remember.

Type of Information Recalled.   The idea units from the problem/solution and comparison texts were divided in half based on their position in the hierarchical content structures for the passages (Meyer, 1975, 1985a). A five factor analysis of variance was conducted on the proportion of idea units recalled from high and low in the content structures of the passages. The factors were group (Strategy, Practice, and Control), age (old and young), passage set (problem/solution and comparison), time (pretest, posttest 1, and posttest 2), and level (high and low in the content structure) with repeated measures on the last three factors. Significant main effects were passage set (F1,69 = 382.81, *p* < .00001), time (F2,68 = 21.32, *p* < .00001), and level (F1,69 = 155.20, *p* < .00001); proportion of ideas recalled was greater for the comparison texts (.32 versus .17), for the posttests (.27 versus .20), and for high level ideas (.28 versus .20). Significant interactions included group by time ($F4,136 = 3.24$, $p < .0143$), group by age ($F2,69 = 3.25$, $p < .0450$), group by level ($F2,69 = 4.76$, $p < .0116$), time by level ($F2,68 = 3.62$, $p < .0321$), passage set by level ($F1,69 = 15.15$, $p < .0002$), and passage set by level by time ($F2,68 = 6.87$, $p < .0019$). The first interaction resulted from slightly poorer performance of the Strategy group on the pretest and substantially superior performance on the posttests. The group by age interaction reflected the fact that summed over testing times the young adults in the Strategy group performed worse than the young adults in the other groups, while the old adults in the Plan group performed better than the old adults in the other groups. The group by level interaction resulted from a greater levels effect (10% difference in recall of high and low information) shown by the Strategy group than the other two groups (7% difference). The three groups performed at similar levels on the low level information, but the Strategy group recalled more high level ideas. The time by level interaction reflects a greater levels effects after the pretest; there was a 6% difference in recall of high and low information on the pretest, while there was a 10% differences on both posttests. The passage set by level by time interaction showed that this increase in the levels effect from pretest to posttests was due to large increases on the problem/solution set with time, not the comparison set. The passage set by level interaction indicated that there was a greater levels effect (11% difference between high–low ideas) on the problem/solution set, than the comparison set (6%). An expected group by time by level interaction was not statistically significant ($F4,136 = 1.25$) nor was this interaction with the addition of age ($F4,136 = .86$). Thus, it appears the age groups showed similar effects of training and similar level effects. The level by group interaction showed that the Strategy group was recalling more main ideas than the other two groups.

Two sets of delayed recall protocols were collected. They were collected primarily because Hultsch, Hertzog, and Dixon (1984) and Meyer and Rice (1988) found greater age deficits for old adults after a delay; however, these findings were with old adults scoring very high on vocabulary or ability measures, while the subjects in the present study scored in the average to high average range. Thus, the 2 week delayed recall for the problem/solution passages and the 30 min delayed recall for the comparison passages were collected to see if greater age deficits occurred with increased distance from presentation time. These comparisons were examined separately for each passage in terms of recall of high and low level information.

A four factor analysis of variance (group, age, time—posttest 1 immediate recall or posttest 2 2 week delayed recall, and level) was calculated, with repeated measures on time and level, for the problem/solution texts. All main effects were statistically significant (group: $F2,73 = 3.46$, $p < .00001$; age: $F1,73 = 5.67$; $p < .0199$; time: $F1,73 = 129.16$, $p < .00001$; level: $F1,73 = 108.93$, $p < .00001$). Greater proportions of ideas were remembered by the Strategy group

(.16 versus .11 for the Control and .13 for the Practice groups), by the young adults (.15 versus .11), for the immediate recall test (.19 versus .08), and from high in the structure (.18 versus .09). The only significant interactions were between level and age ($F1,73 = 8.22$, $p < .0054$) and between time and level ($F1,73 = 29.71$, $p < .00001$). Young adults recalled more main ideas than old adults (.21 versus .16), while they recalled nearly equivalent proportions of details (.09 versus .08). These findings are compatible with findings of the lower verbal adults in the study by Dixon, Hultsch, Simon, and von Eye (1984). The time by level interaction resulted from a larger levels effects (8%, .20 high–.12 low) immediately after reading the text than two weeks later (3%, .06 high–.03 low). There was no evidence for greater age deficits over time.

A five factor analysis of variance was conducted for the immediate and 30 min delayed recall of the comparison texts; the factors were group, age, delay interval (immediate versus 30 min delayed recall), time (pretest, posttest 1, posttest 2), and level. Again, no support was found for greater age deficits over time. Significant main effects and interactions included age ($F1,61 = 5.53$, $p < .0219$ with young performing better), delay interval ($F1,61 = 55.19$, $p < .00001$ with superior immediate recall), time ($F2,60 = 5.75$, $p < .0052$ with the posttests superior to pretests), level ($F1,61 = 46.22$, $p < .00001$ with high ideas recalled better), delay interval by time by condition interaction ($F4,120 = 2.90$, $p < .025$ where the Strategy group showed the largest pretest to posttest gains for the immediate rather than delayed recall test and the other groups small, but similar gains at both delay intervals), and a five factor interaction ($F4,120 = 3.33$, $p < .0126$ which appears uninterpretable).

Type of Question Answered Correctly.   On the second posttest subjects read the parakeet text (Meyer, 1975) and answered short answer questions coming from high (13 points) and low (13 points) in the content structure of the passage. These data are summarized in Table 4.9. A three factor (group, age, level) analysis of variance with repeated measures on level was conducted. Significant effects and interactions included age ($F1,73 = 6.06$, $p < .02$), level ($F1,73 = 133.25$, $p < .00001$), and level by age ($F1,73 = 7.81$, $p < .007$). An expected level by group by age interaction was not found ($F2,73 = 2.04$, $p < .1380$) although as seen in Table 4.9 the old adults in the Strategy group look more like the young adults than old adults in the other groups. The parakeet text is descriptive with little signaling; thus, with this less organized text little effects from training are seen. In addition, the superior performance on detail questions by old adults found by Meyer and Rice (1981) with these questions answered by high verbal adults were not found by this sample of average verbal adults. The level by age interaction indicated that a larger levels effect was found for young adults than old adults on these questions; young and old adults correctly answered about the same number of detail questions, but young adults answered more main idea questions correctly.

TABLE 4.9
Number of Questions From High and Low in the Content Structure
Answered Correctly by the Strategy, Practice, and Control Groups
After Reading the Parakeet Passage

Age	Group		Type of Questions	
			High Level	Low Level
Old	Strategy	M	10.00	6.36
		S.D.	(1.97)	(2.50)
	Practice	M	8.23	5.54
		S.D.	(3.37)	(2.50)
	Control	M	8.56	6.22
		S.D.	(3.15)	(3.25)
Young	Strategy	M	10.89	7.22
		S.D.	(2.47)	(3.11)
	Practice	M	11.50	5.50
		S.D.	(1.37)	(3.15)
	Control	M	11.50	7.00
		S.D.	(1.62)	(3.38)

Type of Information Selected as Most Important.   Subjects underlined the 10 most important things to remember from the problem/solution texts. The percentage of a subject's underlining that came from high in the content structure of the texts was analyzed with a three factor analysis of variance (group, age, time). The only statistically significant finding was a time by group interaction ($F2,71 = 4.04$, $p < .0219$). The Practice (61%) and Control (61%) group tended to underline more main ideas on the pretest than the Strategy group (59%), while this was reversed on the posttest (66%, 58%, and 58% for the Strategy, Practice and Control groups, respectively). Thus, on the underlining task there was evidence that training with the plan strategy resulted in changes in the type of information readers believed to be important to remember. After training they placed more emphasis on main ideas and less on details; this is a strategy evident for more expert, highly verbal readers (Meyer, 1984; Rice & Meyer, 1985).

To further explore these changes of emphasis, the number of items high in the structure that were underlined by subjects were analyzed as a percentage of the total high items in the passages. In light of the previous analysis, it was most interesting to find no main effects of group nor age nor time, and no significant interactions of any of these variables. Another analysis using the same three factors was then done on the percentage of all low level items that subjects underlined. Again, no main effects were observed, but the interaction of group with test time was significant ($F4,138 = 3.36$, $p < .02$). Analysis of simple effects showed no group differences on the pretest or final posttest, but on posttest 1 they did differ ($F2,69 = 3.8$, $p < .03$). The Practice group on posttest 1 showed a large increase in the percentage of low level items they considered important (up 13%), while the other groups showed no such increase.

Subjects were also asked to select the most important items from a passage about supertankers (Meyer, 1985a; Meyer et al., 1980) that they read on the second posttest. The percentage of items they underlined, which were actually high in the content structure, was analyzed with a group by age ANOVA. The main effect of group was the only significant finding ($F2,68 = 4.66, p < .02$): Tukey multiple comparisons among the groups revealed that the Strategy group differed significantly from the Practice group (74% and 61%, respectively). The Control group (scoring between the other two at 69%) did not differ from either of the other two groups.

As with the other problem/solution set of passages, these data were re-analyzed as a percentage of all the items high in the structure. Again, no effects of group or age were significant. The same type of analysis on the percentage of all low items underlined showed a main effect of group ($F2,68 = 4.36, p < .02$) which was due to a significant difference between the Strategy and Practice groups (21% and 34%, respectively). The Control group (24%) did not differ significantly from the other two.

These findings from the underlining tasks taken as a whole lead to an interesting conclusion. Subjects in the Strategy group became somewhat better after training at rejecting details as unimportant, while subjects in the Practice group tended to do the opposite and see the details as more important after their training.

Two questions on a questionnaire administered on posttest 2 relate to this issue of changes in the type of information subjects' sought to remember after training. These questions and corresponding data are displayed in Table 4.10. As seen in the table, the old and young adults in the Strategy group as well as the

TABLE 4.10
Responses of Old and Young Adults in the Strategy, Practice, and Control Groups to Questions About Observing Differences in the Types of Information They Remember Since the Pretest

	Strategy		Practice		Control	
	Old	Young	Old	Young	Old	Young
Do you feel that you remember different kinds of information from your reading in our testing sessions than you did the first time we met?						
Yes	16	8	5	5	6	3
No	2	1	5	1	8	7

$$\chi^2 = 16.85, \text{ d.f. } = 5, p < .01.$$

	Strategy		Practice		Control	
Do you feel that you remember different kinds of information from your reading in everyday life than you did before you volunteered for this project?						
Yes	17	7	3	5	6	0
No	3	2	7	1	9	12

$$\chi^2 = 29.32, \text{ d.f. } = 5, p < .001.$$

young adults in the Practice group felt that there was a change in the type of information they remembered from the pretest to the posttests. In contrast, the old and young adults in the Control group did not observe any change. The old Practice group did not differ significantly from the old Strategy group (chi-square = 3.32, d.f. = 1, $p < .1$) nor from the old Control group (chi-square = .01, d.f. = 1, n.s.). The old and young adults in the Strategy group did not differ significantly from each other in the type of information stated to vary from pretest to posttests (chi-square = 2.33, d.f. = 3). Of the 22 responses from the old and young adults in the Strategy group that explained the differences observed 45% said they now found problems and solutions or other structures, 27% said they now recalled details, 14% said they recalled the important information, and another 14% listed an assortment of other things.

In response to the second question about changes observed in their everyday reading, group differences also were found. The old adults in the Strategy group and the young adults in both the Strategy and Practice groups felt that they remembered different kinds of information from their everyday reading after completion of the project than they did before it; however, this was not the case for the other three groups. The three groups that reported changes did not differ in the kinds of information that changed (chi-square = 8.89, d.f. = 10). Of the 29 responses from these subjects 45% reported that this different information remembered in everyday life was connecting information, conclusions or the important rather than trivia. This change in information remembered was identified as facts by 14%. It was characterized as scientific information by 7%. Seventeen percent listed assorted types of information and the final 17% listed that they simply recalled more information. Thus, the questionnaire data indicated some changes in the type of information remembered by adults in the Strategy group.

DID TRAINING AFFECT OTHER MEASURES OF READING COMPETENCY OR ENJOYMENT?

Although we expected the training to influence use of the strategy and free recall, we also administered measures to test for unexpected outcomes of the training. These measures included performance on a standardized reading comprehension test, parts of another reading test, recognition of topics read, ability to answer thought questions, and a questionnaire about interest and enjoyment of reading.

Reading Tests. The Metropolitan Survey Battery in Reading is a timed multiple choice test. A three factor (group, age, and time) analysis of variance was conducted on standard scores obtained by the subjects on the pretest and posttest 1. The only statistically significant finding from this analysis was an age effect ($F1,74 = 11.29; p < .0012$). Young adults (893.6) performed better than old adults (833.9). There was a trend for improvement from pretest to posttest

(F1,74 = 3.32, p < .0724). Although the old Strategy group showed over two times the improvement of the other groups, this difference was not significant. Thus, training effects were not found on this timed standardized test with multiple choice questions. The same findings held for the questions selected from the Davis Reading Test that we thought measured sensitivity to the author's structure; our forms turned out to vary significantly so centered scores were used in the analysis. The only significant effect was age (F1,73 = 4.45, p < .0384). Thus, age deficits and no training effects were also found for these multiple choice questions.

Thought Questions.   Problem solving thought questions were designed for four texts read with problem/solution structures. Eight points were possible on the task. Although the Strategy group performed slightly better (5.9 versus 4.5 for the Control and 4.6 for the Practice groups), the differences were not statistically significant (F2,73 = 2.22, p < .1155). Age deficits were almost significant (F2,73 = 3.94, p < .051). Thus, training effects were not found for the thought questions.

Recognition of Topics Read.   On the final posttest, subjects were given a list of 24 topics, 12 of which they had read as a passage at some point in the testing sessions, and were asked to circle those they recognized. The number of topics correctly recognized was analyzed with a two factor ANOVA (group by age) and a significant age effect resulted (F1,73 = 8.53, p < .005). Young subjects correctly identified more topics than old subjects (10.8 and 9.2, respectively). Then, a second analysis with the same factors was conducted on the number of false alarms subjects made (circling a topic which was not one that was read). A significant age effect in this analysis (F1,73 = 4.96, p < .03) indicated that older subjects were responding somewhat more conservatively, committing less false alarms (.50) than the young subjects (.93). In light of this, each subjects' proportion correct and proportion of false alarms were reinterpreted as d-prime (a measure of sensitivity) and beta (a measure of conservation in response criterion) according to signal detection theory (Pastore & Scheirer, 1974). Analysis of d-prime with two factors (group and age) showed no main effects or interactions, demonstrating that old and young subjects were equally adept at recognizing previously encountered topics. Differences in the strictness of their recognition criterion was evident by a main effect of age on beta (F1,73 = 7.14, p < .01). Older subjects recognized fewer topics correctly because they were less willing to make false alarms, reflected in their higher criterion (6.01 versus 3.05 for young subjects). Others have also found greater cautiousness (Botwinick, 1959; Okun, 1976; Zabrucky, Moore, & Schultz, 1987) or less risk taking with increasing age (Okun & Elias, 1977; Reese & Rodeheaver, 1985).

Questions About Reading.   Five questions administered on the last posttest queried any observed changes in reading, memory from reading, and interest

TABLE 4.11
Questions About Changes in Reading, Memory From Reading, and
Reading Interest and Enjoyment Answered by Old and Young
Adults in the Strategy, Practice, and Control Groups Two
Weeks After Instruction

	Strategy		Practice		Control	
	Old	Young	Old	Young	Old	Young
Have you been reading more since you began working with us?						
Yes	5	3	3	3	0	2
No	14	6	10	3	17	10
Chi-square = 8.86, d.f. = 5, n.s.						
Do you feel that you remember more from your reading in our testing sessions than you did the first time we met?						
Yes	18	9	8	4	5	6
Probably/ slightly	2	0	2	2	4	0
No	1	0	2	0	7	6
Chi-square = 27.48, d.f. = 10, $p < .01$.						
Do you feel that you remember more from your reading in everyday life than you did before you volunteered for this project?						
Yes	16	7	4	3	4	1
Somewhat	4	0	3	3	3	1
No	2	2	5	0	8	10
Chi-square = 32.71, d.f. = 10, $p < .001$.						
Has your interest in reading increased since you began this project?						
Yes	13	3	4	3	3	4
No	7	6	8	3	13	8
Chi-square = 9.08, d.f. = 5, n.s.						
Has your enjoyment of reading increased since you began this project?						
Yes	17	7	4	3	5	4
No	2	3	8	3	11	8
Chi-square = 18.11, d.f. = 5, $p < .01$.						

and enjoyment of reading. These questions and their corresponding data are
found in Table 4.11. With regard to the first question, training did not appear to
have increased their reading outside the classroom. In response to the second
question, nearly all of the adults in the Strategy and Practice groups felt that they
could remember more in the latter testing sessions than they did on the pretest.
However, only about half of the adults in the Control group thought they had
improved, while the other half reported no improvement. There were no signifi-

cant differences in appraisal of improvement in the testing sessions between the Strategy group and the Practice group (chi-square = 7.53, d.f. = 6, n.s.). In addition, as noted in the next question listed in Table 4.11, the old and young adults in the Strategy group noted more reading improvement in their everyday lives than did subjects in the other groups.

The only statistically significant data dealing with changes in interest in reading were between the old adults in the Strategy group and the old adults in the Control group. Those in Strategy group claimed that their interest in reading had increased, while those in the Control group claimed no such increase (chi-square = 8.28, d.f. = 2, $p < .02$). Both old and young adults in the Strategy group claimed that their enjoyment of reading had increased since they began the project, while this was not the case for the adults in the other two groups.

Thus, the Strategy and Practice subjects felt that the training had improved their memory for recalling text in the laboratory. However, only the Plan group reported corresponding memory improvement in everyday life, increased interest in reading, and more enjoyment of reading.

CASE STUDIES OF ONE YOUNG AND ONE OLDER ADULT

Briefly, we examine the progress of one young adult and one old adult from the Strategy group. Table 4.12 describes the characteristics of these two learners.

First, we look at the progress of the young adult who we call Jennifer. On the pretest Jennifer did not use problem/solution nor comparison top-level structures to organize any of her four recalls; however, she could use the easier descriptive top-level structure on the practice passage. On the pretest she recalled an average of 10% of the idea units from the passages and answered 38% of the questions correctly. On the first posttest Jennifer used the top-level structures of the texts in all of her recalls, recalled an average of 27% of the idea units, and answered 75% of the questions correctly. Two weeks after instruction Jennifer again used the top-level structure for all recalls, recalled 23% of the idea units, and answered 100% of the questions correctly. On the passage sorting tasks 2 weeks after instruction, Jennifer correctly sorted into the five basic plans 17 out

TABLE 4.12
Characteristics of One Young and Old Adult in the Strategy Group

| | Age | Vocabulary Quick WAIS | | | Education | Metropolitan Survey Reading Advanced 2 | |
		raw	scaled			% Rank (grade 12)	Instructional Reading Level
young	22	38%	42	10	13	48	11+
old	69	43%	55	13	15	36	9 - 10

of 17 selections taken from magazines, newspapers, and the Bible. The amount of information she could remember more than doubled on the free recall task. This increase in the amount of information remembered from texts also showed comparable increases on questions answered. The improvement was maintained at the delayed testing session two weeks after completion of instruction. In addition, a 6% increase in percentile rank on the Metropolitan Reading Test was found in comparing her pretest and posttest performance.

We also examine changes in Jennifer's performance on the problem/solution set of passages. On the pretest she read the reactor passage; in this passage problems (the need to generate electrical power, the need to clean up pollution, and finite reserves) were discussed and fast breeder reactors presented as the solution and then described. Jennifer's recall simply lists some ideas from the passage and misses the plan as can be seen below.

> Breeder reactors are the fast growing idea of how to carry feul [sic]. It was talking about how important gas is becoming because we are getting low on it.

Compare that recall to her recall of the other problem/solutions texts after instruction.

> *Posttest 1:* Schizophenic [sic] is a problem to physchitrists [sic] and they need to change it with the possible solution being that they use anti-s-proteins. These help the brain calm down after a crisis. They keep a people in a normal state of mind. It can help the Schizophenic [sic] stop seeing allussions [sic] and bring him out of his fanisy [sic] world. *Posttest 2:* There has been a problem about how to divide the money up when a person dies without having a will.
>
> If you go to probate court to try to settle it. It might take up to 6 years to get your money plus all the court costs.
>
> A solution to this problem is to make a trust. This is a substitute for a will. It avoids going to court. Trusts can never die. The trustor can divide up his money the way he wants and it will stay that way unless he changes his mind.

The same changes in her approach to reading and remembering texts can be seen by looking at her recall of both sets of comparison passages. By the end of the instruction Jennifer became very proficient at using the plan strategy and recalled 68% of the idea units from the comparison passage on the topic of railroads.

In summary, Jennifer mastered this strategy for utilizing the structure in text and showed dramatic increases in her memory of what she read. By the end of the third session Jennifer appeared to have acquired that strategy; in the last two sessions she refined it using it with less signaling and more muddled texts. When asked which plans were hardest and easiest for her, she explained that they were all easy and that once you catch on you can see the signaling words. In evaluating changes in reading over the program, Jennifer said the following: "I feel I remember more and think more about what I'm reading. I try to figure out the plan and the main idea sentence in the testing sessions and in everyday reading. I like reading more than before the sessions and I read more magazines.''

Next, we look briefly at the performance of an older adult in the Strategy group who we call Christina. Like the young adult, simply learning the definitions of the plans was not sufficient. The last three sessions were necessary to model and practice how to use the plan to search memory and write about or tell what was remembered. By the beginning of the fourth session Christina had mastered description and sequence, but still needed work on causation, problem/solution, and comparison. By the end of that session she had also mastered causation and problem/solution, but still needed to work on comparison. By the end of the final session she showed mastery of all five plans. After instruction she sorted 12 out of 17 passages correctly into the five plans. On the pretest she used the plan strategy on none of the problem/solution or comparison text, but could use it on the descriptive practice text; on the two posttests she used the plan on all of the texts. Her performance of the Metropolitan Reading Test went up 2% after the instruction. Christina's recall and response to questions improved. For example, her recall on the pretest of the comparison text completely missed the comparison and yielded recall of 16% of the idea units, while posttest recall employing the strategy was up to 59%.

Christina reported that her memory was much better after the program and that she was enjoying reading more and looking for problem/solutions in everything she read. In addition, she stated, ''I believe that this memory improvement program is very valuable to the older person. It makes you more aware of details of what you are reading. Your recall is stimulated by using the methods given in this program. I feel that a little longer period or more classes would have been helpful.'' When the program was offered to the control group after the conclusion of the experiment, Christina volunteered to go through the program a second time.

5 Discussion of the Findings

EVALUATION OF TRAINING WITH THE STRUCTURE STRATEGY

In evaluating the training program we consider three factors (Willis, 1985). First, the size or magnitude of the effect will be examined. Second, consideration is given to any differential patterns in transfer of training across near and far transfer tasks. Third, maintenance of the training over time is discussed.

Magnitude of Effects. The converging evidence from the various tasks examining the ability to use the plan strategy clearly point out that the subjects in the Strategy group learned this strategy. For example, on the problem/solution texts the subjects rose from 0% using the strategy on the pretest to 90% to 100% using it on the posttests. The magnitude of change was not as great on the comparison texts, but it was still substantial. On the comparison texts recalled 30 min after reading, use of the strategy rose from 33% on the pretest to 95% to 100% on the posttests. In addition, on the culturally salient comparison texts use of the top-level structure in text to organize recall rose from 57% to 70% on the pretest to 95% to 100% for the two age groups of adults in the Strategy group. These greater effects on the problem/solution passages were surprising since the comparison structure was thought to be a more difficult structure (Meyer & Freedle, 1984). Hiebert, Englert, and Brennan (1983) found the comparison structure more difficult for college students than structures of sequence, enumeration (listing), or description; however, they did not examine problem/solution structures. The greater length and difficulty of the problem/solution materials may account for the poorer performance on the pretest and availability for enormous improvement on the posttest.

Also, the Strategy group was superior to the other groups in describing the structure of texts and sorting them according to structure. Evidence from the questionnaire data indicated that the Strategy group increased their knowledge or metacognition (Flavell, 1981) about the plan strategy through the instruction. Members of the Strategy group reached stage six in the six operational levels of using the plan strategy that are depicted in Fig. 5.1. In summary, instruction with the plan strategy did significantly and dramatically increase the use of this strategy by both young and old adults deficient in the use of this strategy prior to instruction.

Instruction with the plan strategy substantially increased the amount of information remembered after reading. Merely giving subjects practice taking the pretest improved free recall performance in the order of .24 to .37 standard deviations. However, this was not due to greater naivete of elderly subjects (Willis, 1985), since the young adults improved as much as the old adults. Practice and perhaps the opportunity for cooperative learning experiences (Larson & Dansereau, 1986) for the Practice group improved their free recall performance in the order of .44 to .63 standard deviations, although differences in gains between the Practice and Control were not significantly different. The effect of practice is not negligible in improving free recall and no doubt the practice component of instruction with the plan strategy contributed to its success, but opportunity for practice alone does not show the dramatic improvement of instruction with the plan strategy. The magnitude of gain in free recall with the plan strategy was in the order of .83 to 1.28 standard deviations. In terms of being able to correctly answer main idea questions, the adults who learned the

Stage 1:   Readers do not use any systematic form of organization in retelling what they have read.

Stage 2:   Readers use different organization without knowing what they have done.

Stage 3:   Readers use the same organization as in the text without knowing what they have done.

Stage 4:   Readers use a different organization thinking it to be the same as that of the text.

Stage 5:   Readers use the same organization as in the text, and know that they have done so.

Stage 6:   Readers consistently use the same organization as in the text, and know that they have done so; or consciously decide not to apply the strategy.

FIG. 5.1.   Six operational levels of using text structure with the plan strategy.

plan strategy clearly outperformed the adults in the other two groups without instruction about the strategy.

There was no evidence to support a slowing in reading speed with instruction in the plan strategy. The only trend for slowing was for the Practice group. Thus, the plan strategy appeared to increase efficiency in reading and remembering text.

Instruction with the plan strategy appeared to cause a shift in subjects' strategies for evaluating the type of information thought to be important to remember. The plan strategy gives a learner a criteria for evaluating the importance of ideas in a text to the overall message of the author. As a result, adults who received this instruction recalled more main ideas and rejected details as important for identification as critical information. Adults in the Strategy group explained that they remembered different types of information after training; they characterized this information as connecting information, conclusions, and important information rather than trivia. In addition, subjects who received instruction about the plan strategy claimed improved reading strategies, superior memory for their reading in the laboratory and everyday life, and increased interest in and enjoyment of reading.

Transfer of Training. On the passages used in instruction and also in the testing sessions the Strategy group showed their greater ability to use the plan strategy over the other groups. In addition, this superiority was evident on the problem/solution texts whose structure came from an article in *Scientific American* magazine. Thus, the adults in the Strategy group could transfer their training to this set of passages that proved to have the most difficult structure to utilize. The Strategy group also transferred the strategy to comparison texts taken from 9th grade social studies books as well as to the experimenter contrived texts with the culturally salient comparison structures. The Strategy group was the only group to make significant pretest to posttest gains on these comparison passages, but their superiority to the other groups was less dramatic on these passages since all subjects tended to find it easier to use the comparison structures to organize their recalls than the problem/solution structure. Transfer of the strategy also was clearly evident in the Strategy group's ability to correctly sort 17 texts taken from everyday reading materials (e.g., *Better Homes & Gardens, U.S. News and World Report, Bible*) according to their top-level structure.

Thus, mastery of the strategy enabled the adults to identify the top-level structure or plan of materials they read and to use these structures to organize their own recall of the information in the reading materials. In addition, it enabled them to recall more information from their reading as well as answer more main idea questions involving problems, solutions, causes, and reasons. Facilitation in recall appeared to be due primarily to the subjects' greater recall of main ideas, rather than details. The facilitation of the strategy for free and cued recall was found for passages organized with problem/solution and comparison structures where these structures were well signaled. Facilitation on questions correctly answered did not appear to transfer to a loosely organized descriptive text with little signaling (the parakeet text). In addition, the strategy did not significantly increase scores on a standardized reading comprehension test, thought questions, nor recognition of topics read.

The plan strategy is thought to be an encoding and retrieval strategy; it gives learners a systematic way of identifying the main ideas in text and provides them with an organized approach to search memory for the information stored about a passage. The reading test and topic recognition tasks both involved recognition rather than recall, the strength of the strategy. The reading test was multiple choice and readers could go back and search a reading selection for the correct answer; the answers involved information taken directly from the texts. Thus, it is not surprising that the mastery of the strategy did not facilitate performance on these recognition measures. It was hoped that instruction with the strategy would aid people in their ability to read a new problem and solve it with knowledge gained from their reading; these thought questions occurred on the second post-test and required memory of the texts read over all the testing conditions spread over the duration of a month. Perhaps a task requiring memory over less time would have been a better test of far transfer to thought questions.

Maintenance Over Time.   On all measures of use of structure, recall, and response to questions there were no declines in the Strategy group's performance from the posttest given 2 days after to instruction to that given 2 weeks after instruction. Thus, gains made through instruction were maintained over time. Also, gains made through practice taking the pretest by the Control group were not added to by practice taking the first posttest. Evidently, facilitation came from the initial opportunity to become familiar with the procedures and require-ments of the recall tasks.

A strong case for the lasting effect of the training comes from the delayed recall of the problem/solution texts. After reading and recalling a text from this set 2 days after instruction, the subjects recalled this passage again 2 weeks later at posttest 2. Eighty-seven percent of the adults in the Strategy group used the plan strategy as evidenced by the problem/solution structure used to organize their recalls; however, only 17% of the adults in the Practice and Control groups used the problem/solution structure to organize their recalls. Thus, instruction helped the Strategy group use the plan strategy to remember what they read weeks before; this was the aim of the instruction, to give people a strategy to remember what they read. Not only did the Strategy group show vast superiority in their use of the strategy to organize recall, but the amount of information they could recall was substantially greater.

AGE EFFECTS

On the pretest there were age deficits in use of the plan strategy to organize recall. These data are compatible with the findings in the literature (Meyer, 1987; Meyer & Rice, 1988) that average verbal old adults are deficient in their use of the top-level structure in text. On the pretest only 12% of the old adults consistently used the top-level structure in text to organize their four recalls from problem/solution and comparison texts, while 33% of young adults used the structure. When these subjects exhibiting mastery were excluded from subsequent analyses, no further age deficits between the young and old adults in any of the three groups were noted. The old adults in the Strategy group increased their use of text structure after instruction as much as the young adults in this group.

There were age deficits found on the passage sorting task. The young adults in all of the groups outperformed the old adults. However, the old adults who received instruction with the strategy performed slightly better than the young adults in the groups without this instruction.

On the free recall tasks there were no age deficits on the problem/solution and culturally salient comparison sets of texts, but there were age deficits on the comparison texts. The two comparison texts were approximately the same length, but perhaps the old adults had more prior knowledge (Hultsch & Dixon, 1983) about the topics in the culturally salient texts; all age groups read these texts on creation versus evolution at a slower rate than the other texts. The literature (Meyer, 1987) indicates that age deficits are less likely to occur from longer than shorter texts; perhaps this factor contributed to the lack of age deficits on the longer and more difficult problem/solution texts. Both age groups recalled 16% of the ideas from the problem/solution texts, while their recall was 36% and 29% for the young and old groups, respectively, on the comparison texts.

There were age deficits on the number of questions which could be correctly answered, both short answer and multiple choice on the standardized reading tests. However, if the performance of the old adults in the Strategy group is examined after instruction substantial gains can be found. In fact, on the questions from the problem/solution texts the performance of the old adults in the Strategy group is well above that for the young adults in the other groups. However, in the free recall data and question data the age by group by time interaction was never significant. This appears to be due to parallel gains made by the young adults in the Strategy group whose pretest performance frequently was as low as the old adults. In the analyses with the level effects, the group by age interaction was significant and indicated that summed over test times the old adults in the Strategy group recalled about the same amount of ideas as the young adults in the other two groups (28%), while the young adults in the Strategy group recalled about the same amount of ideas as the old adults in the other groups (22%). Thus, although the young groups looked equivalent on subject characteristics collected prior to instruction, the young adults in the Strategy group were lower in recall performance on the pretest than the other young groups, particularly the Control group. The young adults in the Strategy group made enormous gains in use of the strategy. The gains of the young and old adults in the Strategy group were equally outstanding. When the old adults in the Strategy group are compared on pretest scores for most tasks to the young adults in the Control group, the old adults were significantly deficient. However, after instruction the old adults in the Strategy group performed as well or better than the young adults in the Control group.

Reading time clearly showed a slowing with age. This slowing is well-established in the literature (Botwinick, 1967, 1978; Reese & Rodeheaver, 1985), but its causes are still under debate (Okun, 1976; Reese & Rodeheaver, 1985). Some of the possible explanations posited include physiological slowing of the nervous system with age, a compensational slowing to make up for declines in processing abilities, and decreased risk taking with age. The data from the recognition task of topics read suggest a decrease in risk taking with age. Further research should control and manipulate presentation time for old and young adults trained with the plan strategy to better test the limits in performance of older adults in comparison to young adults.

Past research (Meyer, 1984, 1987; Meyer & Rice, 1988) has noted that text variables such as signaling have large effects on highly verbal old adults, but negligible effects on older adults with average to high average scores on vocabulary tests. In an attempt to determine factors underlying verbal ability that affect reading comprehension, Rice and Meyer (1985) administered questionnaires about reading behaviors to young and old adults of high and average verbal ability. Certain reading behaviors were related to success on prose learning tasks for both age groups, and old adults with average vocabulary scores reported the lowest incidence of these behaviors. These data were compatible with a practice explanation which was further explored with a diary study (Rice, 1986a, 1986b; Rice & Meyer, 1986). Total time spent reading in everyday life correlated with recall in the laboratory (Rice & Meyer, 1986); four reading categories (technical journals, science books, textbooks, and the Bible) accounted for 40% of the variance in recall. However, the study indicated that it is not only quantity of practice, but quality as well. Time spent reading the newspaper was positively correlated with recall for high verbal old adults, but negatively correlated for average verbal old adults. Thus, there does not appear to be a simple linear relation between practice in reading and recall, but instead, a certain skill level may be necessary before practice is effective. High verbal old adults are proficient in using the plan strategy (Meyer & Rice, 1988), while average verbal old adults are not.

The current study trained this later group of older adults to use the plan strategy. Use of the strategy and recall rose dramatically. Improvement in recall was also found for the groups receiving practice only through participating in the pretest or the pretest plus practice reading the same materials as the strategy group, but without instruction on the strategy. These groups did not improve as much as the strategy group. Thus, support was found for the position that some age deficits result from ineffective strategies. These ineffective strategies could result from cohort differences; the reading behavior of average verbal adults is probably determined more by schooling practices than high scoring adults who probably pick up the plan strategy without instruction. Alternatively, the ineffective strategies could result from disuse of the plan strategy and subsequent loss of brain circuitry (Cotman & Holets, 1985) which could be regenerated with training. As suggested by Cohen (in press) ineffective strategies could result from reduced cognitive capacity with aging (Cohen. 1979; Hasher & Zacks, 1979; Petros et al., 1983; Spilich, 1983). However, this explanation seems less plausible since the plan strategy could be readily learned over a relatively short time interval.

IMPLICATIONS

This study joins others (Denney, 1982; Labouvie-Vief & Gonda, 1976; Robertson-Tchabo, Hausman, & Arenberg, 1976; Schmitt, Murphy, & Sanders, 1981; Sterns & Sanders, 1980; Willis et al., 1981) in pointing to the plasticity of older adults and their potential for learning effective strategies. In a society with rapid technological change older adults will be called upon to update their knowledge and skills. This strategy can help them to better grasp the main ideas posited in texts and to better remember what they read. It appears to be readily acquired by older adults with a relatively small investment of time.

6

Instructional Materials for the Structure Strategy

TEACHER'S MANUAL

Session 1: Rationale for Strategy and Definitions and Examples of Five Basic Text Structures.

INSTRUCTOR'S PROGRAM FOR SESSION 1

goal: To increase your memory of what you read by using the structure in reading materials.

1. Introduction to Group

We are delighted to have you here and participating in this project. Please answer the questions at the top of page 1 of your program on the scale provided. Also, please write your name on the top of page 1.

Objectives of the program are outlined.

(a) For me: We are studying learning and memory from reading materials by young, middle-aged, and old adults. Over the last 6 years this research has been supported by grants from the National Institute of Mental Health and the National Institute on Aging.

From our studies we have found that for all age groups successful readers employ a deliberate plan or strategy for remembering what they read. Successful readers identify and utilize the writing plan used in their reading materials; they use this plan to help them remember what they have read when they discuss the information with others or write down what they remember about their reading.

In this program you will learn how to use this strategy for reading and remembering.

Our research indicates that with practice people can learn to use this strategy effectively and increase the amount of information they can remember. We have discovered that while a man may never be too old to learn, it's a lot easier for him if he is in practice. In other words, when it comes to reading comprehension skill, use it or lose it.

All participants will be able to increase the amount of information remembered from reading materials after this instruction. Not only will the amount of information be increased, but this strategy will help you to identify and remember the most important information you read. Your participation and hard work will be greatly appreciated.

(b) Your goal is to improve your learning and memory by identifying and using an organizational plan in reading materials.

2. Introduction to Session 1

Aim 1: To establish a rationale for using the reading strategy.

Communication.   If we learn and remember important information effectively, it is likely that we will perform well and feel better about the task. Over the next five sessions I will show you a way to increase this ability to get information from what you read. This will involve using a strategy, deliberate plan, for remembering. Our strategy involves two steps. In reading, we find the organizational plan used by the writer. In remembering, we use the same organizational plan. This is a strategy to improve memory. The strategy is called *using the plan.*

I will give you an analogy to help you better understand our strategy. Scientists have discovered two kinds of light: regular daylight or lamp light and laser light. In regular light photons are scattered indiscriminately like strollers meandering through a mall. However, with lazer light photons are organized into a solid beam; the strollers are organized and marching like soldiers through the mall. Lazer light can accomplish amazing feats over regular light, such as removing cataracts from the eyes of blind people. The strategy that you will learn will enable you to organize your attention and memory. It will give you a powerful learning and memory aid.

We have taught others to use this strategy. A trained group of readers could remember twice as much information from their reading materials after instruction (both 1 day and 3 weeks after) than they could before; and they outperformed an untrained group by twice the amount recalled. Moreover, readers in both groups who found and used the author's plan remembered more information from texts than those who did not find the plan.

Aim 2: To specify learning and teaching tasks of the program.

Communication.   Your job will be to listen attentively to the ways in which this strategy for remembering is applied to reading, to apply it to reading materials, and, after you leave each day, to apply it to your own reading. Our job will be to show you how to use the strategy and to check on your efficiency in using it.

3. Principles: Session 1

Communication.   We know five facts about reading for information.

1. The writer wants to tell you something.
2. You must be told in writing.
3. There are only a small number of possible plans in which to organize information about a topic.
4. The writer should organize his or her main ideas about a topic with a plan.
5. To find this organizational plan is the key to getting the writer's main ideas or message.

Figure 6.1 is shown on the overhead. This strategy is a good one to use under certain conditions, but not others. Use it when you want to know what a writer is trying to tell you; use it when you want to tell someone or write them a letter about what you read in an article. It is not a good strategy to follow if you are just reading to find out a particular detail, such as the number of electoral votes cast in the last election, and don't have any interest in the point the writer is trying to make.

4. Discussion: Session 1

Three instructional goals were set for this session:

1. To guide the students to devise a strategy for remembering based on the organizational plan of a passage.
2. To communicate the common existence of five organizational plans found in expository text.
3. To describe characteristics of the five organizational plans.

Step 1.   The group discusses the five principles outlined above and depicted in Fig. 6.1. Ask them why they think that finding the plan might be an effective approach to understanding what they have read. They examine them as a basis for devising a strategy for organized recall. Students are guided to discover that

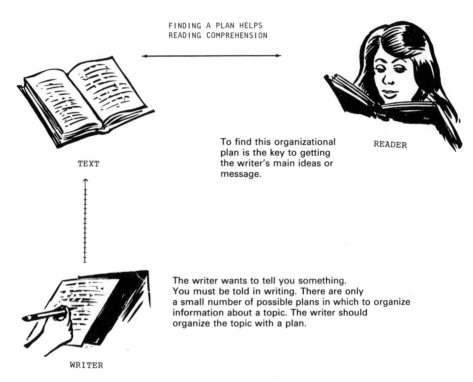

FIG. 6.1. The organizational plan is a key to finding the writer's message.

finding the organizational plan of the passage and using this plan to organize their recall of the passage would yield efficient memory. The most general level of structure is discussed as the most efficient target for identification. The strategy is named using the *plan*. It's use is exemplified in Fig. 6.2. In review, our strategy involves two steps. In reading, we find the plan the writer used. In recalling, we use the same organization. This is a strategy to improve memory. The strategy is called *using the plan*.

Test. Students complete two test items on page 159 of their booklets. The responses are marked and corrective feedback given where necessary.

1. A strategy for remembering what I read has two steps. In reading, I will _____ (search for and identify the author's plan). In remembering, I will _____ (use the same plan to recall and organize what I remember).

2. This strategy is called *Using* _____ (the plan).

A Plan
for
READING

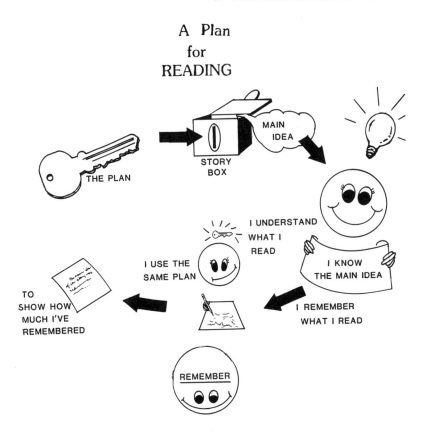

Do these things -

(1) Find the plan when you read

(2) Use the same plan to tell what you can remember

FIG. 6.2. A plan for reading.

Step 2.   Students learn about five basic plans for organizing expository text. In order to use a plan for reading and remembering text, it will be helpful to learn about five commonly used plans in reading materials. These plans are described in Table 6.1. The five plans are designated as follows: *description, sequence, causation, problem/solution,* and *comparison.* Table 6.1 presents the five plans and signals that can cue you into these plans. (Talk through the table as the students examine it.)

These are the five plans we will be working with every day that we meet. We will begin working with them in short advertisements and paragraphs and gradu-

TABLE 6.1
Five Basic Writing Plans and Signals that Cue Readers to These Plans

Writing Plan and Definition	Signals
Description Descriptive ideas that give attributes, specifics, or setting information about a topic. The main idea is that attributes of a topic are discussed.	for example; such as; for instance e.g., a newspaper article describing who, where, when and how
Sequence Ideas grouped on the basis of order or time. The main idea is the procedure or history related.	to begin with; as time passed; later e.g., recipe procedures, history of Civil Was battles, growth from birth to 12
Causation Presents causal or cause and effect-like relationships between ideas. The main ideas are organized into cause and effect parts. The effect comes before the reason (cause) in explanations.	because; so; caused; reasons if..., then... e.g., directions: if you want to take good pictures, then you must...
Problem/Solution The main ideas are organized into two parts: a <u>problem</u> part and a <u>solution</u> part that responds to the problem by trying to eliminate it, or a <u>question</u> part and an <u>answer</u> part that responds to the <u>question</u> by trying to answer it.	need to prevent; problem; solution; question; answer e.g., scientific articles often first raise a question or problem and then seek to give an answer or solution
Comparison Relates ideas on the basis of differences and similarities. The main idea is organized in parts that provide a comparison, contrast, or alternative perspective on a topic.	instead; on the other hand; however; in contrast e.g., political speeches, particularly where one view is clearly favored over the other

ally work with more complicated materials. This first session you should get the general ideas about these plans, but don't worry about mastering them the first day because we will continually go over them on each day that we meet.

Follow along in Table 6.1 as we discuss each plan. Another copy of Table 6.1 can be found on the last page of your booklet; tear it out and keep it in front of you. Examples of these plans are readily identifiable in everyday life and can be found in advertisements. The main captions of advertisements in magazines can often be easily categorized into one of these plans. To help you understand the definitions of the plans, I will show you some examples of their use by advertisers.

Description

Description gives more information about a topic by presenting an attribute, specific, or setting. For example, on the topic of whales, descriptive passages could be generated by describing the physical characteristics of whales as a group, by describing one particular type of whale, by describing the environment of whales, and so forth. Articles are often organized as a group or list of descriptions about a topic. This listing of descriptions about a topic may be signaled in an article by such words as "three attributes" of whales will be discussed . . . "first, . . . second . . . . . third. . . . . ." Newspaper articles often follow the descriptive plan, telling us about who, where, how, and when.

We will examine some plans of *description* in two advertisements taken from magazines.

Example 1. "EVEREADY" DOUBLE GUARANTEE (Fig. 6.3)

Guarantee #1. The Eveready "Skipper" Flashlight. A switch so durable, so dependable . . . we gave it a 10 year guarantee.

Guarantee #2. "Eveready" Flashlight Batteries. They're guaranteed against damaging your flashlight in any way. And they cost less than alkaline batteries. Two great guarantees from the most trusted brand name in the business. "Eveready."

"Double" in the title of this advertisement signals us to the possibility of two descriptions about the topic, "Eveready guarantees." The two guarantees follow and are explicitly signaled for us as #1 and #2. The two descriptions give us specific information about the guarantees: A 10 year guarantee on the flashlight and batteries guaranteed against damaging our flashlights. The last sentence again signals the plan for this advertisement with the words "two guarantees." Further descriptions about the topic "Eveready" guarantees are given in the last sentence (the guarantees are great and "Eveready" is trusted). Thus, the plan for this advertisement is description.

Example 2. OH THE LOVELY NUTTY THINGS YOU CAN DO WITH DIAMOND WALNUTS. CHOCOLATE CHIP COOKIES: CALIFORNIA WALNUT PIE: CALIFORNIA WALNUT BREAD: CHEWY WALNUT SQUARES (courtesy of Diamond Walnut Growers, Inc.) (Fig. 6.4.)

In this advertisement we see four descriptions that specify the lovely nutty things you can do with walnuts. The overall plan for this advertisement is description. Within each of the four separate descriptions of things to do with walnuts we can find the next plan we will discuss, *sequence.* The sequence plan

FIG. 6.3.   Description shown with Eveready double guarantee.

FIG. 6.4. Description depicted with advertisement about walnuts (Advertisement reproduced with the permission of Diamond Walnut Growers, Inc.).

is used to give the order for mixing the ingredients and preparing the pan and oven in the recipes.

Sequence

As seen in Table 6.1, the plan for a text based on order or time is called *sequence*. For this plan a number of items are ordered and presented serially in a continuous progression as they relate to a particular topic or process. Examples of this plan include procedures in a recipe, stages in development from birth to twelve months, and the history of the Civil War battles.

Examine the following example of a sequence typical in magazines for young parents.

Example 3.

More than likely, an infant's **first** tooth will be one of the two lower front teeth. These two will be **followed in a few months** by the four upper front teeth. On an average, a baby will have these six teeth **by the time** he is a year old and his complete set of 20 primary teeth **by the time** he is 2½ years old.

In this paragraph the sequence plan is used to order the increasing number of teeth and the increasing age of the child. The words in bold face help to tell us that a sequence plan is used to organize the information given by the author. Also, in this example the ordering of the quantity of teeth and the ordering of the child's age is related to ordering of the teeth in the mouth, the location of the teeth. Ordering ideas by time and also by location falls under the sequence plan.

Causation

The *causation* plan is aimed at presenting causal relationships (like the ''if/then'' of antecedent/consequent statements in logic). In using this plan the reader should look for the *cause* part of the causation plan and the *effect* part of this plan. Directions often follow the causation plan. If you want a certain outcome, such as good pictures, then you will follow a certain sequence of procedures; following those procedures (the cause) will give you the desired effect. Explanations also follow the causation plan; they give the reasons or causes for an effect.

The following advertisement exemplifies the causation plan.

Example 4.   (Fig. 6.5).

Four good **reasons why** Johnson's Baby Lotion is the best ''grownup'' body lotion you can buy. Thicker and richer than other lotions. Absorbs fast. Goes to work

Four good reasons why *Johnson's* Baby Lotion is the best "grownup" body lotion you can buy.

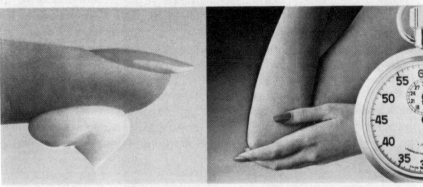

Thicker and richer than other lotions.

Absorbs fast. Goes to work instantly.

Unique combination of 10 skin softeners.

Leaves you feeling beautifully soft all over.

When it comes to keeping skin soft, JOHNSON'S Baby Lotion has everything you want in a body lotion and more. Its super-rich formula gives a new beauty to your skin and leaves it with a healthy, youthful glow. In short, JOHNSON'S Baby Lotion is a terrific body lotion. We've told you four good reasons why. But don't take our word for it. Just give it a try.

It's a perfect lotion for grownup skin.

Johnson & Johnson

Johnson's
baby
lotion

© J&J 1980

FIG. 6.5. Causation shown with baby lotion advertisement (Advertisement reproduced with the permission of Johnson and Johnson).

instantly. Unique combination of 10 skin softeners. Leaves you feeling beautifully soft all over.

Reasons why in the advertisement signal us to the causal plan. This advertisement is an explanation of why this lotion is the best; the effect is given before the causes or reasons. So you see for the causation plan you can have the information organized in either the cause/effect order or the effect/cause order. The effect in the causal plan is that Johnson's Baby Lotion is the best "grownup" body lotion you can buy. The cause in the plan is composed of a listing of four reasons as signaled in the advertisement. The advertisers want us to assume that these four statements are true: Thicker and richer, fast, unique, and leaves you soft, and that it thus follows that the product is the best you can buy. As can be seen by the causation's use in this and other advertisements, the constraints of formal logic are not necessary to use the causation plan in writing. The ideas can be related in a quasi-causal fashion.

Problem/solution

The *problem/solution* plan has two parts, a problem part and a solution part; the solution part has to respond to the ideas in the problem part. This plan also has a *question/answer* form; here a question is raised in one part and in the other part an answer is given to the question. Scientific articles often adhere to the problem/solution or question/answer plan, first raising a problem or a question and then seeking to give a solution or answer.

The first example of this plan in the following advertisement uses the question and answer format.

Example 5
YOUR SHISH KABOBS LOOK SO TANTALIZING. SHOULD YOUR GLASSES BE SPOTTY? GET THE CASCADE LOOK. . . . VIRTUALLY SPOTLESS (courtesy Proctor & Gamble) (Fig. 6.6)

The details of this advertisement expand on the question and the answer segments of this plan. The first paragraph below from this advertisement repeats and expands on the question that appeared in the bold face title of the advertisement; the second paragraph explains why Cascade is the solution to the spotty glass problem.

> Your guests will rave when they see this dish. But what about your glasses? You don't want spots at a time like this, or anytime. (Here the question is answered "NO" and the problems of spots emphasized.)
>
> The spotty glass shows that plain water alone can leave dulling spots. (Here we see that the problem of spots is caused by plan ordinary water.) So it's good to know that Cascade's sheeting action fights drops that spot . . . give your guests glasses with the Cascade look! (Here Cascade is identified as the suggested solution because it fights water drops.) (courtesy Proctor & Gamble)

FIG. 6.6. Problem/solution with question/answer format depicted with an advertisement about spotty glasses (advertisement reproduced courtesy of Proctor and Gamble).

Better Homes and Gardens has run a feature entitled "Tips, Tools, and Techniques" that explicitly signals the problem/solution plan to its readers. The next example was taken from this column.

Example 6.

Reprinted from *Better Homes and Gardens* magazine. PROBLEM: After you've waxed the car, dried residue lingers around the grill. SOLUTION: A flagged-tip nylon paintbrush will remove the polish from crevices without scratching the paint (H. G., Springville, TN). Copyright Meredith Corporation, 1983

Comparison

Again look at Table 6.1 as we discuss the final plan, *comparison*. This plan organizes on the basis of similarities and differences. The number of matching relationships and issues compared varies with the complexity and kind of comparative text (e.g., comparison of deodorant brands, to beliefs about God, to highly structured legal arguments).

An analogy is a type of comparison plan; for example, an advertisement on Diamond Walnuts stated the following.

Example 7. THE ART OF BEING A SHREWD DIAMOND BUYER (courtesy Diamond Walnuts Growers, Inc.) (Fig. 6.7)

Here an analogy is drawn between the care exercised in selecting diamonds and the care in selecting this brand of walnuts (Diamond).

With the comparison plan an author may equally recommend the compared views or she may favor one view over another. Political speeches are often of the comparison type, particularly where one view is clearly favored over the other.

Example 8. HEAVY DUTY REYNOLDS WRAP GIVES YOU 2 JUICY OPTIONS. JUICY AND WRAPPED. JUICY AND TENTED (courtesy Reynolds Metals Company) (Fig. 6.8)

In this advertisement alternative ways to prepare turkey with Reynolds Wrap are presented. The options are equally desirable from the author's viewpoint. The word option in this advertisement helps to signal us that a comparison plan is being used. For the comparison plan look for issues on which options are compared; in this example the issues are (1) how to use the foil and (2) the end result. We see differences in use of the foil, wrap or tent, and similarities in the end result, roasted to perfection.

Example 9. MOST WRAPS JUST WRAP. REYNOLDS WRAP WRAPS, MOLDS AND SEALS TIGHTLY (courtesy Reynolds Metals Company) (Fig. 6.9)

Diamond® Walnuts are picked at their prime so they're never green with youth or too old.

Diamond Walnuts are pleasingly plump and full of fresh, crunchy nutmeat.

You won't see spots before your eyes because Diamond Walnuts are checked for sunburn.

Smooth skin outside means more delicious crunchiness inside.

Like all healthy Californians, Diamond Walnuts have a golden tan.

The art of being a shrewd Diamond buyer.

This isn't an ad about walnuts. It's an ad about Diamonds.

And if you think they're the same thing, take a closer look at the Diamond above.

Long before you ever crack open a beauty like this, we've put it through the world's toughest inspections.

And by the time you lay eyes on a shelled Diamond Walnut, as many as 40 expert eyes have checked it for virtually every imperfection.

But there's a lot more to Diamond's high standards than meets the eye.

We also pack our walnuts at their peak. To give you the freshest, crunchiest nutmeats.

Then we zip them to cold storage to seal in the freshness and flavor.

If you don't think all this nitpicking by our nut pickers pays off, take another look at the walnut on this page.

Of course, there is an easier way to be a shrewd Diamond buyer.

Just look for our package.

DIAMOND OF CALIFORNIA

In a nutshell, Diamond's the best.

FIG. 6.7. Comparison: analogy shown with a diamond buyer (Advertisement reproduced with the permission of Diamond Walnut Growers, Inc.).

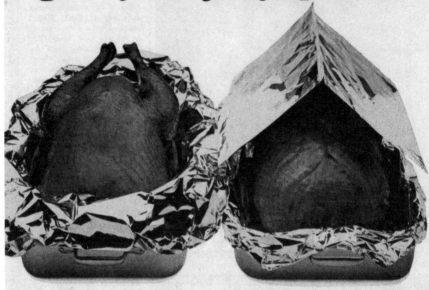

Heavy Duty Reynolds Wrap®
gives you 2 juicy options.

Juicy and Wrapped

You just wrap bird completely in Heavy Duty Reynolds Wrap and roast. When turkey is almost done, turn back foil to brown the bird. This method roasts turkey evenly, keeps in juices and flavor, reduces oven spattering.

Many women say this is the best way to roast a turkey to perfection. And they're right.

Juicy and Tented

To start, line roasting pan with Heavy Duty Reynolds Wrap. Then take a sheet of Heavy Duty Reynolds Wrap and "tent" it over lightly browned bird and roast. This method roasts turkey evenly, keeps in juices and flavor, reduces oven spattering.

Many women say this is the best way to roast a turkey to perfection. And they're right.

Bake your dressing separately during the last hour of roasting. Just place dressing in sheet of Heavy Duty Reynolds Wrap, bring up ends and twist to form a bundle.

What wrap can you use to...line a pan, cook in, store leftovers in, then cook in again? Reynolds Wrap? You're right.

Complete turkey roasting instructions on box, or write for turkey recipe booklet, "All About Turkey," to Reynolds Metals Co., A.D.C., P.O. Box 27003, Richmond, Va. 23261.

Reynolds Wrap Aluminum Foil 37½

The Best Wrap Around.

FIG. 6.8. Comparison with equally weighted alternatives depicted in an advertisement about Reynolds Wrap (Permission to reproduce the advertisement given by Reynolds Metals Company).

FIG. 6.9. Comparison with unequally weighted format depicted in an advertisement about Reynolds Wrap (Permission to reproduce the advertisement given by Reynolds Metals Company).

In contrast, in this advertisement one product is contrasted to others and favored as superior. The word "just" in this advertisement cues us into the comparison plan with one product favored over another. Usually this form of comparison is more prevalent with advertisements because the advertisers want to convince you that their product is superior so that you will buy it.

The following advertisement uses the unequally weighed version of the comparison plan to urge your support of the Save the Children Federation.

Example 10.   YOU CAN HELP SAVE BO SUK FOR $15 A MONTH. OR YOU CAN TURN THE PAGE (Fig. 6.10)

As mentioned before, these five basic plans are familiar in various contexts. Political speeches are often of the comparison type, particularly where one view is clearly favored over the other. Newspaper articles are often of the descriptive type, telling us who, where, how, and when. Scientific articles often adhere to the problem/solution type, first raising a question or problem and then seeking to give an answer or solution. History texts frequently follow the sequence plan with chronological ordering.

Many texts will reflect more than one of these basic five plans. For example, folktales contain much description, causation, and events sequenced in time within an overall problem/solution plan where the protagonist confronts and resolves a problem. Folktales may carry an overall comparison plan, such as demonstrating the contrast between good and evil. For example, an Aesop fable about a genie and two woodsmen was comprised of two substories: one about an honest woodsman and the other about a dishonest woodsman. The overall plan for the story was comparison with emphasis on the honest woodsman as explicitly signaled by the author in the moral "Honesty is the best policy." Our strategy for reading and remembering will focus on the **overall plan** used in the text rather than plans used to organize details in a text.

You can practice using the strategy even when watching television. For example, there is a television show on public television called the Nature of Things. This program showed a 15 min segment with a problem/solution format. The problem was the rejection of organs transplanted into the body, such as liver and heart transplants. The solution was psychosporin, a drug effective in preventing organ rejection. The program described the problem and solution with examples taken from the lives of people. To remember the message of this show so that you could later discuss it with friends, you could jot down problem = organ rejection; solution = psychosporin.

Just as traffic signs signal you to attend to important aspects of your driving, there are signaling words in reading materials that signal the different plans. Some signaling words are listed below. In the space provided write the name of the plan that best corresponds to each signaling word; you can refer to Table 6.1 for assistance.

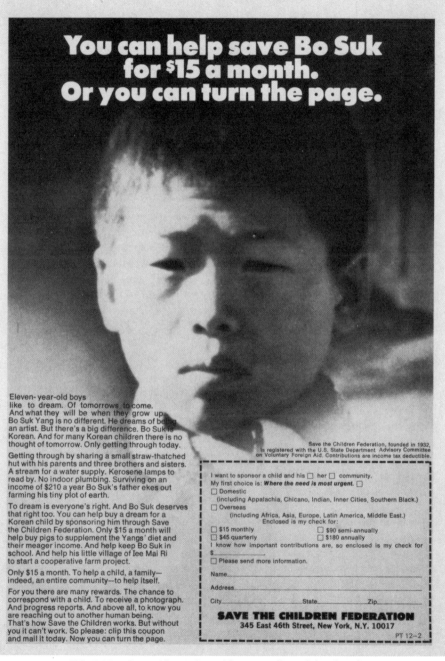

FIG. 6.10. Comparison plan with unequally weighted options.

to start with _____ (sequence) _____ specifically _____ (description)

_____ in explanation _____ (causation) _____ in opposition _____

(comparison) _____ to satisfy the problem _____ (problem/solution) _____

the reason _____ (causation) _____ more recently _____ (sequence) _____

attributes of _____ (description) _____ compared to _____ (comparison)

_____ years ago _____ (sequence) _____ in describing _____ (description)

_____ in response to your puzzlement _____ (problem/solution) _____

To review the five basic plans for reading and remembering, we will examine the test advertisements found in your packets. Please pair up with a partner; each member of the pair should read the advertisement and determine the overall plan used to organize the information. Write down the name of the plan and then, share your plan with your partner. Progress in this manner one by one through the sample advertisements. When you have finished we will go over the plans for the advertisements as a group and discuss any disagreements or problems.

Copies of the advertisements used in the review can be found in the materials for students that were used in session 1.

Review Ad. #1

WANT A TOUGH STAIN OUT? SHOUT IT OUT!

The plan used is problem/solution with the question/answer format. The problem is the mess the family is in due to stains. The solution is using Shout to wash the clothes because Shout gets out stains.

Review Ad. #2

HAPPY CAT STAYS MOIST AND MEATY TASTING ALL DAY, SO CATS STAY HAPPY ALL DAY.

The so in the advertisement cues us into the causation plan. The cause is Happy Cat's moist and meaty taste lasting all day and the effect is that cats stay happy all day.

Review Ad. #3

"WITH EIGHT BROTHERS AND SISTERS, BIRTHDAYS USED TO BE A PROBLEM." NOW I SEND THE BIRTHDAY PARTY BOUQUET FROM BY FTD FLORIST. IT'S MORE THAN A GIFT. IT'S A CELEBRATION.

Problem in this advertisement signals us to the problem/solution plan. The problem is thinking of gifts for so many relatives and Olsen's solution is sending them special birthday flowers.

FIG. 6.11. Review advertisement #1. By permission of S. C. Johnson & Son, Inc., Racine, Wisconsin.

FIG. 6.12. Review advertisement #2. Happy Cat is a registered trademark of Ralston Purina Company. Reproduced with permission. Copyright Ralston Purina Company, 1984.

"With eight brothers and sisters, birthdays used to be a problem." Now I send the Birthday Party* Bouquet from my FTD* Florist. It's more than a gift, it's a celebration.

Merlin Olsen

Send your thoughts with special care.™

*Registered trademark of Florists' Transworld Delivery Association.

FIG. 6.13. Review advertisement #3. Advertisement for the FTD Birthday Party Bouquet furnished by the 24,000 Member Florists of FTD. Copyright 1987 FTDA.

Review Ad. #4

COMPARE NEW VO5 TO OTHER LEADING HAIRSPRAYS. THE DIFFERENCE IS—CRYSTAL CLEAR.

The signaling word **compare** in this advertisement cues us to the comparison plan. VO5 is favored over the other hairsprays.

Review Ad. #5

CLUB MED SHOULD FEEL THIS FREE. HEDONISM II. CLUB MED SHOULD BE THIS GOOD.

The plan used is comparison. Hedonism II and Club Med are compared and Hedonism II is favored.

Discuss any problems the students had with these advertisements. We are focusing on the plan the author used to write the advertisement. Once you figure out what the author is telling you then you can evaluate his or her message. For example, consider the Hedonism II advertisement. If I don't smoke or drink, then Hedonism II may be a bad choice for me because I will end up paying for

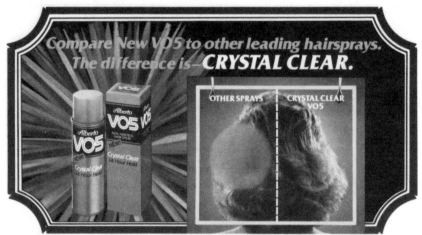

FIG. 6.14. Review advertisement #4. Courtesy Alberto Culver Company.

the "free cigarettes and drinks" of the other vacationers. I would need to check and see if Hedonism II is more expensive than Club Med.

Remember this strategy is to be used when you want to remember a lot from your reading and you want to know what the author said. You probably would not use it when casually looking over the newspaper for enjoyment.

Next you and your partner will write advertisements in two different writing plans to sell your new invention, the safety pin. The writing plans you will use are specified in your materials. After writing the advertisements in their packets, have volunteers share advertisements with different plans with the class.

Example of possible advertisements: *Comparison*—compare the straight pin with the favored safety pin; *Problem/solution*—pricking your finger due to the sharp end of the straight pin; solution is the safety pin with the sharp end hidden; *Description*—sharp for entering fabric, a cap which covers end after material has been penetrated, etc.; *Sequence*—first the invention of steel, then the invention of the straight pin, now the invention of the safety pin; *Causation*—due to the use of two safety pins, Robert's diapers stay on securely.

Finally, have the students turn to the picture of the tiger at the end of their packets (also show tiger on overhead). Have each student write about the picture using two of the plans; these will be two different plans than those used for the advertisement (see p. 172).

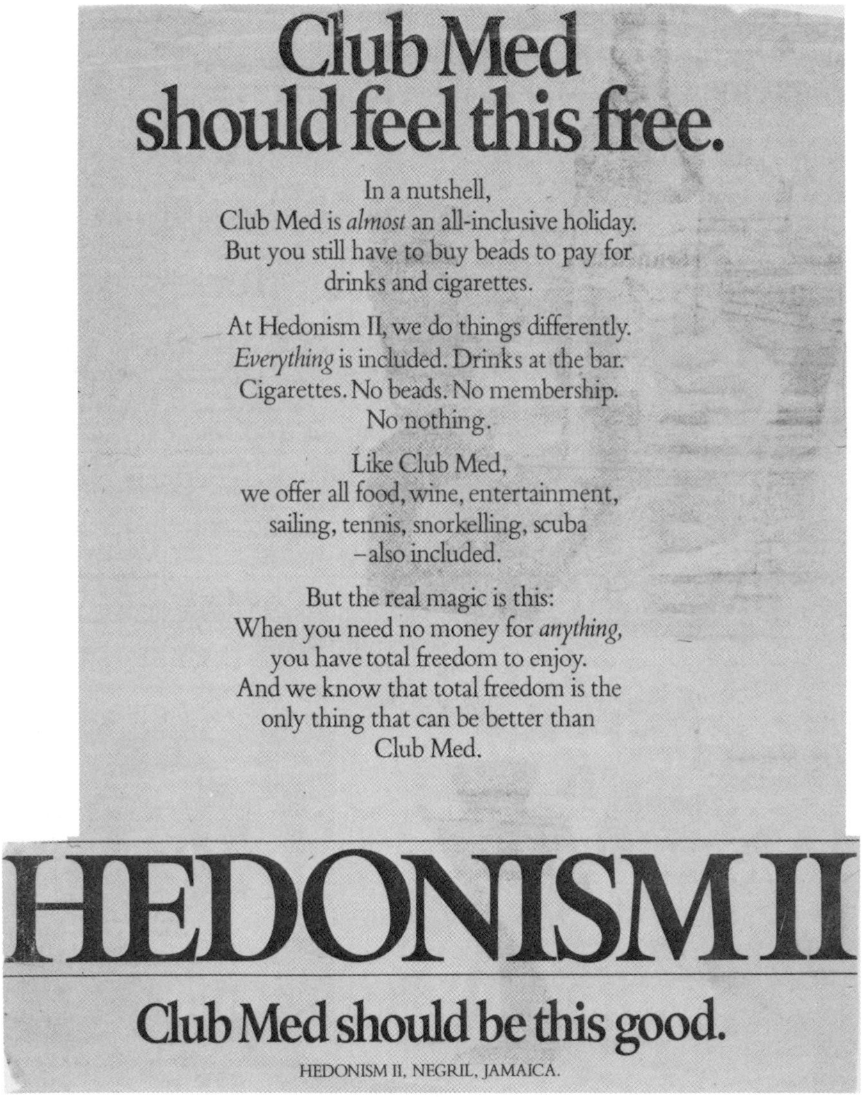

FIG. 6.15. Review advertisement #5.

Take your copy of Table 6.1 home with you to review what we have learned today. During the next couple of days as you read materials, look for these plans and signals used to cue them. Please leave your packets with me so that I can check your progress. (Check their tiger texts for the different plans and select good examples to use for the next session).

Session 2: Signaling Words for Five Text Structures and Identification of Structures in Short Texts.

INSTRUCTOR'S PROGRAM FOR SESSION 2

1. Introduction to the Group

Review program objectives: To improve recall by identifying and using the writing plans in reading materials.

Check whether (a)   students thought of the five types of plans after they left our first session.

(b)   students encountered any of these plans in their reading.

Review session 1 by Let's Check 1. Have students fill in the following:

Five Plans   *One Signaling Word*

1. _____   _____

2. _____   _____

3. _____   _____

4. _____   _____

5. _____   _____

Have students check their work by looking at Table 6.2; make any needed corrections.

At this point go over the tiger articles written by the class last session. Show the tiger overhead and have seven students (cover each of the five plans) read the article you specify. Let the class try to figure out which plan was used to write the article and verify it with the writer.

2. Introduction to Session 2

Aim 1: To teach other signaling words and the idea that listing can occur with any of the five plans.

Communication.   Signaling words can cue you into that plan used by an author to organize his or her main ideas. Remember that we are looking for the overall writing plan that organizes all the information presented; signals will probably be found for plans that organize just parts of the information too, but we will focus on the plans that organize all of the information into a whole. The information organized by this overall plan is the main idea the author is trying to tell you.

Go through Table 6.2 reviewing the plans and discussing the signaling words. Also discuss listing and its signals given at the bottom of that Table. Keep Table

TABLE 6.2

Five Basic Writing Plans and Signals that Cue Readers to These Plans

Writing Plan and Definition	Signals
Description Descriptive ideas that give attributes, specifics, or setting information about a topic. The main idea is that attributes of a topic are discussed. E.g., newspaper article describing who, where, when and how.	for example, which was one, this particular, for instance, specifically, such as, attributes of, that is, namely, properties of, characteristics are, qualities are, marks of, in describing,_____
Sequence Ideas grouped on the basis of order or time. The main idea is the procedure or history related. E.g., recipe procedures, history of Civil War battles, growth from birth to 12 months.	afterwards, later, finally, last, early, following, to begin with, as time passed, continuing on, to end, years ago, in the first place, before, after, soon, more recently,_____
Causation Presents causal or cause and effect-like relations between ideas. The main idea is organized into cause and effect parts. E.g., directions: if you want to take good pictures, then you must ....; explanations: the idea explained is the effect and the explanation is its cause.	as a result, because, since, for the purpose of, caused, led to, consequence, thus, in order to, this is why, if/then, the reason, so, in explanation, therefore,_____
Problem/Solution The main ideas are organized into two parts: a problem part and a solution part that responds to the problem by trying to eliminate it, or a question part and an answer part that responds to the question by trying to answer it. E.g., scientific articles often first raise a question or problem and then seek to give an answer or solution.	problem: problem, question, puzzle, perplexity, enigma, riddle, issue, query, need to prevent, the trouble_____ solution: solution, answer, response, reply, rejoinder, return, comeback, to satisfy the problem, to set the issue at rest, to solve these problems,_____

(continued)

115

(table 6.2 continued)

Writing Plan and Definition	Signals
Comparison Relates ideas on the basis of differences and similarities. The main idea is organized in parts that provide a comparison, contrast, or alternative perspective on a topic. E.g., political speeches, particularly where one view is clearly favored over the other.	not everyone, but, in contrast, all but, instead, act like, however, in comparison, on the other hand, whereas, in opposition, unlike, alike, have in common, share, resemble, the same as, different, difference, differentiate, compare to, while, although,
Listing can occur with any of the five writing plans. Listing simply groups ideas together. Passages are often organized as a listing of descriptions about a topic. A sequence always contains a listing of ideas, but the ideas are ordered sequentially. A listing can occur when groups of causes are presented, groups of effects are listed, groups of solutions are posited, groups of ideas are contrasted to another idea, and so forth.	common signals include: and, in addition, also, include, moreover, besides, first, second, third, etc., subsequent, furthermore, at the same time, another, and so forth,

6.2 with you to remind you of the five plans and their signals. Spaces are provided in the Table for you to fill in signaling words that you discover in our work in class and in your home reading.

LET'S CHECK

For each of the passages underline the signaling words that cue us into the author's plan. Write the name of the plan used in the space provided. Share your answers with your partner as you finished each item.

1. Martha worried continually about her health; *as a result* she acquired ulcers.

_____ causation _____ Plan

2. Pollution is a *problem* for our rivers. Polluted rivers are eyesores. They are also health hazards. *One solution* is to stop the dumping of industrial waste.

_____ problem/solution _____ Plan

3. Luxury cars yield comfort, safety, style and excellent resale values; examples of such cars include *include* Buick Riviera, Cadillac Deville, Cadillac Eldorado, Cadillac Seville, Lincoln Continental, Mark IV, Lincoln Versailles, Mercedes-Benz 2400, Mercedes-Benz 300D and 280SE, and Oldsmobile Toronado.

_____ description _____ Plan

4. *Despite* the argument that smoking is harmful, *not everyone agrees.* Certainly, smoking has been related to lung cancer, high blood pressure, and loss of appetite. *But,* for some people smoking relieves tension.

_____ comparison _____ Plan

5. In *1901* Alveretta Bonita Hyde was born in Kellogg, Idaho. In *1921* she married Zona Hiram Smith. *Two years later* Phyllis June Smith was born. *Over nine years later* the *second* and *final* child appeared. Zona died in *1976*. *Four years later* at *80* years old Alveretta married Otto Kessler, a delightful 82 year old. In *1987* at the ages of *86* and *88* Alveretta and Otto were merrily traveling around the country spreading joy to friends and relatives.

_____ sequence _____ Plan

6. **Youths Turn Off on Drugs.** (Copyright, 1984, *U.S. News & World Report.* Excerpted from the issue of February 20, 1984, p. 18.) Back at the schoolyard, the young people are turning away from drugs and alcohol. A new survey for the National Institute on Drug Abuse says that the percentage of high-

school seniors using marijuana 20 or more times a month dropped to 5.5% last year, from 6.3 in 1982. The survey found that daily alcohol use also dipped in 1983—to 5.5%, from 5.7% in '82. One big *reason* for the shift to clean living: concern about health.

_____ causation _____ Plan

Discuss the students' response to the above items. Ask for (1) the plan identified, (2) the signals identified, and (3) the main idea organized by the plan. Use the diagrams seen in Fig. 6.16 (shown on overhead and copies for students) to help them to understand the idea of this overall organizational plan. The diagrams also will point out the hierarchy of major logical relationships in the passage.

At this point a formative evaluation packet was administered. It included sorting 17 short articles from magazines or the Bible into the five types of plans. It also included reading and recalling two short articles, one organized with the causation plan and the other organized with the comparison plan. It also included the following five articles to read, underline the signaling, and identify the plan. All materials were collected to monitor the students' progress. Feedback from these tasks was given during the subsequent sessions.

For each of the passages—   *Underline* the signaling words that cue you into the author's plan.

Write the name of the plan used in the space provided.

1. **Watch the Gestures.** (Copyright, 1984, *U.S. News & World Report.* Excerpted from issue of June 11, 1984, p. 83). An innocent gesture at home can take on a completely *different* meaning in a foreign country, warns Paul Ekman, a professor of psychology at University of California-San Francisco, who has done a study on the subject. The "O.K." sign—thumb and forefinger formed into a circle means you did a great job and everything is A-okay in the U.S.A. *However,* it means "you're worth zero" in France and Belgium, and is a vulgar insult in Italy, Greece and Turkey.

_____ comparison _____ Plan

2. **ABC's of How America Chooses a President.** (Copyright, 1984, *U.S. News & World Report.* Excerpted from issue of Feb. 20, 1984, p. 45.)

How is Election Day established? Federal law places it on the Tuesday following the first Monday in November, in the fourth year after the previous election of a President.

_____ problem/solution-question/answer _____ Plan

3. **Safety Breaker.** (Copyright, 1984, *U.S. News & World Report.* Excerpted from issue of March 19, 1984, p. 80).

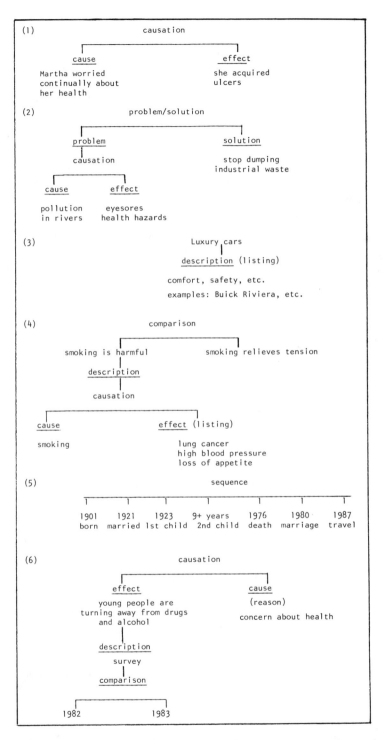

FIG. 6.16. Diagrams of structures for the first short passages examined in session 2.

A simple and inexpensive *way to reduce* the chances of electrocution in the home is to install ground-fault circuit interrupters—devices that detect electrical leaks and shut off the current before serious injury or death—says the Consumer Product Safety Commission.

_____ problem/solution _____Plan

4. **How to Complain.** (Copyright 1984, U.S. News & World Report. Excerpted from issue of March 19, 1984, p. 80.)

When something goes wrong with a product or service you have just bought, how do you get the *problem resolved?* The office of Consumer Affairs recommends these steps: First, complain to the person who sold the item or performed the service. *If* you're still not satisfied, write to the company's headquarters, perhaps even its president. *After that,* contact the appropriate trade association, local, state or federal agency or the Better Business Bureau. *Final resort:* A small-claims court or private lawyer.

_____ problem/solution (sequence & causation embedded) _____ Plan

5. *Since 1782* the bald eagle has been the national emblem of the United States. *At that time* bald eagles nested throughout most of North America. *In the late 1960s* bald eagles had almost disappeared from the eastern United States. *Now* they can be found again, especially in the Great Lakes region, around Chesapeake Bay, and in Maine and Florida.

_____ sequence _____ Plan

Session 3: Modeling Use of the Strategy to Encode and Retrieve Information from Reading Materials.

INSTRUCTOR'S PROGRAM FOR SESSION 3

Feedback: Hand back student's paper identifying the plans and signaling for the short articles from last session's formative evaluation packet. Go through each item discussing which ones were difficult and easy for the group. Use the visual hierarchies seen in Figure 6.17 to explain the ones that proved difficult.

This will take about 20 min. Have extra copies of Table 6.2 available for students to use throughout the session in case they forgot to bring their copy from last session.

Aim 1: To coordinate the act of writing a recall protocol with that of identifying the author's plan in the reading material.

Communication. Choosing the plan is only the first of two steps in helping us remember what we read. Once we have found it, we must use it ourselves. If

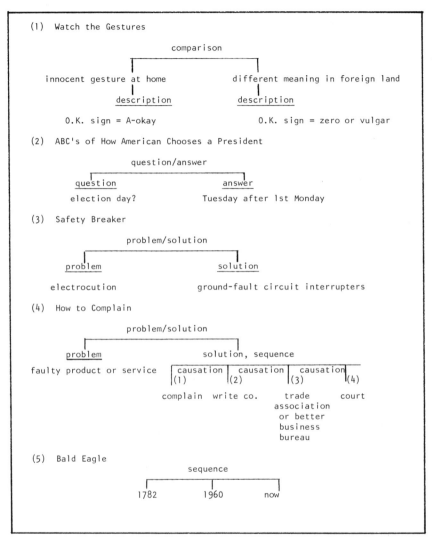

FIG. 6.17. Diagrams of structures for short passages examined in session 2 and discussed in session 3.

the overall plan in what you read is *description*, then you must use description in what you write. If it is *sequence*, then you must use sequence. If it is *causation*, then you must use cause and effect. If it is *problem/solution*, then you must organize your recall as problem and solution. If it is *comparison*, then that is the organization to use in writing down what you remember from your reading. You choose it, use it, or lose it.

Aim 2: To give rationale for the coordination.

Communication.   Researchers over the past 10 years have shown a dramatic finding. Learners who perform well in school in reading are those who use our strategy. Those who pick the article's plan and use it themselves to organize recall remember more of what they have read. And, they remember it longer. One more thing. What they remember always includes the most important parts of a message. Learners who use a different plan don't get as much meaning from what they read. Nor, do they remember for very long. However, this strategy can be taught to learners. As a result they can nearly double the amount of information they can remember.

There is a message in these findings. If you want to improve your ability to remember what you read, use a strategy to help organize yourself. Use the strategy of finding the plan. Find out what overall plan a writer used and use it yourself as a pattern for your thinking, speaking, or writing.

Aim 3: To operationalize the coordination.

Communication.   You need to be attentive at similar times (before, while, and after) for both reading and writing parts of the strategy.

Before you READ: —ask two questions—
WHAT IS THE PLAN FOR THIS PASSAGE?
WHAT IS THE MAIN IDEA THAT FITS THIS PLAN?

These questions will help you to approach your reading in a more organized way. They will help you to concentrate on the most important information in the passage.

While you READ: —find answers to the questions—
After you READ: —remind yourself what plan you found—
Before you WRITE: —ask the questions—
WHAT PLAN DID I FIND WHEN I READ?
HOW WILL I USE THIS FORMAT TO ORGANIZE WHAT I WRITE?
While you WRITE: —use the same plan to organize your writing—
After you WRITE: —check that you used the same plan—

Principles: Session 3

Communication.   For best recall of what we read there are six steps to take.

1. We find the plan in what we read.
2. We write its name at the top of the page, just before we recall.
3. We write the main idea sentence.

4. We use the plan to organize what we recall.

5. We check to see that we have used it.

6. We add anything else that we have just remembered.

If you CHOOSE it and USE it, then you won't LOSE it!

Discussion: Session 3

One instructional goal was set for this session:

1. To have students apply the strategy to passages extracted from everyday reading materials.

Step 1. The principles outlined above were discussed with the object of consolidating the usage phase of strategic behavior. The group discusses what type of information might be expected to follow the main idea sentence if a passage were organized in a given format (e.g., favored view vs opposite view). The functional purpose of the plan is to be stressed in this discussion (e.g., to organize the main idea into competing arguments.) Demonstration passages from everyday reading materials were used to illustrate this function. Discussion was repeated for each of the five common plans.

Demonstration Passages.   Here an adult model is to model the strategy with each type of plan. All students read the passage asking themselves our two important questions: what is the plan? and what is the main idea that fits this plan? Then, the model recalls the plan using the overhead projector. After modeling reading and recall of one plan, the above discussion takes place. A young adult served as model for three passages (recalling in writing on the overhead two passages for the group and showing recall of the third with a pretyped recall on the overhead) and an old adult served as model for the two other passages (one free recalled in writing on the overhead and one talked through with a pretyped recall on the overhead).

Description

The Anatomy of a Mollusk

Mollusks have a solid, unsegmented body which can be divided into four main parts unless greatly modified.

First is the head, bearing tentacles, eyes, and other sense organs. The mouth opens close to the front end and is often armed with teeth. The brain is internal.

The visceral sac is the next distinct part and it houses the gut, heart, and reproductive organs.

The foot is a muscular structure used for locomotion and burrowing.

The mantle is the fourth region of the body and is a fold of skin which develops from the back part and folds over, enveloping the visceral mass and separating it from the shell. The anus and excretory ducts open into the mantle cavity inside which the gills develop. (Adapted—some easier vocabulary & few details omitted from D'Angelo, 1980, p. 113 taken from *The Animal Kingdom* (Fetham, England: Hamlyn Publishing Group Ltd., p. 183).

Sample Model Recall

Description

The mollusk is described by examining its four main parts: head, visceral sac, legs and mantle. First, the head contains the eyes, tentacles, other sense organ, brain and mouth; the mouth is in the front and usually has teeth. Next, the visceral sac contains the digestive and reproductive organs. The legs are used for moving and burrowing. Fourth, the mantle is a covering that start at the back and envelops the visceral mass; the anus and excretory ducts open into the mantle and the gills develop there.

Go through the questions you ask before you read and the two you ask before you write. Also go through the six steps for best recall. For step 6—add something else you remember—e.g., above—the heart is also in the visceral sac.

Sequence

How Snakes Shed Their Skins

When a snake has grown a new epidermis and is about to shed its skin, it secretes a thin layer of fluid between the old and new skin (which are no longer touching), giving the snake a clouded milky appearance. This can be seen especially at the eyes, for the milky fluid covers the pupils and makes the snake almost, if not completely, blind. This condition may last for as much as a week, during this period, snakes normally remain in hiding.

A day or two after the cloudiness has cleared, the snake will shed its skin. This is accomplished by opening and stretching the mouth and rubbing it on surrounding objects until the old skin at the edges of the lips begins to split. Rubbing continually, the snake starts to wriggle out of its skin. This is usually sloughed off in one piece from head to tail, turned inside out in the process by the emerging snake. Sometimes the skin will break up, however, and come off in pieces, as during the shedding of lizards.

The sloughed-off skin is a perfect cast of the snake. The large belly scales, the pattern of scales on the back, the eye spectacle and even casts of facial pits can all be seen. It is completely devoid of color as the pigment cells remain in the dermis, which is never shed. The shed skin is transparent with a white tinge. After it has been detached from the snake for a while, it usually becomes brittle. The sloughed-off skin is not especially attractive, but the newly emerged snake is seen at its best. Most species show their best bright colors in the days immediately following molting; as the upper skin gets older, the colors do not show through as well. (From D'Angelo, 1980, p. 221 taken from *Snakes of the World*. (Feltham, England: Hamlyn Publishing Group Ltd., p. 221).)

Causation

Changes Brought about by the Automobile

The advent of the automobile has caused profound changes in the American way of life. The petroleum industry, the steel industry, and the rubber industry have all grown to tremendous proportions in the past half century. Highway construction is at an all-time peak, and many roads recently completed are already becoming obsolete, requiring government intervention and expenditure. The number of people whose occupations are directly or indirectly influenced by automobiles—the traffic policemen, the garage mechanic, the automobile salesman—is staggering. But perhaps the most noticeable changes brought about by our being a nation on wheels may be found in our social practices. In the first place, we have become more transient as distance has ceased to be a consideration, and we drive anywhere, anytime. Second, and probably more important, the automobile has replaced the parlor for dating purposes. Today a young lady seldom receives "gentleman callers" at home; more likely, her home is only a "pit stop" in a continuous marathon race. (from Malcolm Moore: *Paragraph Development*. Copyright © 1975 by Houghton Mifflin Company. Used by permission.)

Problem/Solution

(For the training program a passage on killer bees was used; however, its source could not be located to obtain necessary permissions. A substitute problem/solution text is provided.)

Teenage Pregnancy

A problem of great concern in this country is the growing number of teenagers who become pregnant. Abortion is certainly not the answer. It kills unborn children and leaves the young mother emotionally and sometimes physically harmed. Delivery of a baby is not always satisfactory either. Babies of teenagers have more problems than babies of mature women in their 20s and 30s. If the young person chooses to raise her child, it is certainly a difficult road for a young girl with limited education and skills. Some high schools are instituting programs to help teenagers continue with school during and after pregnancy.

However, these programs help with the consequences of the problem, but do not get to the cause of the problem. The cause of the difficulty is sex before marriage. A new movement is gaining momentum that encourages teenagers to abstain from sex prior to marriage. Speakers, such as Josh McDowell, take this stand and draw large crowds of young people. The best way to get young people to follow this standard is to talk to them while they are preteens and prepare them for the years ahead. Also, studies have shown that the earlier a girl dates the more likely it is that she will have sex before marriage. Parents need to stress abstinence to their preteens and teenagers and only let teens date when they have the courage and maturity to say no under pressure. Parents also must give their teenagers plenty of love, attention, and hugs at home.

Comparison

Advantages of Each Side in the Civil War

Both the North and South sides had certain advantages at the beginning of the Civil War. The North possessed approximately three-fourths of the nation's wealth and had more than twice the manpower of the South. In addition to its vast farmlands, the North also operated almost all the factories in the country. The Navy, which was solely in the hands of the North, assured control of the entire coastline of the Confederacy. The South, on the other hand, was fighting a defensive war and did not have to carry the fighting to Northern soil. It was blessed with splendid officers and a fighting breed of men accustomed to riding and the use of firearms. Moreover, its cause was popular with many of the European powers. (from Malcolm Moore: *Paragraph Development*. (Copyright © 1975 by Houghton Mifflin Company. Used by permission.)

Recapitulation.   To use the plan strategy we need to know how it should be used. It must serve as a framework for the words we write. If it is *description,* we must set out a list of sentences that describe the main idea. If it is *sequence,* we must write a list of ordered sentences. If it is *causation,* we must have a cause part and an effect part in our writing. If it is a *problem/solution* plan, again we have two parts in what we write. One tells about the problem; its cause and effects. The other tells about the solution; this solution should block one of the causes of the problem. If it is a *comparison* plan, then once more we should use different parts in our written recall—one for each of the views.

Test.   Some test items: a multiple choice test and two recall tests are to be completed to assess the students' progress on this step. Feedback should be given after each task.

Choose the Best Answer for the Following Questions

In writing down what I remember from a passages using a comparison plan, I should **first**

a. write the name comparison at the top of the paper.*
b. start writing what I remember right away before I forget.
c. use sentences that tell the problem and then those that tell the solution.

second, I should

a. write the names and numbers down quickly before I forget them.
b. write down the main idea sentence.*
c. write one thing and then what ever else it reminds me to write next.

then, I should

a. finish up.

b. check to see I have used the comparison plan.

c. use sentences that tell one argument, then sentences that tell the other argument.*

next, I should

a. finish.

b. check to see that I have used the comparison plan to write my recall.*

c. add anything else that I have just remembered.

finally, I should

a. say or write comparison several times.

b. check to see that I have used the comparison plan to write my recall.

c. add anything else that I have just remembered.*

Review the two questions to ask before reading and the two to ask before writing. WHAT IS THE PLAN FOR THE PASSAGE? WHAT IS THE MAIN IDEA THAT FITS THIS PLAN? WHAT PLAN DID I FIND WHEN I READ: HOW WILL I USE THIS FORMAT TO ORGANIZE WHAT I WRITE? Then review the six steps for best recall. (1) CHOOSE THE PLAN IN WHAT YOU READ, (2) WRITE ITS NAME ON THE TOP OF THE PAGE BEFORE YOU RECALL THE TEXT, (3) WRITE THE MAIN IDEA SENTENCE, (4) USE THE PLAN TO ORGANIZE WHAT YOU RECALL, (5) CHECK TO SEE THAT YOU HAVE USED THE PLAN, (6) ADD ANYTHING ELSE YOU CAN REMEMBER FROM WHAT YOU READ. REMEMBER CHOOSE IT, USE IT, OR LOSE IT. Next have the students read and recall the following passage. Encourage them to have Table 6.2 in front of them and use it to help them identify plans and signaling words.

Slimming Down a Plump Pet

An overweight dog or cat could be courting serious health problems. Excess weight makes pets sluggish, puts extra strain on the cardiovascular system, and in the long run tends to shorten their life span. Your veterinarian or any good pet-care manual can tell you the approximate healthy weight for your pet, so that you can determine if you need to do something to help your pet slim down.

Here are some tips you can use if your animal is overweight. Gradually reduce the size of your pet's meals, starting with approximately a 5% reduction and working up to as much as 25% if it's necessary. You could begin using pet food designed for inactive pets, which has about 10 to 20% fewer calories than regular pet food. If your pet is allowed to eat whenever it wishes, you might switch to feeding it only at specific mealtimes. Also, eliminate snacks and table scraps (which are loaded with calories) from your pet's diet, and gradually increase its exercise routine. If you follow these suggestions, look for improvement in your pet's appearance and general health after about 2 months.

Write the name of the plan used in the passage. *Use* it to write down what you remember. Write down as much as you can remember from the passage you have just read. Use complete sentences. You can use the words in the passage or your own words. Do not turn back to the passage after you start writing.

_____

_____

_____

Let's check how well you used the strategy.

DID YOU . . . .

1. Correctly pick the plan ( )
2. Write its name as a reminder at the top of the page ( )
3. Write the main idea sentence ( )
4. Use the same plan in your recall ( )
5. Check that you've used it ( )
6. Add (or try to) anything you'd just remembered. ( )
   (If you didn't remember anything extra, score as correct.)

SCORE:
0–2 OH NO!
3–4 TUT, TUT!
 5   NOT BAD!
 6   GREAT!

Discuss any problems or comments after their first recall attempt. Explain that for the final passages on Chicken-Hawks the six steps will not be listed on the recall page. They will need to remember and follow the six steps. Emphasize that it is extremely important to choose a plan; it is good to have the right plan, but the critical aspect of this strategy is that you choose and use a plan rather than write an unrelated list of sentences about the passage you read.

Chicken-Hawks

In one district, farmers began to kill the chicken-hawks. Large parties of men would go on bird-shoots. They not only shot adult birds, but also destroyed nests and breeding areas used by the hawks. Any young found in the nests were killed immediately. As a result of these hunts the farmers' chickens were not eaten. But, the farmers found something else wrong. Their store of grain in the barns was eaten by rats. Soon the rats were overrunning the farms. There was nothing to stop the spread of the rats. The farmers had removed a natural enemy of the rats—the chicken-hawk. (From BIOLOGY: PATTERNS IN THE ENVIRONMENT (Teaching-Learning Strategies) by Evelyn Morholt and Paul F. Brandwein, Copyright © 1972 by Harcourt Brace Jovanovich, Inc. p. 184. Reprinted by permission of the publisher.)

Write down as much as you can remember from the passage you have just read. Use complete sentences. You can use the words in the passage or your own words. Do not turn back to the passage after you start writing.

_____

_____

_____

Let's check how well you used the strategy.

DID YOU . . . .

1. Correctly pick the plan	( )
2. Write its name as a reminder at the top of the page	( )
3. Write the main idea sentence	( )
4. Use the same plan in your recall	( )
5. Check that you've used it	( )
6. Add (or try to) anything you'd just remembered.	( )

(If you didn't remember anything extra, score as correct.)

SCORE:
0–2   OH NO!
3–4   TUT, TUT!
 5   NOT BAD!
 6   GREAT!

Again discuss their recall and progress using the strategy.

Conclusion: Session 3

Today you used the strategy. You first picked out the plan of the passage you read, asking yourself (1) What is the plan for the passage? and (2) What is the main idea that fits this plan? Then you used the same plan to write down what you remembered. To help you use the strategy you should do six things:

1. Find the plan.
2. Write its name on the top of the recall page.
3. Write the main idea sentence.
4. Use the plan to write what you remember.
5. Check that it has been used.
6. Add anything just remembered.

Usually, the plan you find and use will be one of five types—description, sequence, causation, problem/solution, or comparison. Today you used problem/solution and causation.

What you did today is an indication that this strategy is effective for improving memory of reading materials. Are there any questions on (a) how to pick the plan, (b) how to use it in recalling?

As you leave today, think of the five types of plans and how each of them is a building framework in which to write words, sentences and paragraphs. Look for them in anything you read.

Session 4: Mastering the Strategy and Using it with Longer and Muddled Texts.

INSTRUCTOR'S PROGRAM FOR SESSION 4

1. Introduction to Session 4

Aim 1: To coordinate the group of work of previous sessions with the individual work of session 4.

Communication. During our previous sessions we have attempted to tell you the benefits of using a strategy for remembering what you read. Also, we have shown you what the strategy is and how to use it. Today, I have some feedback or information on how well you are doing. Each of you has a personal progress report included in today's materials.

Aim 2: To outline Session 4.

Communication. During today's session we will speak with each of you about the strategy and your progress in learning it so far. Overall, the group has done marvelously and we are very pleased to be able to provide the personal performance information. During this session each of you will work reviewing all that you know about how to use the strategy and eliminating any problems that may have occurred. Also, we will make suggestions for coping with passages that are muddled or do not clearly follow the pattern of a particular plan.

2. Principles: Session 4

We know **three** things about the strategy of **using the plan.**

1. It helps you remember **more** of what you read.
2. It helps you to remember **more of the important information** in what you read.
3. It helps you to remember this information **longer.**

3. Discussion: Session 4

Three instructional goals were set for this part of the session.

1. To remediate problems in students' acquisition of the strategy.

2. To have students apply the strategy to passages (a) with less signaling than those of earlier sessions, and (b) with less direction than for those of previous sessions.

3. To have students correctly differentiate writing plans with less cuing than for similar tasks of previous sessions.

Step 1. The group is to discuss the likely truth value of the three principles in terms of the nature of the strategy. Point out that the strategy provides a framework for facts and relations which appear in a passage of text and that for longer passages and, ever increasing time delay, this would serve recall better than a random listing of information remembered.

Discussion to be brief and recapitulation to involve a restatement of the principles.

Test. Turn to the next page and fill in the blanks. Then check your responses against the three points listed on the first page. Using the plan strategy has three advantages:

It helps you:

1. ＿＿＿＿＿＿＿＿＿＿

2. ＿＿＿＿＿＿＿＿＿＿

3. ＿＿＿＿＿＿＿＿＿＿

Step 2. A check-list is provided of the individual's progress and comments evaluating performance and specifying procedures to be followed to remedy deficiencies and to assist one another. Against a list of 17 items, marks are made indicating success, or lack of it, as evidenced by the student's performance on exercises and tests for Sessions 1, 2, and 3. The student's current level of proficiency is indicated, and where applicable, problem areas are listed.

Students are to be paired prior to class by the instructor such that a more proficient student could work with one who needs more help. If the pairing and this form of remedial structure is acceptable to both members, the pair rework steps of the previous sessions. Particular attention is required from both for areas indicated as problematic by the progress report and self-appraisal by the student. For students preferring to work alone, the same remedial procedure is to be followed. Have each student read carefully through the Performance Check List as a review and then examine their progress report.

Performance Check List

During the past three session, you have found that:

1. To choose the organization in what you read is a key to understanding.
2. A strategy to improve memory is called *using the plan.*
3. The strategy has *two* parts—*to choose* the organization, and *to use* this organization.
4. *To choose* the plan needs your attention *before, while,* and *after* reading.
5. *To choose* the organizational plan, you **ask** two questions before reading:

What is the plan for this passage?
What is the main idea that fits this plan?

You **answer** these questions while you read, and **check** your answers after reading.

6. The five common plans are:

description
sequence
causation
problem/solution
comparison

7. Signaling words in the passage can help you to **choose** the plan.
8. Each of the plans has a *special way to pattern* the sentences in a passage.

9. The pattern of the *Description* plan is that most of the sentences are arranged to describe the person, place, things, event, or quality in the main idea.

10. The pattern of the *Sequence* plan is that main idea sentences follow in a certain order.

11. The pattern of the *Causation* plan is that there is a cause and an effect organization. The main idea involves two main parts. In one part sentences tell about the **cause,** and in the other part sentences tell about the **effect.** In the explanation form of causation, the effect is given first and its cause, the explanation, follows.

12. The pattern of *Problem/solution* plan is that there is part of the passage that tells about a problem (question, puzzle, concern), and another that tells about its solution (answer, reply). In the question/answer version the answer must deal with the ideas discussed in the question and provide some answer. In the problem/solution version often the causes and effects of the problem are discussed first; then, a solution follows that should attempt to block or eliminate at least one of the causes of the problem.

13. The contrastive pattern of the *Comparison* plan is that different points of view are shown in different parts of the passage. It may be that one view tells what did happen and the other tells what did not happen; or, one might tell what exists and the other what does not exist; or each part might tell opposing arguments. Often when opposing views are compared they are compared on many of the same issues, for example, one political candidate's views on abortion, taxes, government spending, and defense, and then the other candidate's views on these same issues. Your memory will be improved if you remember that a comparison plan was used and the number and name of the issues compared; for the above example remember that the candidates were compared on four issues: abortion, taxes, government spending, and defense.

14. Once you have chosen the plan you must *use it to organize your written recall.* Remember: Choose it, Use it, or Lose it!

15. *To use* the plan requires your attention *before, while,* and *after* you write your recall.

16. *While* you write put your ideas into sentences and paragraphs that follow the pattern of the plan identified.

17. *After* you write, check that you used the correct organization, correctly.

18. To *use it*— *write its name* on the top of the page where you'll be writing your recall (to help you get organized).
    — *write the main idea sentence* (to set up the plan).
    — *arrange sentences and paragraphs* to match the plan (keep thinking about how the plan works).
    — *check* that you've used it (Ask "Have I discussed the main idea the same way as in the passage?")

— *write* down anything you've only just remembered (It often happens that you think of more information as you are checking).

Your skill in using this information has shown that you can:

(a) still learn more about using the strategy.
(b) find the main idea in a passage.
(c) pick the plan of the passage.
(d) use the same plan to arrange you recall.
(e) use the strategy effectively.

These seem to be your problem areas (The numbers correspond to those on the above check list; check what the numbers mean and see if you agree with our analysis of your progress.)

If you can fix these problems you will be able to use the strategy perfectly. Work on your own reading and recalling the next two passages. Use your table with definitions of writing plans and signaling words to help you; if you find other signaling words add them to your table. After you recall each passage check your progress with the *feedback* forms provided.

Passage 1

People with arthritis are one of the groups most exploited by health fraud in the United States. They spend approximately one billion dollars a year on worthless or harmful treatments, such as copper bracelets and cow manure. The reasons are understandable and clear. Arthritis has no cure, and treatment requires you to exert effort and have patience. Results are usually good with time, but still the illness often remains and can flare without warning. (From Arthritis Foundation Booklet: *Rheumatoid Arthritis* Courtesy Arthritis Foundation.)

Write the name of the plan used in the passage. *Use* it to write down what you remember.
Write down as much as you can remember from the passage you have just read. Use complete sentences. You can use the words in the passage or your own words. Do not turn back to the passage after you start writing.

Feedback

1. Did you pick out the organization as *causation?*
   If so, _____ great!
   If not, _____ did you ask the two questions before reading?
   _____ did you look for the plan? (reasons why people with arthritis are exploited by fraud: effect part = tricking people with arthritis; cause part = explanation that there is no cure for arthritis and treatment takes hard work and patience)
   _____ did you find the main idea organized by the plan? (People with arthritis fall for worthless or harmful, fraudulent treatments because arthritis has no cure and is hard to treat.)

2. Did you write the name of the plan at the top of the recall page?
   If so, _____ so far, so good!
   If not, _____ mmmmmmm!

3. Did you write down the main idea as the first sentence?
   If so, _____ keep it up!
   If not, _____ oh no!

4. Did you have two parts in arranging your sentences (an effect part followed by the cause or explanation part)?
   If so, _____ not far to go now!
   If not, _____ tut, tut!

5. Were there two parts: one discussing people with arthritis being fooled by health frauds; and one giving the reasons they are fooled: no cure and difficult treatment?
   If so, _____ I bet you remembered a lot!
   If not, _____ Oh rats!

6. Did you check to see if you remembered any other facts?
   If so, _____ double smiles!
   If not, _____ don't be so overconfident!

Passage 2

Kindness Cures Rat Allergies

Psychologists who work with rats and mice in experiments often become allergic to these creatures. This is a real hazard for these investigators who spend hours a week running rats in experiments. These allergies are a reaction to the protein in the urine of these small animals.

At a meeting sponsored by the National Institutes of Health, Dr. Andrew J. M. Slovak, a British physician, recommended kindness to rats and mice by the experimenters. Psychologists who pet and talk softly to their rats are less often splattered with urine and the protein that causes the allergic reaction.

Write the name of the plan used in the passage. *Use* it to write down what you remember.

Write down as much as you can remember from the passage you have just read. Use complete sentences. You can use the words in the passage or your own words. Do not turn back to the passage after you start writing.

_____

_____

_____

Feedback

1. Did you pick out the organization as *problem/solution?*
    If so, _____ great!
    If not, _____ did you ask the two questions before reading?
    _____ did you look for the plan? (hazard of allergies to rats, evidence about the cause and suggestion to help eliminate exposure to the cause of the problem: protein in the urine)
    _____ did you find the main idea organized by the plan? (the problem of allergies to rats and mice may be solved by kindness to them since kindness reduces exposure to the cause of the problem: protein in urine)

2. Did you write the name of the plan at the top of the recall page?
    If so, _____ so far, so good!
    If not, _____ mmmmmmm!

3. Did you write down the main idea as the first sentence?
    If so, _____ keep it up!
    If not, _____ oh no!

4. Did you have two parts in arranging your sentences?
    If so, _____ not far to go now!
    If not, _____ tut, tut!

5. Were the two parts: one for the problem and one for the solution
    If so, _____ I bet you remembered a lot!
    If not, _____ Oh rats!

6. Did you check?
    If so, _____ double smiles!
    If not, _____ don't be so overconfident!

Aim 3: To make suggestions for coping with muddled passages.

Communication.   Some writers just don't organize their writing well. Others use an organization but muddle its use. If you can pick a plan but see that its use by a writer is muddled, that is an excellent perception. What do you do? Just unmuddle it when you write, but keep the same organization. Let's work through how a learner did just that. Then you can try one for yourself.

Examine the following advertisement that appeared in *Better Homes & Gardens* magazine (see Figure 6.18).

THIS IS WHERE A WRINKLE COULD START. . . . THIS IS WHAT COULD STOP IT.

I'm Lynda Carter. And I don't want wrinkles any more than you do. That's why I use Moisture Whip Moisturizer by Maybelline. Because unlike the leading moisturizers, Moisture Whip contains Padimate O, a protective ingredient that screens out harmful light rays that cause our skin to age and wrinkle before its time. Moisture Whip is also dermatologist tested and fragrance free. So use Moisture Whip every day and do more than moisturize your face. Help protect it from wrinkles. I do.''

Here is a recall written by a learner for this passage.

Problem / Solution

The problem of premature wrinkles is presented and traits of a potential solution are discussed. The problem is wrinkles on our face. No one wants wrinkles and we all want to avoid them as long as possible. We can get wrinkled before our time by harmful rays from the sun.

A solution to premature wrinkling of the facial skin is the use of Moisture Whip by Maybelline because it contains Padimate O, an ingredient that blocks the sun's harmful rays. In addition, Moisture Whip is dermatologist tested, a moisturizer, and used by Lynda Carter to prevent premature wrinkling.

See if the learner:

1. Picked the plan (problem/solution).
2. Wrote the name of the plan before writing a recall.
3. Wrote the main idea as a first sentence.
4. Used two parts to organize the other sentences.
5. Used one part to put all the information together about the *problem* and its cause and another part for that about the *solution*.

The recall mentions everything that the learner could remember about the problem of wrinkling first: a description of the problem and its cause. Then

FIG. 6.18. Clarifying a text by using the plan strategy (advertisement copyrighted © 1981 Maybelline Company).

everything remembered about the solution was given: How it can prevent the cause of the problem and a description of the qualities of the solution. It is better organized in terms of the problem part and solution part than the original advertisement where the solution to the problem was presented earlier in the sentence than the cause of the problem. Text is often a little muddled, but we can use our reading strategy to clarify the text and our understanding of it. You try it with a passage on aspirin.

> How to relieve a headache is a problem. Lots of people take aspirin. Headache is a very common condition. Nobody likes to have a headache. One help for relief of a headache is aspirin.

_____

_____

_____

Compare your recall and reorganization to that of another student as listed below.

Problem/Solution

Headache is a very common human illness. How to cure it is a problem because nobody likes to have a headache. A solution is to take aspirin whan you have a headache. Lots of people do.

Notice that the student _used_ the correct plan _and_ organized the recall in a _less-muddled_ way than the author. As a result, she has recalled all of the information even though she changed some words and the order of the sentences.

Next examine the following article from the _Chicago Tribune_. Write down the name of the plan used in the space provided.

Can molecules be ambidextrous?
by Jon Van

One way to see if a person is right- or left-handed is to have him toss you a pencil and note which hand he uses, and now chemists have found a way to do something like that with molecules. Molecules don't have hands, of course, but they do have characteristics analogous to hand preference. That is, molecules may be composed of exactly the same atoms yet be mirror images of each other. In some drugs this can be important. The common blood pressure medication propranolol is an example. One form of the drug is 100 times as potent as the other. "Ideally, you'd like to treat a patient with just the left-handed form of propranolol," said Thomas Doyle, a member of the American Chemical Society and a research chemist for the U.S. Food and Drug Administration. Unfortunately, the manufacturing process produces left- and right-handed molecules all mixed together in one batch.

_____ plan

Discuss the answers posited by the class. The question/answer plan is a likely incorrect answer due to the question in the title. Explain the misleading title: (1) ambidextrous is using both hands well—the examples of people and molecules in the article shows preference for one hand over the other, not facility with both hands; (2) the questions focus on ambidextrous instead of hand preference brings up the wrong analogy to the mind of the reader; (3) the question format also brings up the wrong writing plan to the mind of the reader—question/answer instead of comparison (analogy subtype) is the plan of the text. The text draws an analogy between hand preference in people and this mirror image phenomenon in molecules and then describes the effects of "hand preference" in molecules with an example—blood pressure medication. The best plan to facilitate memory of this article would be comparison/analogy.

I have asked _____ to work with you on using the strategy for the remainder of tonight's session and for the next session. You will read some passages that clearly show a well-organized writing plan, while others will be more muddled. You and your partner will take turns stating the plan and telling the other person what you remember from the passage. The person listening to the recall should use the *Feedback* form to check whether or not this partner found the writing plan and the main ideas. For some of the passages you will be asked to tell all you can remember, while for most of the passages you will just be asked to tell the plan and the main idea. Take turns recalling the passages; if you recalled the first passage, then let your partner recall the second passage while you fill out his *feedback* form. Try to help each other with any problems; we will be available to consult with you about your questions. Use your table with definitions of writing plans and signaling words to help you; if you find other signaling words add them to your table. Remember to look for the overall writing plan; you may find signaling words for plans that organize small parts of the passage, but the overall writing plan will relate all the information together.

Passage 1: Tell Your Partner the Plan and All You Remember.

Beauty and the Beast
by Bunnie Corwith (appeared in the Lake Forest, Illinois *News Voice*)

I look out the window; our beautiful trees, majestic in their bareness, lean against the blue sky.
T.V. news is discussing the latest terrorist activities.

New snow gently falls, giving the old snow a clean cover; it glistens playfully in the back yard spotlights.

A radio bulletin announces another gang murder.

Our youngest grandchild, a year old, beams at our Golden Retriever and pats him lovingly; she is not afraid.

The neighbors change their door locks every few months, there have been so many burglaries in the area. They are afraid.

As I walk down the street, watching winter birds flit from feeders to trees, a car careens around the corner, going three times as fast as it should. An empty six-pack is thrown from a window on the way by.

Two ducks, a male and a female, fly over the creek, happily together for life.

A friend calls to say that her husband is divorcing her after 25 years of marriage.

I help our daughter pick out a new suit for her job.

A magazine on the newsstand quotes a young woman as saying, of course she takes off all her clothes for a center-fold; Why shouldn't she? Everyone does things like that.

An elderly grandmother, who is ready to join the Lord, dies peacefully in her sleep. The 16-year-old girl with an unwanted pregnancy, kills her unborn infant via an abortion.

God looks down and cries.

Feedback

1. Did you choose the organization *comparison?*
   If so, _____ great!
   If not, _____ did you ask the two questions before reading?
   _____ Did you look for the plan? (contrast between beauty and ugly aspects of life today or good and evil)
   _____ Did you find the main idea organized by the plan? (the author and God favor the good and beautiful and cry out to people to contrast the evil in our world with the peace, order, and beauty God intended)
2. Did you give the main idea as your first statement?
   If so, _____ keep it up!
   If not, _____ oh, no!
3. Did you have two parts in telling what you remembered? In this essay we see a different way to format the comparison plan than previously studied; other examples have given all the information dealing with one view together and then the information from the other view together, while this example alternates views as each issue is mentioned. In the essay the

poetic effect would be spoiled by stating all the good together, followed by a listing of all the bad. However, you could adequately recall the passage that way. Either way and for all comparison plans you should determine the issues covered by both views in order to increase your memory of the material. The issues to remember that were contrasted in this essay were: (1) peace/terror, (2) gentle/violence, (3) fear, (4) order, (5) marital stability, (6) propriety in dress, and (7) death.

4. Did you add anything else you could remember at the end?
    If so, _____ double smiles!
    If not, _____ don't be so overconfident!

Passage 2: Tell Your Partner the Plan and All You Can Remember.

Where you live affects how fast your eyesight will deteriorate from age. A recent study found that people in warmer countries develop age-related farsightedness earlier than those who endure a colder climate. The British ophthalmologist who came to this conclusion says that the temperature of the eye's lens is not well maintained by the body, but is highly influenced by the external environment. Thus, heat may somehow cause changes in the lens that lead to farsightedness. (*Science Digest*, August 1982, p. 94)

Feedback

1. Did you choose the organization *causation?*
    If so, _____ great!
    If not, _____ did you ask the two questions before reading?
    _____ did you look for the plan? (hotter climates cause greater deterioration of the eye; cause part = where you live—warmer or colder climate; effect part = deterioration of the lens—farsightedness)
    _____ did you find the main idea organized by the plan? (hotter climates lead to earlier onset of farsightedness)
2. Did you tell the main idea in your first statement?
    If so, _____ keep it up!
    If not, _____ oh no!
3. Did you have two parts in arranging your sentences (the cause followed by the effect)?
    If so, _____ not far to go now!
    If not, _____ tut, tut!
4. Were there two parts: one discussing the weather conditions where you live; and one discussing the age-related farsightedness?
    If so, _____ I bet you remembered a lot!
    If not, _____ Oh rats!

5. Did you check to see if you remembered any other facts?
   If so, _____ double smiles!
   If not, _____ don't be so overconfident!

Passage 3: Tell Your Partner the Plan and Main Idea.

Psalm 1
(*Holy Bible,* New International Version, 1978)

Blessed is the man who does not walk in the counsel of the wicked or stand in the way of sinners or sit in the seat of mockers. But his delight is in the law of the LORD, and on his law he meditates day and night. He is like a tree planted by streams of water, which yields its fruit in season and whose leaf does not wither. Whatever he does prospers.

Not so the wicked! They are like chaff that the wind blows away. Therefore the wicked will not stand in the judgment, nor sinners in the assembly of the righteous. For the LORD watches over the way of the righteous, but the way of the wicked will perish.

Feedback

1. Did you pick out the organization as *comparison?*
   If so, _____ great!
   If not, _____ did you ask the two questions before reading?
   _____ did you look for the plan? (contrast between the righteous and the wicked)
   _____ did you find the main idea organized by the plan? (the good that comes to the righteous and the bad to the wicked)
2. Did you have two parts in arranging your main idea?
   If so, _____ not far to go now!
   If not, _____ tut, tut!
3. Were the two parts: one for the righteous group and one for the wicked group?
   If so, _____ I bet you remembered a lot!
   If not, _____ Oh rats!

Passage 4: Tell Your Partner the Plan and Main Idea.

A Graceful Creature
(*Basic Reading Comprehension-*#R-7, ESP, Inc. 1975)

The grace and beauty of the swan has fascinated man for centuries. Swans appear often in fairy tales, poetry, and mythology. In 15th century England they were even designated as royal birds.

The stately water birds are found in diverse parts of the world, such as the arctic regions, the southern parts of South America, and the United States. The best known wild swans in the United States are the whistling and trumpeter swans.

A long, slender neck is the most striking feature of the swan. Swans use their long necks to dive for food. They like to eat seeds, roots, and fish eggs. Swans weigh about 40 pounds and measure up to 4½ feet long. Wild swans travel in flocks and are able to fly long distances in spite of their size and weight.

Feedback

1. Did you pick out the organization as *description?*
    If so, _____ great!
    If not, _____ did you ask the two questions before reading?
    _____ did you look for the plan? (description of swans)
2. _____ did you find the main idea organized by the plan? (descriptions of swans' fascination for man, domain in the world, features, habits and dimensions)

Passage 5: Tell Your Partner the Plan and Main Idea.

Noah Puts God First

It is interesting to note that Noah thought of the Lord before he thought of worldly things. After the dove returned with the olive twig and the ark settled on Mt. Ararat, Noah immediately built an altar and offered sacrifices of thanksgiving to Jehovah for the safe delivery of his family from the flood waters. Then he planted a vineyard, harvested his crop, and made some wine. When he had finished, he drank quite a bit more of the wine than was good for him, an act for which he might have been forgiven, considering the amount of time he had spent in the ark with all those animals. (Malcolm Moore: *Paragraph Development.* Copyright © 1975 by Houghton Mifflin Company, p. 37)

Feedback

1. Did you pick out the organization as *sequence?*
    If so, _____ great!
    If not, _____ did you ask the two questions before reading?
    _____ did you look for the plan? (sequence of Noah's activities)
2. _____ did you find the main idea organized by the plan? (in the sequence of Noah's activities Noah put God before worldly tasks)
3. If you recalled the passage would you have arranged the sentences in chronological order from the first thing Noah did to the last?
    If so, _____ good work!
    If not, _____ remember next time!

Passage 6: Tell Your Partner the Plan and Main Idea

Wisdom from Theodore Roosevelt

It is not the critic who counts, nor the man who points how the strong man stumbled, or where the doer of deeds could have done better. The credit belongs to the man who is actually in the arena, whose face is marred by the dust and sweat and blood; who strives valiantly; who errs and comes short again and again; who knows the great enthusiasms, the great devotions, and spends himself in a worthy cause; who at the best, knows in the end the triumph of high achievement; and who, at the worst, if he fails, at least fails while daring greatly, so that his place shall never be with those cold and timid souls who know neither victory nor defeat.

Feedback

1. Did you pick out the organization as *comparison?*
    If so, _____ great!
    If not, _____ did you ask the two questions before reading?
    _____ did you look for the plan? (contrast between courageous doer and the cold and timid onlooker or critic)
2. _____ did you find the main idea organized by the plan?
    (Theodore Roosevelt favors the courageous, active proponent for worthy pursuits regardless of successful outcome over the person who criticizes, yet does not try himself)
3. Did you have two parts in arranging your main idea?
    If so, _____ not far to go now!
    If not, _____ tut, tut!
4. Were the two parts: one for the active, daring souls and one for the critical, timid ones?
    If so, _____ I bet you remembered a lot!
    If not, _____ Oh rats!

Passage 7

Try the next passage taken from *Tufts University Diet & Nutrition Letter* (Vol. 1, No. 9, Nov. 23, 1983, p. 1); it is somewhat muddled. Tell your partner the best plan for this article and the main idea.

Colicky Babies and Breast Milk

Contrary to popular opinion, mother's milk is not always "perfect" for infants. A recent report in *Pediatric* showed that some infants may actually be allergic to their own mother's milk if the mother is drinking cow's milk. It is known that substances the mother eats can pass through her breast milk to cause allergic reactions in the baby.

Physicians Irene Jakobsson and Tor Lindberg wanted to determine if the consumption of cow's milk on the part of the mother might be causing the problem in some babies with infantile colic. They found that when 66 breast-feeding mothers of colicky babies gave up cow's milk for one week, the symptoms of abdominal pain, gas, and excessive crying disappeared in 35 of the infants. When cow's milk was added back to the mothers' diets, 23 of the ''cured'' infants became sickly again. To see if whey, which contains the most allergenic of cow's milk proteins, was at fault, the mothers of about half of the reactive babies were challenged with whey protein capsules and placebo capsules. All but one infant became colicky in response to whey, while no reactions occurred when a placebo was used.

The researchers conclude that in one-third of the breast-fed infants with colic, the problems are related to cow's-milk consumption by the mother. Before switching to a commercial formula, they suggest that the mother give up cow's milk to see how that works. (Reprinted with permission, *Tufts University Diet and Nutrition Letter*. 475 Park Ave. South, 30th Fl. New York, NY 10016.)

Evaluate your partner on the following points:
When reading:

1. I asked what the plan was for the passage.
2. I chose the main idea discussed by the plan.
3. I picked a plan.
4. I picked the problem/solution plan (even though the comparison plan is hinted at in the first sentence).

When retelling:

5. I told the name of the plan.
6. I said *problem/solution.*
7. I gave a main idea sentence.
8. I said something similar to:

> **The problem of colic in breast-fed babies was presented; some physicians did some studies to identify its cause as whey drunk by mothers in cow's milk; the proposed solution for many colicky babies was switching the moms off cow's milk.**

RESULTS:

0–OH OH!
1–2   mmmmmmm!
3–4   Better than mmmmmm!
5–6   Much better,—good job!
7–8   You're there—great work!

The *five* common types of plans are:

description
sequence
causation
problem/solution
comparison

Which of these five is the easiest for you to pick? (If they're all easy, say so.)

_____

Why?

_____

Which of these five is the *most difficult* for *you* to pick? (If they are all difficult, write the hardest first, then the next, etc.)

_____

Why?

_____

Complete the following:
For passages muddled or not, long or short,

1. A strategy for remembering what I read has two parts. In reading, I will
_____ (find the plan). In recalling (writing, speaking, or thinking about what I have read), I will _____ (use the plan).
   2. The strategy is called: Using _____ (the plan).
As you leave today, think of what you might do to further improve how well you use the strategy. Look for the *five* types of plans in your reading outside our classroom. Please bring any passages you have found in your reading to the next session. These passages should have one of the *five* organizational plans that we have been discussing in the last four sessions. It doesn't matter what the passage is about, nor how short or long the passage is. Just bring the book, magazine or other material in which it is contained.

Session 5: Remediation of Difficulties and Use of the Strategy with Everyday Reading Materials

INSTRUCTOR'S PROGRAM FOR SESSION 5
1. Introduction to Session 5

Aim 1:   To update personal progress report.
Aim 2:   To remediate difficulties in students' use of the strategy for particular writing plans.

Aim 3:   To have students identify examples of plans in reading materials that they read in their daily life.

Communication.   First, please complete the scale on the first page of your packet (motivation check). "Do you want to improve your reading comprehension?"

1	2	3	4	5	6	7
not at all	don't care	maybe	I have no feeling one way or the other	yes, some	yes, lots	I would work *very* hard to improve this ability

At the beginning of our last session, you received a report of progress in acquiring the strategy. Since then you have made further progress and we have revised your personal report. Turn to your report and we will work through it. Notice the special comments beside numbers 9, 10, 11, 12, and 13. These indicate strengths you have in using each of the five plans as well as aspects to work on today.

I would like to have you work with the same partner that you worked with during the last session. We will come around and check you on problem areas.

Performance Check List

During the past sessions, you have found that:

1. To choose the organization in what you read is a key to understanding.

2. A strategy to improve memory is called *using the plan.*

3. The strategy has *two* parts—*to choose* the organization, and *to use* this organization.

4. *To choose* the plan needs your attention *before, while,* and *after* reading.

5. *To choose* the organizational plan, you **ask** two questions before reading:

What is the plan for this passage?
What is the main idea that fits the plan?
You **answer** these questions while you read, and **check** your answers after reading.

6. The five common plans are:

description
sequence

causation
problem/solution
comparison

7. Signaling words in the passage can help you to **pick** the plan.

8. Each of the plans has a **special way to pattern** the sentences in a passage.

9. The pattern of the *Description* plan is that most of the sentences are arranged to describe the person, place, things, event, or quality in the main idea.

10. The pattern of the *Sequence* plan is that main idea sentences follow in a certain order.

11. The pattern of the *Causation* plan is that there is a cause and an effect organization. The main idea involves two main parts. In one part sentences tell about the **cause,** and in the other part sentences tell about the **effect.** In explanations we see the effect first followed by the cause, or explanation part.

12. The pattern of *Problem/solution* plan is that there is part of the passage that tells about a problem (question, puzzle, concern), and another that tells about its solution (answer, reply). In the question/answer version the answer must deal with the ideas discussed in the question and provide some answer. In the problem/solution version often the causes and effects of the problem are discussed first; then, a solution follows that should attempt to block or eliminate at least one of the causes of the problem.

13. The contrastive pattern of the *Comparison* plan is that different points of view are shown in different parts of the passage. It may be that one view tells what did happen and the other tells what did not happen; or, one might tell what exists and the other what does not exist; or each part might tell opposing arguments. Often when opposing views are compared they are compared on many of the same issues; for example, one political candidate's views on abortion, taxes, government spending, and defense, and then the other candidate's views on these same issues. Your memory will be improved if you remember that a comparison plan was used and the number and name of the issues compared; for the above example remember that the candidates were compared on four issues: abortion, taxes, government spending and defense.

14. Once you have chosen the plan you must *use it to organize your written recall.*

15. *To use* the plan requires your attention *before, while,* and *after* you write your recall.

16. *While* you write put your ideas into sentences and paragraphs that follow the pattern of the plan identified.

17. *After* you write, check that you used the correct organization, correctly.

18. To *use it* — *write its name* on the top of the page where you'll be writing your recall (to help you get organized).

    — *write the main idea sentence* (to set up the plan)
    — *arrange sentences and paragraphs* to match the plan (keep thinking about how the plan works).
    — *check* that you've used it (Ask "Have I discussed the main idea the same way as in the passage?")
    — *write* down anything you've only just remembered (It often happens that you think of more information as you are checking).

Your skill in using this information has shown that you can:

(a) still learn more about using the strategy.
(b) find the main idea in a passage.
(c) pick the plan of the passage.
(d) use the same plan to arrange your recall.
(e) use the strategy effectively.

These seem to be your problem areas (The numbers correspond to those on the above check list; check what the numbers mean and see if you agree with our analysis of your progress).

_____

_____

If you can fix these problems you will be able to use the strategy perfectly.

I would like to have you work with the same partner that you worked with during the last session. We will come around and check you on problem areas.

You and your partner will be reading and recalling some passages. Then you will read each other's recall and fill out the **feedback** forms for each other; try to help each other with any problems; we will be available to consult with you about your questions.

First, fill out the test item below and check your answers with your partner and the progress report form. Then, work through the following set of passages to read recall, and to evaluate your progress.

Let's Check

Fill in the blanks: For the plan strategy we *choose* it, _____ it, or _____ it!

Two questions to ask yourself before you read and write or tell what you remember are:

1. What is the _____?
2. What is the _____ that fits the _____?

Passage 1

Read and recall the passage and write down all you can remember from it.

The Steamboat

The steam boat came of age in the 1825–50 generation. Early steam vessels were built to operate on eastern rivers. They had deep hulls, and carried most of their cargo below decks. They were able to operate with low-pressure steam engines, and frequently carried sails also. Steamboats built for western rivers were considerably different. Their hulls were flat and shallow, and the superstructure—the part of the vessel above deck—sometimes was three stories high. Low-pressure engines could not be used: The far more powerful (and dangerous) high-pressure engines were installed above the waterline, and fuel, cargo, and passengers all were carried on the main deck and the superstructure. (From *The American Adventure: Expansion, Conflict, and Reconstruction (1825–1880),* Copyright 1975 by Allyn & Bacon.)

Write down as much as you can remember from the passage you have just read. Use complete sentences. You can use the words in the passage or your own words. Do not turn back to the passage after you start writing.

_____

_____

_____

Feedback

1. Did you pick out the organization as *comparison?*
   If so, _____ great!
   If not, _____ did you ask the two questions before reading?
   _____ did you look for the plan? (contrast between eastern and western steamboats)
   _____ did you find the main idea organized by the plan?
Differences in the eastern and western steamboats on the following aspects: hull depth, extent of superstructure, cargo location, type of pressure engine.)
2. Did you write the name of the plan at the top of the recall page?
   If so, _____ so far, so good!
   If not, _____ mmmmmmm!
3. Did you write down the main idea as the first sentence?
   If so, _____ keep it up!
   If not, _____ oh no!

4. Did you have two parts in arranging your sentences?
   If so, _____ not far to go now!
   If not, _____ tut, tut!

5. Were the two parts: one for the eastern steamboat and one for the western steamboat.
   If so, _____ I bet you remembered a lot!
   If not, _____ Oh rats!

6. Did you check?
   If so, _____ double smiles!
   If not, _____ don't be so overconfident!

Passage 2

Hold the Eggs and Butter

This year began with the announcement by the Federal Government of the results of the broadest and most expensive research project in medical history. Its subject was cholesterol, the vital yet dangerous yellowish substance in the blood-stream. . . Among the conclusions: (1) Heart disease is directly linked to the level of cholesterol in the blood. (2) Lowering cholesterol levels markedly reduces the incidence of fatal heart attacks. Basil Rifkin, project director of the study, believes that research "strongly indicates that the more you lower cholesterol and fat in your diet, the more you reduce your risk of heart disease." (Copyright 1984 Time Inc. All rights reserved. Reprinted by permission from TIME.)

Write down as much as you can remember from the passage you have just read. Use complete sentences. You can use the words in the passage or your own words. Do not turn back to the passage after you start writing.

_____

_____

_____

Feedback

1. Did you pick out the organization as *causation?*
   If so, _____ great!
   If not, _____ did you ask the two questions before reading?
   _____ did you look for the plan? (cause: lower cholesterol, effect: less incidence of fatal heart attacks)
   _____ did you find the main idea organized by the plan? (reducing cholesterol will result in less risk of heart disease)

2. Did you write the name of the plan at the top of the recall page?
   If so, _____ so far, so good!
   If not, _____ mmmmmmm!
3. Did you write down the main idea as the first sentence?
   If so, _____ keep it up!
   If not, _____ oh no!
4. Did you have two parts in arranging your sentences? (One part describing the cause: cholesterol, what it is and the study investigating it; the other part describing the effect on heart disease)
   If so, _____ not far to go now!
   If not, _____ tut, tut!
5. Did you check?
   If so, _____ double smiles!
   If not, _____ don't be so overconfident!

Passage 3

Caffeine and Birth Defects

Pregnant women needn't be as cautious about caffeine consumption as had been thought, according to a new study by the Food and Drug Administration. A 1980 study, in which caffeine was injected directly into the stomachs of pregnant rats, resulted in a high incidence of birth defects in the offspring. In the new study, caffeine was put into rats' drinking water—to more closely approximate the way humans ingest the stimulant—and few birth defects were found. (Copyright, 1984, U.S. New & World Report. Excerpted from issue of spring, 1984.)

Write down as much as you can remember from the passage you have just read. Use complete sentences. You can use the words in the passage or your own words. Do not turn back to the passage after you start writing.

_____

_____

_____

Feedback

1. Did you pick out the organization as *comparison?*
   If so, _____ great!
   If not, _____ did you ask the two questions before reading?
   _____ did you look for the plan? (contrast between old and new study on caffeine)

_____ did you find the main idea organized by the plan? (the new more ecologically valid study didn't show a high incidence in birth defects from caffeine, while the older study did)

2. Did you write the name of the plan at the top of the recall page?
   If so, _____ so far, so good!
   If not, _____ mmmmmmm!

3. Did you write down the main idea as the first sentence?
   If so, _____ keep it up!
   If not, _____ oh no!

4. Did you have two parts in arranging your sentences?
   If so, _____ not far to go now!
   If not, _____ tut, tut!

5. Were the two parts: one for the old study and one for the new one?
   If so, _____ I bet you remembered a lot!
   If not, _____ Oh rats!

6. Did you check?
   If so, _____ double smiles!
   If not, _____ don't be so overconfident!

Passage 4

Infectious arthritis refers to the arthritis that some people develop as a complication of another disease caused by a virus, bacterium, or fungus. The infectious agent first causes one disease but then spreads into one or more joints, causing arthritis. For example, one common cause of infectious arthritis is the bacterium that causes gonorrhea. In some people, this bacterium escapes from the genital organs and gets into the bloodstream, which carries it into the joints and leads to arthritis.

Drug treatment to get rid of the infection usually clears up the arthritis completely, if it is begun soon after the joint symptoms began. After the swelling has gone down and the infection is gone, some people may need special exercises to rebuild strength in the affected area. (Arthritis Foundation booklet: *Arthritis, Basic Facts,* pp 25–26, Courtesy the Arthritis Foundation).

Write down as much as you can remember from the passage you have just read. Use complete sentences. You can use the words in the passage or your own words. Do not turn back to the passage after you start writing.

_____

_____

_____

Feedback

1. Did you pick out the organization as *problem/solution?*
   If so, _____ great!
   If not, _____ did you ask the two questions before reading?
   _____ did you look for the plan? (the problem is infectious arthritis caused by a virus, bacterium, or fungus, and the solution is immediate drug treatment and for some exercise too)
   _____ did you find the main idea organized by the plan? (infectious arthritis can be cured with drug treatment)

2. Did you write the name of the plan at the top of the recall page?
   If so, _____ so far, so good!
   If not, _____ mmmmmmm!

3. Did you write down the main idea as the first sentence?
   If so, _____ keep it up!
   If not, _____ oh no!

4. Did you have two parts in arranging your sentences?
   If so, _____ not far to go now!
   If not, _____ tut, tut!

5. Were the two parts: one for the problem and one for the solution.
   If so, _____ I bet you remembered a lot!
   If not, _____ Oh rats!

6. Did you check?
   If so, _____ double smiles!
   If not, _____ don't be so overconfident!

Passage 5

Birding Tips: How to Tell the Difference Between Geese and Ducks (from *Joy of Nature,* Copyright © 1977, The Reader's Digest Association, Inc., p. 187).

Male and female geese have identical plumage. Large birds with long necks, geese are good walkers. Geese, which molt only once a year, look the same at all times of the year. Nests are placed in hollows on grassy or marshy ground. Geese usually feed on land, grazing on grass and grain; brant, a sea-going species, feed on ellgrass. Though geese are powerful swimmers, they do not dive. Geese are strong fliers. They often form precise V's or long, irregular lines. They are quite noisy in flight.

Male ducks are more colorful than females of the species. Small, plump birds with short necks, ducks have stubby legs and walk clumsily. Ducks molt body feathers twice a year. Most kinds have two plumages—breeding and nonbreeding. Males in eclipse (non-breeding) plumage look like females. Ducks nest in various sites—some even in tree holes. All ducks can dive. Some species dive to obtain fish; others eat mollusks or aquatic plants. In flight, most ducks form loose flocks.

Write down as much as you can remember from the passage you have just read. Use complete sentences. You can use the words in the passage or your own words. Do not turn back to the passage after you start writing.

_____

_____

_____

Feedback

1. Did you pick out the organization as *comparison?*
   If so, _____ great!
   If not, _____ did you ask the two questions before reading?
   _____ did you look for the plan? (contrast between geese and ducks in appearance and habits)
   _____ did you find the main idea organized by the plan? (geese and ducks differ in plumage between male and female and in breeding plumage in males, necks, walking ability, number of molting periods per year, location of nests, diet, diving ability, and flying behavior)

2. Did you write the name of the plan at the top of the recall page?
   If so, _____ so far, so good!
   If not, _____ mmmmmmm!

3. Did you write down the main idea as the first sentence?
   If so, _____ keep it up!
   If not, _____ oh no!

4. Did you have two parts in arranging your sentences?
   If so, _____ not far to go now!
   If not, _____ tut, tut!

5. Were the two parts: one for the geese and other for the ducks?
   If so, _____ I bet you remembered a lot!
   If not, _____ Oh rats!

6. Did you check?
   If so, _____ double smiles!
   If not, _____ don't be so overconfident!

Use of Outside Reading Materials

Students examine materials which they had collected from outside reading during the training period. One sample should be selected by each student and exchanged with that of their partner. Students read and recall the material and receive feedback from their partner. Additional collected materials should be discussed between the pairs.

For students who did not bring outside materials, passages were provided. They included: (1) "Parents Urged to Boil Rubber Nipples," *FDA Consumer,* March 1984, pp. 17–18, (2) "Fabled 'skipper effect' on Iceland fishing industry a myth, scientists find," *Chicago Tribune,* May 20, 1984, Section 6, p. 7, (3) "ABC's of How America Chooses a President," *U.S. News & World Report,* 1984—reprints at 35 cents each with minimum order of 5 copies: Reprints, U.S. News & World Report, 2400 N. Street, N.W., Washington, D.C., (4) "Bird-Care Basics" by Judy Crawford, *Better Homes and Gardens,* September, 1983, pp. 76–78, (5) "When Time Began," by Fred Hoyle, *The Saturday Evening Post,* from D'Angelo pp. 191–192, (6) "Planetary Flights," by David Morrison. *Astronomy,* September 1983, p. 6 . The plans for these examples are (1) and (2) organized with problem/solution; (3) organized with question /answer; (4) structured with description; (5) structured as comparison/analogy; (6) organized as a sequence.

Recapitulation.   Many of you brought examples of writing organized with a plan now familiar to you. Others found such examples but forgot to bring them today. In any case, it is important to remember that what you learn *in* this class must be used in your reading and recall *outside* the class. Otherwise you will soon forget all that you have accomplished. When you read something that you want to remember—use the plan strategy. You can use the strategy to write down what you remember, to retell a friend what you remember about an article, or to think about the article by yourself.

Conclusion.   During the five sessions that we've been together you have done several things important to your role as a learner. Particularly, you have acquired a strategy which will help you better organize your memory for what you read. The work you have done in the sessions has shown how well you've learned the strategy. The next step is up to you. You must take what you have learned away from this setting and use it—otherwise our time together will have been wasted. Congratulations on your achievement in our class and best wishes for what's ahead.

STUDENT'S MANUAL AND WORKBOOK

Session 1: Rationale for Strategy and Definitions and Examples of Five Basic Text Structures.

_____

name

STUDENT'S PROGRAM FOR SESSION 1

goal: To increase your memory of what you read by using the structure in reading materials.

Do you want to improve your ability to remember what you have read?

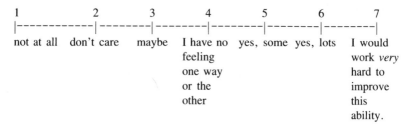

1	2	3	4	5	6	7
not at all	don't care	maybe	I have no feeling one way or the other	yes, some	yes, lots	I would work _very_ hard to improve this ability.

1. Objectives

(a) _For me:_ We are studying learning and memory from reading materials by young, middle-aged, and old adults. Over the last 6 years this research has been supported by grants from the National Institute of Mental Health and the National Institute on Aging.

From our studies we have found that for all age groups successful readers employ a deliberate plan or strategy for remembering what they read. Successful readers identify and utilize the writing plan used in their reading materials; they use this plan to help them remember what they have read when they discuss the information with others or write down what they remember about their reading. In this program you will learn how to use this strategy for reading and remembering.

Our research indicates that with practice older adults can use this strategy effectively and increase the amount of information they can remember. We have discovered that while a man may never be too old to learn, it's a lot easier for him if he is in practice. In other words, when it comes to reading comprehension skill, use it or lose it.

All participants will be able to increase the amount of information remembered from reading materials after this instruction. Not only will the amount of information be increased, but this strategy will help you to identify and remember the most important information you read. Your participation and hard work will be greatly appreciated.

(b) *For you:* To improve your learning and memory by identifying and using an organizational plan in reading materials.

2. Introduction to Session 1

Aim 1: To establish a rationale for using the reading strategy.

Over the next five sessions I will show you a way to increase this ability to get information from what you read. This will involve using a strategy, deliberate plan, for remembering. Our strategy involves two steps. In reading, we find the organizational plan used by the writer. In remembering, we use the same organizational plan. This is a strategy to improve memory. The strategy is called *using the plan.*

We have taught others to use this strategy. A trained group of readers could remember twice as much information from their reading materials after instruction (both 1 day and 3 weeks after) than they could before; and they outperformed an untrained group by twice the amount recalled. Moreover, readers in both groups who found and used the author's plan remembered more information from texts than those who did not find the plan.

Aim 2: To specify learning and teaching tasks of the program.

Communication. Your job will be to listen attentively to the ways in which this strategy for remembering is applied to reading, to apply it to reading materials, and, after you leave each day, to apply it to your own reading. My job will be to show you how to use the strategy and to check on your efficiency in using it.

3. Principles: Session 1

Communication. We know five facts about reading for information.

1. The writer wants to tell you something.

2. You must be told in writing.

3. There are only a small number of possible plans in which to organize information about a topic.

4. The writer should organize his or her main ideas about a topic with a plan.

5. To find this organizational plan is the key to getting the writer's main ideas or message.

You will want to use this strategy when you want to remember what the writer is trying to tell you. You will not want to use the strategy when you are reading for the purpose of finding a particular fact.

Test

1. A strategy for remembering what I read has two steps. In reading, I will _____. In remembering, I will _____.

2. This strategy is called *Using* _____.

In order to use a plan for reading and remembering text, it will be helpful to learn about five commonly used plans in reading materials. These plans are described in Table 6.1. The five plans are designated as follows: *description, sequence, causation, problem/solution,* and *comparison.* Table 6.1 presents the five plans and signals that can cue you into these plans.

These are the five plans we will be working with every day that we meet. We will begin working with them in short advertisements and paragraphs and gradually work with more complicated materials. This first session you should get the general ideas about these plans, but don't worry about mastering them the first day because we will continually go over them on each day that we meet together.

Follow along in Table 6.1 as we discuss each plan. Examples of these plans are readily identifiable in everyday life and can be found in advertisements. The

TABLE 6.1
Five Basic Writing Plans and Signals that Cue Readers to These Plans

Writing Plan and Definition	Signals
Description Descriptive ideas that give attributes, specifics, or setting information about a topic. The main idea is that attributes of a topic are discussed.	for example; such as; for instance e.g., a newspaper article describing who, where, when and how
Sequence Ideas grouped on the basis of order or time. The main idea is the procedure or history related.	to begin with; as time passed; later e.g., recipe procedures, history of Civil Was battles growth from birth to 12
Causation Presents causal or cause and effect-like relationships between ideas. The main ideas are organized into cause and effect parts. The effect comes before the reason (cause) in explanations.	because; so; caused; reasons if..., then... e.g., directions: if you want to take good pictures, then you must...
Problem/Solution The main ideas are organized into two parts: a problem part and a solution part that responds to the problem by trying to eliminate it, or a question part and an answer part that responds to the question by trying to answer it.	need to prevent; problem; solution; question; answer e.g., scientific articles often first raise a question or problem and then seek to give an answer or solution
Comparison Relates ideas on the basis of differences and similarities. The main idea is organized in parts that provide a comparison, contrast, or alternative perspective on a topic.	instead; on the other hand; however; in contrast e.g., political speeches, particularly where one view is clearly favored over the other

main captions of advertisements in magazines can often be easily categorized into one of these plans. To help you understand the definitions of the plans, I will show you some examples of their use by advertisers.

Description

Description gives more information about a topic by presenting an attribute, specific, or setting. For example, on the topic of whales, descriptive passages could be generated by describing the physical characteristics of whales as a group, by describing one particular type of whale, by describing the environment of whales, and so forth.

Articles are often organized as a group or list of descriptions about a topic. This listing of descriptions about a topic may be signaled in an article by such word as "three attributes" of whales will be discussed . . . "first, . . . second . . . . third. . . . . ." Newspaper articles often follow the descriptive plan, telling us about who, where, how, and when.

We will examine some plans of *description* in two advertisements taken from magazines.

Example 1. "EVEREADY" DOUBLE GUARANTEE (Fig. 6.3)

Guarantee #1. The Eveready "Skipper" Flashlight. A switch so durable, so dependable . . . we gave it a 10 year guarantee.

Guarantee #2. "Eveready" Flashlight Batteries. They're guaranteed against damaging your flashlight in any way. And they cost less than alkaline batteries. Two great guarantees from the most trusted brand name in the business. "Eveready."

"Double" in the title of this advertisement signals us to the possibility of two descriptions about the topic, "Eveready guarantees." The two guarantees follow and are explicitly signaled for us as #1 and #2. The two descriptions give us specific information about the guarantees: A 10 year guarantee on the flashlight and batteries guaranteed against damaging our flashlights. The last sentence again signals the plan for this advertisement with the words "two guarantees." Further descriptions about the topic "Eveready" guarantees are given in the last sentence (the guarantees are great and "Eveready" is trusted). Thus, the plan for this advertisement is description.

Example 2

OH THE LOVELY NUTTY THINGS YOU CAN DO WITH DIAMOND WALNUTS. CHOCOLATE CHIP COOKIES: CALIFORNIA WALNUT PIE: CALIFORNIA WALNUT BREAD: CHEWY WALNUT SQUARES (courtesy of Diamond Walnut Growers, Inc.) (Fig. 6.4)

In this advertisement we see four descriptions that specify the lovely nutty things you can do with walnuts. The overall plan for this advertisement is description. Within each of the four separate descriptions of things to do with walnuts we can find the next plan we will discuss, *sequence*. The sequence plan is used to give the order for mixing the ingredients and preparing the pan and oven in the recipes.

Sequence

As seen in Table 6.1, the plan for a text based on order or time is called *sequence*. For this plan a number of items are ordered and presented serially in a continuous progression as they relate to a particular topic or process. Examples of this plan include procedures in a recipe, stages in development from birth to twelve months, and the history of the Civil War battles. Examine the following example of a sequence typical of articles in magazines for young parents.

Example 3

More than likely, an infant's **first** tooth will be one of the two lower front teeth. These two will be **followed in a few months** by the four upper front teeth. On an average, a baby will have these 6 teeth **by the time** he is a year old and his complete set of 20 primary teeth **by the time** he is 2½ years old.

In this paragraph the sequence plan is used to order the increasing number of teeth and the increasing age of the child. The words in bold face help to tell us that a sequence plan is used to organize the information given by the author. Also, in this example the ordering of the quantity of teeth and the ordering of the child's age is related to ordering of the teeth in the mouth, the location of the teeth. Ordering ideas by time and also by location falls under the sequence plan.

Causation

The *causation* plan is aimed at presenting causal relationships (like the "if/then" of antecedent/consequent statements in logic). In using this plan the reader should look for the *cause* part of the causation plan and the *effect* part of this plan. Directions often follow the causation plan. If you want a certain outcome, such as good pictures, then you will follow a certain sequence of procedures; following those procedures (the cause) will give you the desired effect. Explanations also follow the causation plan; they give the reasons or causes for an effect.

The following advertisement exemplifies the causation plan.

Example 4 (Fig. 6.5).

Four good **reasons why** Johnson's Baby Lotion is the best "grownup" body lotion you can buy. Thicker and richer than other lotions. Absorbs fast. Goes to work instantly. Unique combination of 10 skin softeners. Leaves you feeling beautifully soft all over. (courtesy Johnson and Johnson)

Reasons why in the advertisement signal us to the causal plan. This advertisement is an explanation of why this lotion is the best; the effect is given before the cause or reasons. So information organization with the causation plan can be in the cause/effect order or the effect/cause order. The effect in the causal plan above is that Johnson's Baby Lotion is the best "grownup" body lotion you can buy. The cause in the plan is composed of a listing of four reasons as signaled in the advertisement. The advertisers want us to assume that these four statements are true: Thicker and richer, fast, unique, and leaves you soft, and that it thus follows that the product is the best you can buy. As can be seen by the causation's use in this and other advertisements, the constraints of formal logic are not necessary to use the causation plan in writing. The ideas can be related in a quasi-causal fashion.

Problem/solution

The *problem/solution* plan has two parts, a problem part and a solution part; the solution part has to respond to the ideas in the problem part. This plan also has a *question/answer* form; here a question is raised in one part and in the other part an answer is given to the question. Scientific articles often adhere to the problem/solution or question/answer plan, first raising a problem or a question and then seeking to give a solution or answer.

The first example of this plan in the following advertisement uses the question and answer format.

Example 5

YOUR SHISH KABOBS LOOK SO TANTALIZING. SHOULD YOUR GLASSES BE SPOTTY? GET THE CASCADE LOOK . . . . VIRTUALLY SPOTLESS. (courtesy Proctor & Gamble) (Fig. 6.6)

The details of this advertisement expand on the question and the answer segments of this plan. The first paragraph below from this advertisement repeats and expands on the question that appeared in the bold face title of the advertisement; the second paragraph explains why Cascade is the solution to the spotty glass problem.

Your guests will rave when they see this dish. But what about your glasses? You don't want spots at a time like this, or anytime. (Here the question is answered "NO" and the problem of spots emphasized.)

The spotty glass shows that plain water alone can leave dulling spots. (Here we see that the problem of spots is caused by plan ordinary water.) So it's good to know that Cascade's sheeting action fights drops that spot . . . gives your guests glasses with the Cascade look! (Here Cascade is identified as the suggested solution because it fights water drops.) (courtesy Proctor & Gamble)

Better Homes and Gardens has run a feature entitled "Tips, Tools, and Techniques" that explicitly signals the problem/solution plan to its readers. The next example was taken from this column.

Example 6   Reprinted from *Better Homes & Gardens* magazine

PROBLEM: After you've waxed the car, dried residue lingers around the grill. SOLUTION: A flagged-tip nylon paintbrush will remove the polish from crevices without scratching the paint (H. G., Springville, TN) (Copyright Meredith Corporation, 1983)

Comparison

Again look at Table 6.1 as we discuss the final plan, *comparison*. This plan organizes on the basis of similarities and differences. The number of matching relationships and issues compared varies with the complexity and kind of comparative text (e.g., comparison of deodorant brands, to beliefs about God, to highly structured legal arguments).

An analogy is a type of comparison plan; for example, an advertisement on Diamond Walnuts stated the following.

Example 7

THE ART OF BEING A SHREWD DIAMOND BUYER. (courtesy Diamond Walnut Growers, Inc.) (Fig 6.7)

Here an analogy is drawn between the care in selecting diamonds and the care used in selecting this brand of walnuts (Diamond).

With the comparison plan an author may equally recommend the compared views or she may favor one view over another. Political speeches are often of the comparison type, particularly where one view is clearly favored over the other.

The following advertisements also utilize the comparison plan.

Example 8

HEAVY DUTY REYNOLDS WRAP GIVES YOU 2 JUICY OPTIONS. JUICY AND WRAPPED. JUICY AND TENTED. (courtesy Reynolds Metals Company) (Fig. 6.8)

In this advertisement alternative ways to prepare turkey with Reynolds Wrap are presented. The options are equally desirable from the author's viewpoint.

The word option in this advertisement helps to signal us that a comparison plan is being used.

Example 9

MOST WRAPS **JUST** WRAP. REYNOLDS WRAP WRAPS, MOLDS AND SEALS TIGHTLY. (courtesy Reynolds Metals Company) (Fig. 6.9)

In contrast, in this advertisement one product is contrasted to others and favored as superior. The word **just** in this advertisement cues us into the comparison plan with one product favored over another. Usually this form of comparison is more prevalent with advertisements because the advertisers want to convince you that their product is superior so that you will buy it.

The following advertisement uses the unequally weighed version of the comparison plan to urge your support of the Save the Children Federation.

Example 10

YOU CAN HELP SAVE BO SUK FOR $15 A MONTH. OR YOU CAN TURN THE PAGE. (Fig. 6.10)

As mentioned before, these five basic plans are familiar in various contexts. Political speeches are often of the comparison type, particularly where one view is clearly favored over the other. Newspaper articles are often of the description type, telling us who, where, how, and when. Scientific articles often adhere to the problem/solution type, first raising a question or problem and then seeking to give an answer or solution. History texts frequently follow the sequence plan with chronological ordering.

Many texts will reflect more than one of these basic five plans. For example, folktales contain much description, causation, and events sequenced in time within an overall problem/solution plan where the protagonist confronts and resolves a problem. Folktales may carry an overall comparison plan, such as demonstrating the contrast between good and evil. For example, an Aesop fable about a genie and two woodsmen was comprised of two substories: one about an honest woodsman and the other about a dishonest woodsman. The overall plan for the story was comparison with emphasis on the honest woodsman as explicitly signaled by the author in the moral "Honesty is the best policy." Our strategy for reading and remembering will focus on the **overall plan** used in the text rather than plans used to organize details in a text.

Just as traffic signs signal you to attend to important aspects of your driving, there are signaling words in reading materials that signal the different plans. Some signaling words are listed below. In the space provided write the name of the plan that best corresponds to each signaling word; you can refer to Table 6.1 for assistance.

to start with _____ specifically _____

in explanation _____ in opposition _____

to satisfy the problem _____

the reason _____ more recently _____

attributes of _____ compared to _____

years ago _____ in describing _____

in response to your puzzlement _____

To review the five basic plans for reading and remembering, we will examine the following advertisements. Please pair up with a partner; each member of the pair should read the advertisement and determine the overall plan used to organize the information. Write down the name of the plan and then, share your plan with your partner. Progress in this manner one by one through the sample advertisements. When you have finished we will go over the plans for the advertisements as a group and discuss any disagreements or problems. Review Ad. #1

WANT A TOUGH STAIN OUT? SHOUT IT OUT!

Review Ad. #2

HAPPY CAT STAYS MOIST AND MEATY TASTING ALL DAY, SO CATS STAY HAPPY ALL DAY. (Happy Cat is a registered trademark of Ralston Purina Company. Reproduced with permission. Copyright Ralton Purina Company, 1984).

Review Ad. #3

"WITH EIGHT BROTHERS AND SISTERS, BIRTHDAYS USED TO BE A PROBLEM." NOW I SEND THE BIRTHDAY PARTY BOUQUET FROM BY FTD FLORIST. IT'S MORE THAN A GIFT, IT'S A CELEBRATION. (Advertisement for the FTD Birthday Party Bouquet furnished by the 24,000 Member Florists of FTD. Copyright 1987 FTDA.)

Review Ad. #4_____ PLAN

COMPARE NEW VO5 TO OTHER LEADING HAIRSPRAYS. THE DIFFERENCE IS —CRYSTAL CLEAR. (courtesy Alberto Culver Company)

Review Ad. #5_____ PLAN

CLUB MED SHOULD FEEL THIS FREE. HEDONISM II. CLUB MED SHOULD BE THIS GOOD.

FIG. 6.11. Review advertisement #1. By permission of S. C. Johnson & Son, Inc., Racine, Wisconsin.

FIG. 6.12. Review advertisement #2. Happy Cat is a registered trademark of Ralston Purine Company. Reproduced with permission. Copyright Ralston Purina Company, 1984.

FIG. 6.13. Review advertisement #3. Advertisement for the FTD Birthday Party Bouquet furnished by the 24,000 Member Florists of FTD. Copyright 1987 FTDA.

FIG. 6.14. Review advertisement #4. Courtesy Alberto Culver Company.

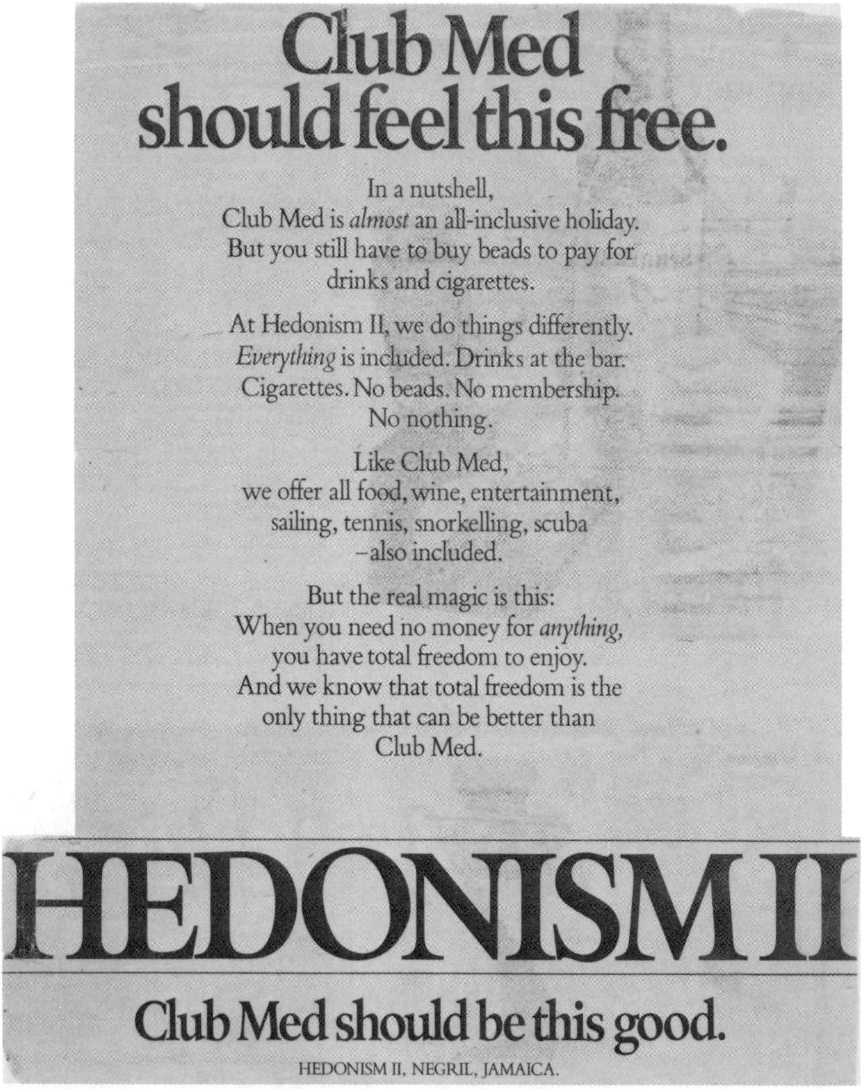

Club Med should feel this free.

In a nutshell,
Club Med is *almost* an all-inclusive holiday.
But you still have to buy beads to pay for
drinks and cigarettes.

At Hedonism II, we do things differently.
Everything is included. Drinks at the bar.
Cigarettes. No beads. No membership.
No nothing.

Like Club Med,
we offer all food, wine, entertainment,
sailing, tennis, snorkelling, scuba
–also included.

But the real magic is this:
When you need no money for *anything*,
you have total freedom to enjoy.
And we know that total freedom is the
only thing that can be better than
Club Med.

HEDONISM II

Club Med should be this good.

HEDONISM II, NEGRIL, JAMAICA.

FIG. 6.15.   Review advertisement #5.

Next you and your partner will write advertisements in two different writing plans to sell your new invention, the safety pin. The two writing plans you will use are circled below.

1. Use the description sequence causation problem/solution comparison plan to think about the MOST IMPORTANT THINGS you would write in your

advertisement about the safety pin. Write your main ideas for your advertisement in the space provided. _____ Plan

_____

_____

_____

_____

2. Use the description sequence causation problem/solution comparison plan to think about the MOST IMPORTANT THINGS you would write in your advertisement about the safety pin. Write your main ideas for your advertisement in the space provided. _____ Plan

_____

_____

_____

_____

Examine the picture of the tiger (Fig. 6.19). Write about the picture in two different ways by using the two plans circled in your packet. This time work along without your partner.

1. DESCRIPTION SEQUENCE CAUSATION PROBLEM/SOLUTION COMPARISON PLAN

_____

_____

_____

_____

2. DESCRIPTION SEQUENCE CAUSATION PROBLEM/SOLUTION COMPARISON PLAN

_____

_____

_____

_____

FIG. 6.19.   Stimulus used to aid writing of short passages with different plans.

Take your copy of Table 6.1 with you to review what we have learned today. During the next couple of days as you read materials, look for these plans and signals used to cue them. Please leave your packet with me so that I can check your progress.

TABLE 6.1
Five Basic Writing Plans and Signals that Cue Readers to These Plans

Writing Plan and Definition	Signals
Description Descriptive ideas that give attributes, specifics, or setting information about a topic. The main idea is that attributes of a topic are discussed.	for example; such as; for instance e.g., a newspaper article describing who, where, when and how
Sequence Ideas grouped on the basis of order or time. The main idea is the procedure or history related.	to begin with; as time passed; later e.g., recipe procedures, history of Civil Was battles growth from birth to 12
Causation Presents causal or cause and effect-like relationships between ideas. The main ideas are organized into cause and effect parts. The effect comes before the reason (cause) in explanations.	because; so; caused; reasons if..., then... e.g., directions: if you want to take good pictures, then you must...
Problem/Solution The main ideas are organized into two parts: a <u>problem</u> part and a <u>solution</u> part that responds to the problem by trying to eliminate it, or a <u>question</u> part and an <u>answer</u> part that responds to the question by trying to answer it.	need to prevent; problem; solution; question; answer e.g., scientific articles often first raise a question or problem and then seek to give an answer or solution
Comparison Relates ideas on the basis of differences and similarities. The main idea is organized in parts that provide a comparison, contrast, or alternative perspective on a topic.	instead; on the other hand; however; in contrast e.g., political speeches, particularly where one view is clearly favored over the other

Session 2: Signaling Words for Five Text Structures and Identification of Structures in Short Texts

name
STUDENT'S PROGRAM FOR SESSION 2

Program Objectives: **To improve recall by identifying and using the writing plans in reading materials.**

Let's Check #1

Fill in the following:

Five Plans   *One Signaling Word*

1. _____   _____

2. _____   _____

3. _____   _____

4. _____   _____

5. _____   _____

Check your work by looking at Table 6.2; make any needed corrections.

Aim 1: To teach other signaling words and the idea that listing can occur with any of the five plans.

Communication.   Signaling words can cue you into that plan used by an author to organize his or her main ideas. Remember that we are looking for the overall writing plan that organizes all the information presented; signals will probably be found for plans that organize just parts of the information too, but we will focus on the plans that organize all of the information into a whole. The information organized by this overall plan is the main idea the author is trying to tell you.

Go through Table 6.2 to review the plans as we discuss the signaling words. Keep Table 6.2 with you to remind you of the five plans and their signals. Spaces are provided in the Table for you to fill in signaling words that you discover in our work in class and in your home reading.

LET'S CHECK #2

For each of the passages underline the signaling words that cue us into the author's plan. Write the name of the plan used in the space provided. Work with your partner comparing your answers after you complete each item.

1. Martha worried continually about her health; as a result she acquired ulcers.

_____ Plan

2. Pollution is a problem for our rivers. Polluted rivers are eyesores. They are also health hazards. One solution is to stop the dumping of industrial waste.

_____ Plan

3. Luxury cars yield comfort, safety, style and excellent resale values; examples of such cars include Buick Riviera, Cadillac Deville, Cadillac Eldorado, Cadillac Seville, Lincoln Continental, Mark IV, Lincoln Versailles, Mercedes-Benz 2400, Mercedes-Benz 300D and 280SE, and Oldsmobile Toronado.

_____ Plan

4. Despite the argument that smoking is harmful, not everyone agrees. Certainly, smoking has been related to lung cancer, high blood pressure, and loss of appetite. But, for some people smoking relieves tension.

_____ Plan

5. In 1901 Alveretta Bonita Hyde was born in Kellogg, Idaho. In 1921 she married Zona Hiram Smith. Two years later Phyllis June Smith was born. Over nine years later the second and final child appeared. Zona died in 1976. Four years later at 80 years old Alveretta married Otto Kessler, a delightful 82 year old. In 1987 at the ages of 86 and 88 Alveretta and Otto were merrily traveling around the country spreading joy to friends and relatives.

_____ Plan

6. **Youths Turn Off on Drugs.** (Copyright, 1984, U.S. News & World Report. Excerpted from issue of February 20, 1984, p. 18.)

Back at the schoolyard, the young people are turning away from drugs and alcohol. A new survey for the National Institute on Drug Abuse says that the percentage of high-school seniors using marijuana 20 or more times a month dropped to 5.5% last year, from 6.3 in 1982. The survey found that daily alcohol use also dipped in 1983—to 5.5%, from 5.7% in '82. One big reason for the shift to clean living; concern about health.

_____ Plan

For each of the passages—   *Underline* the signaling words that cue you into the author's plan.

Write the name of the plan used in the space provided.

1. **Watch the Gestures.** (Copyright, 1984, *U.S. News & World Report.* Excerpted from issue of June 11, 1984, p. 83). An innocent gesture at home can take on a completely different meaning in a foreign country, warns Paul Ekman, a professor of psychology at University of California-San Francisco, who has done a study on the subject. The "O.K." sign—thumb and forefinger formed into a circle means you did a great job and everything is A-okay in the U.S.A. However, it means "you're worth zero" in France and Belgium, and is a vulgar insult in Italy, Greece and Turkey.

_____ Plan

2. **ABC's of How America Chooses a President.** (Copyright, 1984, *U.S. News & World Report.* Excerpted from issue of Feb. 20, 1984, p. 45.)

How is Election Day established? Federal law places it on the Tuesday following the first Monday in November, in the fourth year after the previous election of a President.

_____ Plan

3. **Safety Breaker.** (Copyright, 1984, *U.S. News & World Report.* Excerpted from issue of March 19, 1984, p. 80).

A simple and inexpensive way to reduce the chances of electrocution in the home is to install ground-fault circuit interrupters—devices that detect electrical leaks and shut off the current before serious injury or death—says the Consumer Safety Commission.

_____ Plan

4. **How to Complain.** (Copyright 1984, U.S. News & World Report. Excerpted from issue of March 19, 1984, p. 80.)

When something goes wrong with a product or service you have just bought, how do you get the problem resolved? The office of Consumer Affairs recommends these steps: First, complain to the person who sold the item or performed the service. If you're still not satisfied, write to the company's headquarters, perhaps even its president. After that, contact the appropriate trade association, local, state or federal agency or the Better Business Bureau. Final resort: A small-claims court or private lawyer.

_____ Plan

5. Since 1782 the bald eagle has been the national emblem of the United States. At that time bald eagles nested throughout most of North America. In the late 1960s bald eagles had almost disappeared from the eastern United States. Now they can be found again, especially in the Great Lakes region, around Chesapeake Bay, and in Maine and Florida.

_____ Plan

Session 3: Modeling Use of the Strategy to Encode and Retrieve Information from Reading Materials

_____

name

STUDENT'S PROGRAM FOR SESSION 3

Review and Feedback. We have returned some of your papers from last session. Check your answers and examine the overall writing plans shown in Fig. 6.17 in your booklet.

Aim 1: To coordinate the act of writing a recall protocol with that of identifying the author's plan in the reading material.

Communication. Finding the plan is only the first of two steps in helping us remember what we read. Once we have found it, we must use it ourselves. If the overall plan in what you read is *description,* then you must use description in what you write. If it is *sequence,* then use must use sequence. If it is *causation,* then you must use cause and effect. If it is *problem/solution,* then you must organize your recall as problem and solution. If it is *comparison,* then that is the organization to use in writing down what you remember from your reading.

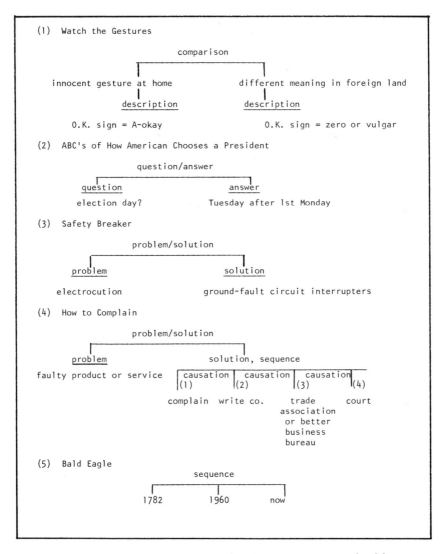

(1) Watch the Gestures

comparison

innocent gesture at home   different meaning in foreign land

description   description

O.K. sign = A-okay   O.K. sign = zero or vulgar

(2) ABC's of How American Chooses a President

question/answer

question   answer

election day?   Tuesday after 1st Monday

(3) Safety Breaker

problem/solution

problem   solution

electrocution   ground-fault circuit interrupters

(4) How to Complain

problem/solution

problem   solution, sequence

faulty product or service   causation | causation | causation
                             (1)   (2)   (3)   (4)

                             complain write co.   trade   court
                                                   association
                                                   or better
                                                   business
                                                   bureau

(5) Bald Eagle

sequence

1782   1960   now

FIG. 6.17. Diagrams of structures for short passages examined in session 2 and discussed in session 3.

Aim 2: To give rationale for the coordination.

Communication.   Researchers over the past 10 years have shown a dramatic finding. Learners who perform well in school in reading are those who use our strategy. Those who pick the article's plan and use it themselves to organize recall remember more of what they have read. And, they remember it longer.

One more thing. What they remember always includes the most important parts of a message. Learners who use a different plan don't get as much meaning from what they read. Nor, do they remember for very long. However, this strategy can be taught to learners. As a result they can nearly double the amount of information they can remember. You must choose it, use it or lose it.

There is a message in these findings. If you want to improve your ability to remember what you read, use a strategy to help organize yourself. Use the strategy of finding the plan. Find out what overall plan a writer used and use it yourself as a pattern for your thinking, speaking, or writing.

Aim 3: To operationalize the coordination.

Communication.   You need to be attentive at similar times for both reading and writing parts of the strategy.

Before you READ: —ask two questions—
WHAT IS THE PLAN FOR THIS PASSAGE?
WHAT IS THE MAIN IDEA THAT FITS THIS PLAN?
These questions will help you to approach your reading in a more organized way. They will help you to concentrate on the most important information in the passage.
While you READ: —find answers to the questions—
After you READ: —remind yourself what plan you found—
Before you WRITE: —ask the questions—
WHAT PLAN DID I FIND WHEN I READ?
HOW WILL I USE THIS FORMAT TO ORGANIZE WHAT I WRITE?
While you WRITE: —use the same plan to organize your writing—
After you WRITE:—check that you used the same plan—

Principles: Session 3

Communication.   For best recall of what we read there are six steps to take. These are listed below.

1. We find the plan in what we read.
2. We write its name at the top of the page, just before we recall.
3. We write the main idea sentence.
4. We use the plan to organize what we recall.
5. We check to see that we have used it.
6. We add anything else that we have just remembered.

IF YOU *CHOOSE* IT AND *USE* IT, THEN YOU WON'T *LOSE* IT.

Discussion: Session 3

One instructional goal was set for this session:

1. To have students apply the strategy to passages extracted from everyday reading materials.

Demonstration Passages.   We will model the strategy with each type of plan; the passages to be read and recalled are listed below.

The Anatomy of a Mollusk

Mollusks have a solid, unsegmented body which can be divided into four main parts unless greatly modified.

First is the head, bearing tentacles, eyes, and other sense organs. The mouth opens close to the front end and is often armed with teeth. The brain is internal.

The visceral sac is the next distinct part and it houses the gut, heart, and reproductive organs.

The foot is a muscular structure and used for locomotion and burrowing.

The mantle is the fourth region of the body and is a fold of skin which develops from the back part and folds over, enveloping the visceral mass and separating it from the shell. The anus and excretory ducts open into the middle cavity inside which the gills develop. (adapted—some easier vocabulary & few details omitted from D'Angelo, 1980, p. 113 taken from *The Animal Kingdom* (Feltham, England: Hamlyn Publishing Group Ltd., p. 183).)

How Snakes Shed Their Skins

When a snake has grown a new epidermis and is about to shed its skin, it secretes a thin layer of fluid between the old and new skin (which are no longer touching), giving the snake a clouded milky appearance. This can be seen especially at the eyes, for the milky fluid covers the pupils and makes the snake almost, if not completely, blind. This condition may last for as much as a week, during this period, snakes normally remain in hiding.

A day or two after the cloudiness has cleared, the snake will shed its skin. This is accomplished by opening and stretching the mouth and rubbing it on surrounding objects until the old skin at the edges of the lips begins to split. Rubbing continually, the snake starts to wriggle out of its skin. This is usually sloughed off in one piece from head to tail, turned inside out in the process by the emerging snake. Sometimes the skin will break up, however, and come off in pieces, as during the shedding of lizards.

The sloughed-off skin is a perfect cast of the snake. The large belly scales, the pattern of scales on the back, the eye spectacle and even casts of facial pits can all be seen. It is completely devoid of color as the pigment cells remain in the dermis, which is never shed. The shed skin is transparent with a white tinge. After it has been detached from the snake for a while, it usually becomes brittle. The sloughed-off skin is not especially attractive, but the newly emerged snake is seen at its best. Most species show their best bright colors in the days immediately following molting; as the upper skin gets older, the colors do not show through as well. (From D'Angelo, 1980, p. 221 taken from *Snakes of the World* (Feltham, England: Hamlyn Publishing Group Ltd, p 221).)

Changes Brought about by the Automobile

The advent of the automobile has caused profound changes in the American way of life. The petroleum industry, the steel industry, and the rubber industry have all grown to tremendous proportions in the past half century. Highway construction is at an all-time peak, and many roads recently completed are already becoming obsolete, requiring government intervention and expenditure. The number of people whose occupations are directly or indirectly influenced by automobiles—the traffic policemen, the garage mechanic, the auto mobile salesman—is staggering. But perhaps the most noticeable changes brought about by our being a nation on wheels may be found in our social practices. In the first place, we have become more transient as distance has ceased to be a consideration, and we drive anywhere, anytime. Second, and probably more important, the automobile has replaced the parlor for dating purposes. Today a young lady seldom receives "gentleman callers" at home; more likely, her home is only a "pit stop" in a continuous marathon race. (from Malcoln Moore: *Paragraph Development*. Copyright © 1975 by Houghton Mifflin Company. Used by permission.)

Teenage Pregnancy

A problem of great concern in this country is the growing number of teenagers who become pregnant. Abortion is certainly not the answer. It kills unborn children and leaves the young mother emotionally and sometimes physically harmed. Delivery of a baby is not always satisfactory either. Babies of teenagers have more problems than babies of mature women in their twenties and thirties. If the young person chooses to raise her child, it is certainly a difficult road for a young girl with limited education and skills. Some high schools are instituting programs to help teenagers continue with school during and after pregnancy.

However, these programs help with the consequences of the problem, but do not get to the cause of the problem. The cause of the difficulty is sex before marriage. A new moment is gaining momentum that encourages teenagers to abstain from sex prior to marriage. Speakers, such as Josh McDowell, take this stand and draw large crowds of young people. The best way to get young people to follow this standard is to talk to them while they are preteens and prepare them for the years ahead. Also, studies have shown that the earlier a girl dates the more likely it is that she will have sex before marriage. Parents need to stress abstinence to their preteens and teenagers and only let teens date when they have the courage and maturity to say no under pressure. Parents must also give their teenagers plenty of love, attention, and hugs at home.

Advantages of Each Side in the Civil War

Both the North and South sides had certain advantages at the beginning of the Civil War. The North possessed approximately three-fourths of the nation's wealth and had more than twice the manpower of the South. In addition to its vast farmlands, the North also operated almost all the factories in the country. The Navy, which was solely in the hands of the North, assured control of the entire coastline of the Confederacy. The South, on the other hand, was fighting a defensive war and did not have to carry the fighting to Northern soil. It was blessed with splendid officers and a fighting breed of men accustomed to riding and use of firearms. Moreover, its cause was popular with many of the European powers. (from Malcolm Moore: *Paragraph Development.* Copyright (© 1975 by Houghton Mifflin Company. Used by permission.)

Recapitulation. To use the plan strategy we need to know how it should be used. It must serve as a framework for the words we write. If it is *description,* we must set out a list of sentences that describe the main idea. If it is *sequence,* we must write a list of ordered sentences. If it is *causation,* we must have a cause and an effect part. If it is a *problem/solution* plan, again we have two parts in what we write. One tells about the problem; its causes and effects. The other tells about the solution; this solution should be aimed at blocking one of the causes of the problem. If it is a *comparison* plan, then once more we should use different parts in our written recall—one for each of the views.

LET'S CHECK #1

Choose the Best Answer for the Following Questions

In writing down what I remember from a passages using a comparison plan, I should **first**

(a) write the name comparison at the top of the paper.

(b) start writing what I remember right away before I forget.

(c) use sentences that tell the problem and then those that tell the solution.

second, I should

(a) write the names and numbers down quickly before I forget them.

(b) write down the main idea sentence.

(c) write one thing and then what ever else it reminds me to write next.

then, I should

(a) finish up.

(b) check to see I have used the comparison plan.

(c) use sentences that tell one argument, then sentences that tell the other argument.

next, I should

(a) finish.

(b) check to see that I have used the comparison plan to write my recall.

(c) add anything else that I have just remembered.

finally, I should

(a) say or write comparison several times.

(b) check to see that I have used the comparison plan to write my recall.

(c) add anything else that I have just remembered.

Now, you will get to try the strategy by reading and remembering two passages. First, read and recall the passage on *Plump Pets;* you can check you performance and we can discuss any problems before your read the last passage. REMEMBER CHOOSE IT, USE IT OR LOSE IT!

Slimming Down a Plump Pet

An overweight dog or cat could be courting serious health problems. Excess weight makes pets sluggish, puts extra strain on the cardiovascular system, and in the long run tends to shorten their life span. Your veterinarian or any good pet-care manual can tell you the approximate healthy weight for your pet, so that you can determine if you need to do something to help your pet slim down.

Here are some tips you can use if your animal is overweight. Gradually reduce the size of your pet's meals, starting with approximately a 5% reduction and working up to as much as 25% if it's necessary. You could begin using pet food designed for inactive pets, which has about 10 to 20% fewer calories than regular pet food. If your pet is allowed to eat whenever it wishes, you might switch to feeding it only at specific mealtimes. Also, eliminate snacks and table scraps (which are loaded with calories) from your pet's diet, and gradually increase its exercise routine. If you follow these suggestions, look for improvement in your pet's appearance and general health after about 2 months.

Find the plan used in the passage. *Use* it to write down what you remember on the next page in your packet.

Write down as much as you can remember from the passage you have just read. Use complete sentences. You can use the words in the passage or your own words. Do not look back at the passage after you start writing.

_____

_____

_____

_____

_____

_____

_____

_____

_____

_____

_____

LET'S CHECK #2

Let's check how well you used the strategy
DID YOU. . . . .

1 point each

1. Correctly pick the plan   ( )
2. Write its name as a reminder at the top of the page   ( )
3. Write the main idea sentence   ( )
4. Use the same plan in your recall   ( )
5. Check that you've used it   ( )
6. Add (or try to) anything you've just remembered.   ( )
   (If you didn't remember anything extra, score as correct.)

SCORE:
0–2   OH NO!
3–4   TUT, TUT!
 5   NOT BAD!
 6   GREAT!

It is good to find the right plan; it is critical to choose and use some plan rather than just listing ideas.

Chicken-Hawks

In one district, farmers began to kill the chicken-hawks. Large parties of men would go on bird-shoots. They not only shot adult birds, but also destroyed nests and breeding areas used by the hawks. Any young found in the nests were killed immediately. As a result of these hunts the farmers' chickens were not eaten. But, the farmers found something else wrong. Their store of grain in the barn was eaten by rats. Soon the rats were overrunning the farms. There was nothing to stop the spread of the rats. The farmers had removed a natural enemy of the rats—the chicken-hawk. (From *BIOLOGY: PATTERNS IN THE ENVIRONMENT* (Teaching-Learning Strategies) by Evelyn Morholt and P. F. Brandwein, Copyright © 1972 by Harcourt Brace Jovanovich, Inc. p. 184. Reprinted by permission of the publisher.)

Turn to the recall sheet and use the strategy to write down what you can remember from the passage. The six steps will not be listed on the recall sheet this time; see how well you can employ the strategy on your own.

Write down as much as you can remember from the passage you have just read. Use complete sentences. You can use the words in the passage or your own words. Do not look at the passage after you start writing.

_____

_____

_____

_____

_____

_____

_____

_____

_____

_____

LET'S CHECK #3

Let's check how well you used the strategy.
DID YOU. . . . .

1 point each

1. Correctly pick the plan   (   )
2. Write its name as a reminder at the top of the page   (   )

3. Write the main idea sentence   (   )
4. Use the same plan in your recall   (   )
5. Check that you've used it   (   )
6. Add (or try to) anything you'd just remembered.   (   )
   (If you didn't remember anything extra, score as correct.)

SCORE:
0–2   OH NO!
3–4   TUT, TUT!
  5   NOT BAD!
  6   GREAT!

Conclusion: Session 3

Today you used the strategy. You first picked out the plan of the passage you read, asking yourself (1) What is the plan for the passage? and (2) What is the main idea that fits this plan? Then you used the same plan to write down what you remembered. To help you use the strategy you should do six things:

1. Choose the plan.
2. Write its name on the top of the recall page.
3. Write the main idea sentence.
4. Use the plan to write what you remember.
5. Check that it has been used.
6. Add anything just remembered.

Usually, the plan you find and use will be one of five types—description, sequence, causation, problem/solution, or comparison. Today you used problem/solution and causation.

What you did today is an indication that this strategy is effective for improving memory of reading materials. Are there any questions on (a) how to pick the plan, (b) how to use it in recalling?

As you leave today, think of the five types of plans and how each of them is a building framework in which to write words, sentences and paragraphs. Look for them in anything you read.

Session 4: Mastering the Strategy and Using it with Longer and Muddled Texts

STUDENT'S PROGRAM FOR SESSION 4

Welcome to Session 4! We have a lot of work to do tonight!

1. Today's Goals:

* To remove problems in use of the plan strategy.
* To apply the strategy with less prompts than during the last session
* To correctly tell the difference among writing plans with less signaling.
* To apply the strategy to muddled passages.

2. Principles: Session 4

We know **three** things about the strategy of **using the plan.**

1. It helps you remember **more** of what you read.
2. It helps you to remember **more of the important information** in what you read.
3. It helps you to remember this information **longer.**

The **plan** strategy provides a framework for facts and relations which appear in a passage. For longer passages and ever increasing delays after reading, the plan strategy will help you remember more than just listing what you remember without a plan.

Test

Using the plan strategy has three advantages:
It helps you:

1. _____
2. _____
3. _____

Check your answers with the three points listed under principles above.

Performance Check List

During the past three session, you found that:

1. To choose the organization in what you read is a key to understanding.

2. A strategy to improve memory is called *using the plan.*

3. The strategy has *two* parts—*to choose* the organization, and *to use* this organization.

4. *To choose* the plan needs your attention *before. while,* and *after* reading.

5. *To choose* the organizational plan, you ask two questions before reading:

What is the plan for this passage?
What is the main idea that fits this plan?

You **answer** these questions while you read, and **check** your answers after reading.

    6. The five common plans are:

description
sequence
causation
problem/solution
comparison

    7. Signaling words in the passage can help you to **choose** the plan.

    8. Each of the plans has a **special way to pattern** the sentences in a passage.

    9. The pattern of the *Description* plan is that most of the sentences are arranged to describe the person, place, things, event, or quality in the main idea.

    10. The pattern of the *Sequence* plan is that main idea sentences follow in a certain order.

    11. The pattern of the *Causation* plan is that there is a cause and an effect organization. The main idea involves two main parts. In one part sentences tell about the **cause,** and in the other part sentences tell about the **effect.** In the explanation form of causation, the effect is given first and its cause, the explanation, follows.

    12. The pattern of *Problem/solution* plan is that there is part of the passage that tells about a problem (question, puzzle, concern), and another that tells about its solution (answer, reply). In the question/answer version the answer must deal with the ideas discussed in the question and provide some answer. In the problem/solution version often the causes and effects of the problem are discussed first; then, a solution follows that should attempt to block or eliminate at least one of the causes of the problem.

    13. The contrastive pattern of the *Comparison* plan is that different points of view are shown in different parts of the passage. It may be that one view tells what did happen and the other tells what did not happen; or, one might tell what exists and the other what does not exist; or each part might tell opposing arguments. Often when opposing views are compared they are compared on many of the same issues; for example, one political candidate's views on abortion, taxes, government spending, and defense, and then the other candidate's views on these same issues. Your memory will be improved if you remember that a comparison plan was used and the number and name of the issues compared; for the above

example remember that the candidates were compared on four issues: abortion, taxes, government spending, and defense.

14. Once you have chosen the plan you must *use it to organize your written recall*. Remember: Choose it, Use it, or Lose it!

15. *To use* the plan requires your attention *before, while,* and *after* you write your recall.

16. *While* you write put your ideas into sentences and paragraphs that follow the pattern of the plan identified.

17. *After* you write, check that you used the correct organization, correctly.

18. To *use it*—   *write its name* on the top of the page where you'll be writing your recall (to help you get organized).

— *write the main idea sentence* (to set up the plan).

— *arrange sentences and paragraphs* to match the plan (keep thinking about how the plan works).

— *check* that you've used it (Ask "Have I discussed the main idea the same way as in the passage?")

— *write* down anything you've only just remembered (It often happens that you think of more information as you are checking).

Your skill in using this information has shown that you can:

(a)   still learn more about using the strategy.
(b)   find the main idea in a passage.
(c)   pick the plan of the passage.
(d)   use the same plan to arrange you recall.
(e)   use the strategy effectively.

These seem to be your problem areas (The numbers correspond to those on the above check list; check what the numbers mean and see if you agree with our analysis of your progress.)

If you can fix these problems you will be able to use the strategy perfectly. Work on your own reading and recalling the next two passages. Use your table with definitions of writing plans and signaling words to help you; if you find other signaling words add them to your table. After you recall each passage check your progress with the *feedback* forms provided.

Passage 1

People with arthritis are one of the groups most exploited by health fraud in the United States. They spend approximately one billion dollars per year on worthless or harmful treatments, such as copper bracelets and cow manure. The reasons are understandable and clear. Arthritis has no cure, and treatment requires you to exert effort and have patience. Results are usually good with time, but still the illness often remains and can flare without warning. (From Arthritis Foundation Booklet: *Rheumatoid Arthritis*)

Write the name of the plan used in the passage. *Use* it to write down what you remember.

Write down as much as you can remember from the passage you have just read. Use complete sentences. You can use the words in the passage or your own words. Do not look at the passage after you start writing.

_____

_____

_____

_____

_____

_____

_____

_____

_____

_____

_____

Feedback

1. Did you pick out the organization as *causation?*
   If so, _____ great!
   If not, _____ did you ask the two questions before reading?
   _____ did you look for the plan? (reasons why people with arthritis are exploited by fraud: effect part = tricking people with arthritis; cause part = explanation that there is no cure for arthritis and treatment takes hard work and patience)
   _____ did you find the main idea organized by the plan? (People with arthritis fall for worthless or harmful, fraudulent treatments because arthritis has no cure and is hard to treat).

2. Did you write the name of the plan at the top of the recall page?
   If so, _____ so far, so good!
   If not, _____ mmmmmmmm!

3. Did you write down the main idea as the first sentence?
   If so, _____ keep it up!
   If not, _____ oh no!

4. Did you have two parts in arranging your sentences (an effect part followed by the cause or explanation part)?
   If so, _____ not far to go now!
   If not, _____ tut, tut!

5. Were there two parts: one discussing people with arthritis being fooled by health frauds; and one giving the reasons they are fooled: no cure and difficult treatment?
   If so, _____ I bet you remembered a lot!
   If not, _____ Oh rats!

6. Did you check to see if you remembered any other facts?
   If so, _____ double smiles!
   If not, _____ don't be so overconfident!

Passage 2

Kindness Cures Rat Allergies

Psychologists who work with rats and mice in experiments often become allergic to these creatures. This is a real hazard for these investigators who spend hours a week running rats in experiments. These allergies are a reaction to the protein in the urine of these small animals.

At a meeting sponsored by the National Institutes of Health, Dr. Andrew J. Slovak, a British physician, recommended kindness to rats and mice by the experimenters. Psychologists who pet and talk softly to their rats are less often splattered with urine and the protein that causes the allergic reaction.

Write the name of the plan used in the passage. *Use* it to write down what you remember.

Write down as much as you can remember from the passage you have just read. Use complete sentences. You can use the words in the passage or your own words. Do not look back at the passage after you start writing.

_____

_____

_____

_____

_____

_____

_____

Feedback

1. Did you pick out the organization as *problem/solution?*
   If so, _____ great!
   If not, _____ did you ask the two questions before reading?
   _____ did you look for the plan? (hazard of allergies to rats, evidence about the cause and suggestion to help eliminate exposure to the cause of the problem: protein in the urine)
   _____ did you find the main idea organized by the plan? (the problem of allergies to rats and mice may be solved by kindness to them since kindness reduces exposure to the cause of the problem: protein in urine)

2. Did you write the name of the plan at the top of the recall page?
   If so, _____ so far, so good!
   If not, _____ mmmmmmm!

3. Did you write down the main idea as the first sentence?
   If so, _____ keep it up!
   If not, _____ oh no!

4. Did you have two parts in arranging your sentences?
   If so, _____ not far to go now!
   If not, _____ tut, tut!

5. Were the two parts: one for the problem and one for the solution
   If so, _____ I bet you remembered a lot!
   If not, _____ Oh rats!

6. Did you check?
   If so, _____ double smiles!
   If not, _____ don't be so overconfident!

Aim 3: To make suggestions for coping with muddled passages.

Communication.   Some writers just don't organize their writing well. Others use an organization but muddle its use. If you can pick a plan but see that its use by a writer is muddled, that is an excellent perception. What do you do? Just unmuddle it when you write, but keep the same organization. Let's work through how a learner did just that. Then you can try one for yourself. Examine the following advertisement that appeared in *Better Homes & Gardens* magazine. (Fig. 6.18)

THIS IS WHERE A WRINKLE COULD START. . . . THIS IS WHAT COULD STOP IT.

I'm Lynda Carter. And I don't want wrinkles any more than you do. That's why I use Moisture Whip Moisturizer by Maybelline. Because unlike the leading moistur-

FIG. 6.18. Clarifying a text by using the plan strategy (Advertisement copyrighted © 1981 Maybelline Company).

izers, Moisture Whip contains Padimate O, a protective ingredient that screens out harmful light rays that cause our skin to age and wrinkle before its time. Moisture Whip is also dermatologist tested and fragrance free. So use Moisture Whip every day and do more than moisturize your face. Help protect it from wrinkles. I do.

Here is a recall written by a learner for this passage.

Problem/Solution

The problem of premature wrinkles is presented and traits of a potential solution are discussed. The problem is wrinkles on our face. No one wants wrinkles and we all want to avoid them as long as possible. We can get wrinkled before our time by harmful rays from the sun.

A solution to premature wrinkling of the facial skin is the use of Moisture Whip by Maybelline because it contains Padimate O, an ingredient that blocks the sun's harmful rays. In addition, Moisture Whip is dermatologist tested, a moisturizer, and used by Lynda Carter to prevent premature wrinkling.

See if the learner:

1. Chose the plan (problem/solution).
2. Wrote the name of the plan before writing a recall.
3. Wrote the main idea as a first sentence.
4. Used two parts to organize the other sentences.
5. Used one part to put all the information together about the *problem* and its cause and another part for that about the *solution*.

The recall mentions everything that the learner could remember about the problem of wrinkling first: A description of the problem and its cause. Then everything remembered about the solution was given: How it can prevent the cause of the problem and a description of the qualities of the solution. It is better organized in terms of the problem part and solution part than the original advertisement where the solution to the problem was presented earlier in the sentence than the cause of the problem. Text is often a little muddled, but we can use our reading strategy to clarify the text and our understanding of it.

You try it with a passage on aspirin.

How to relieve a headache is a problem. Lots of people take aspirin. Headache is a very common condition. Nobody likes to have a headache. One help for relief of a headache is aspirin.

_____

_____

Compare your recall and reorganization to that of another student as listed below.

Problem / Solution

Headache is a very common human illness. How to cure it is a problem because nobody likes to have a headache. A solution is to take aspirin when you have a headache. Lots of people do.

Notice that the student *used* the correct plan *and* organized the recall in a *less-muddled* way than the author. As a result, she has recalled all of the information even though she changed some words and the order of the sentences.

Next examine the following article from the *Chicago Tribune*. Write down the name of the plan used in the space provided.

Can molecules be ambidextrous?
by Jon Van

One way to see if a person is right- or left-handed is to have him toss you a pencil and note which hand he uses, and now chemists have found a way to do something like that with molecules. Molecules don't have hands, of course, but they do have charactistics analogous to hand preference. That is, molecules may be composed of exactly the same atoms yet be mirror images of each other. In some drugs this can be important. The common blood pressure medication propranolol is an example. One form of the drug is 100 times as potent as the other. "Ideally, you'd like to treat a patient with just the left-handed form of propranolol," said Thomas Doyle, a member of the American Chemical Society and a research chemist for the U.S. Food and Drug Administration. Unfortunately, the manufacturing process produces left- and right-handed molecules all mixed together in one batch. © Copyrighted 1984, Chicago Tribune Company, all rights reserved, used with permission.

_____ plan

I have asked _____ to work with you on using strategy for the remainder of tonight's session and for the next session. You will read some passages that clearly show a well-organized writing plan, while others will be more muddled. You and your partner will take turns stating the plan and telling the other person what you remember from the passage. The person listening to the recall should use the *Feedback* form to check whether or not his partner found the writing plan and the main ideas. For some of the passages you will be asked to tell all you can remember, while for most of the passages you will just be asked to tell the plan and the main idea. Take turns recalling the passages; if you recalled the first passage, then let your partner recall the second passage while you fill out his *feedback* form. Try to help each other with any problems; we will be available to consult with you about your questions. Use your table with definitions of writing plans and signaling words to help you; if you find other signaling words add them to your table. Remember to look for the overall writing plan; you may find signaling words for plans that organize small parts of the passage, but the overall writing plan will relate all the information together.

Passage 1: Tell Your Partner the Plan and All You Remember

Beauty and the Beast

by Bunnie Corwith (appeared in the *News Voice*)

I look out the window; our beautiful trees, majestic in their bareness, lean against the blue sky.
T.V. news is discussing the latest terrorist activities.

New snow gently falls, giving the old snow a clean cover; it glistens playfully in the back yard spotlights.
A radio bulletin announces another gang murder.

Our youngest grandchild, a year old, beams at our Golden Retriever and pats him lovingly; she is not afraid.
The neighbors change their door locks every few months, there have been so many burglaries in the area. They are afraid.

As I walk down the street, watching winter birds flit from feeders to trees, a car careens around the corner, going three times as fast as it should. An empty six-pack is thrown from a window on the way by.

Two ducks, a male and a female, fly over the creek, happily together for life.
A friend calls to say that her husband is divorcing her after 25 years of marriage.

I help our daughter pick out a new suit for her job.
A magazine on the newsstand quotes a young woman as saying, of course she takes off all her clothes for a center-fold; Why shouldn't she? Everyone does things like that.

An elderly grandmother, who is ready to join the Lord, dies peacefully in her sleep. The 16-year-old girl with an unwanted pregnancy, kills her unborn infant via an abortion.

God looks down and cries.

Feedback

1. Did you choose the organization *comparison?*
    If so, _____ great!
    If not, _____ did you ask the two questions before reading?
    _____ did you look for the plan? (contrast between beauty and ugly aspects of life today or good and evil)

_____ did you find the main idea organized by the plan? (the author and God favor the good and beautiful and cry out to people to contrast the evil in our world with peace, order, and beauty God intended)

2. Did you give the main idea as your first statement?
   If so, _____ keep it up!
   If not, _____ oh no!

3. Did you have two parts in telling what you remembered? In this essay we see a different way to format the comparison plan than previously studied; other examples have given all the information dealing with one view together and then the information from the other view together, while this example alternates views as each issue is mentioned. In the essay the poetic effect would be spoiled by stating all the good together, followed by a listing of all the bad. However, you could adequately recall the passage that way. Either way and for all comparison plans you should determine the issues covered by both views in order to increase your memory of the material. The issues to remember that were contrasted in this essay were: 1) peace/terror, 2) gentle/violence, 3) fear, 4) order, 5) marital stability, 6) propriety in dress, and 7) death.

4. Did you add anything else you could remember at the end?
   If so, _____ double smiles!
   If not, _____ don't be so overconfident!

Passage 2: Tell Your Partner the Plan and all You Can Remember

Where you live affects how fast your eyesight will deteriorate from age. A recent study found that people in warmer countries develop age-related far-sightedness earlier than those who endure a colder climate. The British ophthal-mologist who came to this conclusion says that the temperature of the eye's lens is not well maintained by the body, but is highly influenced by the external environment. Thus, heat may somehow cause changes in the lens that lead to farsightedness. (*Science Digest,* August 1982, p. 94)

Feedback

1. Did you choose the organization *causation?*
   If so, _____ great!
   If not, _____ did you ask the two questions before reading?
   _____ did you look for the plan? (hotter climates cause greater deteri-oration of the eye; cause part = where you live—warmer or colder climate; effect part = deterioration of the lens—farsightedness)
   _____ did you find the main idea organized by the plan? (hotter cli-mates lead to earlier onset of farsightedness)

2. Did you tell the main idea in your first statement?
    If so, _____ keep it up!
    If not, _____ oh no!
3. Did you have two parts in arranging your sentences (the cause followed by the effect)?
    If so, _____ not far to go now!
    If not, _____ tut, tut!
4. Were there two parts: one discussing the weather conditions where you live; and one discussing the age-related farsightedness?
    If so, _____ I bet you remembered a lot!
    If not, _____ Oh rats!
5. Did you check to see if you remembered any other facts?
    If so, _____ double smiles!
    If not, _____ don't be so overconfident!

Passage 3: Tell Your Partner the Plan and Main Idea

Psalm 1
(Holy Bible, New International Version, 1978)

Blessed is the man who does not walk in the counsel of the wicked or stand in the way of sinners or sit in the seat of mockers. But his delight is in the law of the LORD, and on his law he meditates day and night. He is like a tree planted by streams of water, which yields its fruit in season and whose leaf does not wither. Whatever he does prospers.

Not so the wicked! They are like chaff that the wind blows away. Therefore the wicked will not stand in the judgment, nor sinners in the assembly of the righteous. For the LORD watches over the way of the righteous, but the way of the wicked will perish.

Feedback

1. Did you pick out the organization as *comparison?*
    If so, _____ great!
    If not, _____ did you ask the two questions before reading?
    _____ did you look for the plan? (contrast between the righteous and the wicked)
    _____ did you find the main idea organized by the plan? (the good that comes to the righteous and the bad to the wicked)
2. Did you have two parts in arranging your main idea?
    If so, _____ not far to go now!
    If not, _____ tut, tut!

3. Were the two parts: one for the righteous group and one for the wicked group?
   If so, _____ I bet you remembered a lot!
   If not, _____ Oh rats!

Passage 4: Tell Your Partner the Plan and Main Idea

A Graceful Creature
(Basic Reading Comprehension—#R-7, ESP, Inc. 1975)

The grace and beauty of the swan has fascinated man for centuries. Swans appear often in fairy tales, poetry, and mythology. In 15-century England they were even designated as royal birds.

The stately water birds are found in diverse parts of the world, such as the arctic regions, the southern parts of South America, and the United States. The best known wild swans in the United States are the whistling and trumpeter swans.

A long, slender neck is the most striking feature of the swan. Swans use their long necks to dive for food. They like to eat seeds, roots, and fish eggs. Swans weigh about 40 pounds and measure up to 4½ feet long. Wild swans travel in flocks and are able to fly long distances in spite of their size and weight.

Feedback

1. Did you pick out the organization as *description?*
   If so, _____ great!
   If not, _____ did you ask the two questions before reading?
   _____ did you look for the plan? (descriptions of swans)
2. _____ did you find the main idea organized by the plan? (descriptions of swans' fascination for man, domain in the world, features, habits and dimensions)

Passage 5: Tell Your Partner the Plan and Main Idea

Noah Puts God First

It is interesting to note that Noah thought of the Lord before he thought of worldly things. After the dove returned with the olive twig and the ark settled on Mt. Ararat, Noah immediately built an altar and offered sacrifices of thanksgiving to Jehovah for the safe delivery of his family from the flood waters. Then he planted a vineyard, harvested his crop, and made some wine. When he had finished, he drank quite a bit more of the wine than was good for him, an act for which he might have been forgiven, considering the amount of time he had spent in the ark with all those animals. (Malcolm Moore: *Paragraph Development.* Copyright © 1975 by Houghton Mifflin Company, p. 37)

Feedback

1. Did you pick out the organization as *sequence?*
    If so, _____ great!
    If not, _____ did you ask the two questions before reading?
    _____ did you look for the plan? (sequence of Noah's activities)
2. _____ did you find the main idea organized by the plan? (in the sequence of Noah's activities Noah put God before worldly tasks)
3. If you recalled the passage would you have arranged the sentences in chronological order from the first thing Noah did to the last?
    If so, _____ good work!
    If not, _____ remember next time!

Passage 6: Tell Your Partner the Plan and Main Idea

Wisdom from Theodore Roosevelt

It is not the critic who counts, nor the man who points how the strong man stumbled, or where the doer of deeds could have done better. The credit belongs to the man who is actually in the arena, whose face is marred by the dust and sweat and blood; who strives valiantly; who errs and comes short again and again; who knows the great enthusiasms, the great devotions, and spends himself in a worthy cause; who at the best, knows in the end the triumph of high achievement; and who, at the worst, if he fails, at least fails while daring greatly, so that his place shall never be with those cold and timid souls who know neither victory nor defeat.

Feedback

1. Did you pick out the organization as *comparison?*
    If so, _____ great!
    If not, _____ did you ask the two questions before reading?
    _____ did you look for the plan? (contrast between courageous doer and the cold and timid onlooker or critic)
2. _____ did you find the main idea organized by the plan? (Theodore Roosevelt favors the courageous, active proponent for worthy pursuits regardless of successful outcome over the person who criticizes, yet does not try himself.
3. Did you have two parts in arranging your main idea?
    If so, _____ not far to go now!
    If not, _____ tut, tut!

4. Were the two parts: one for the active, daring souls and one for the critical, timid ones?
   If so, _____ I bet you remembered a lot!
   If not, _____ Oh rats!

Passage 7

Try the next passage taken from *Tufts University Diet & Nutrition Letter* (Vol. 1, No. 9, Nov. 23, 1983, p. 1); it is somewhat muddled. Tell your partner the best plan for this article and the main idea.

Colicky Babies and Breast Milk

Contrary to popular opinion, mother's milk is not always "perfect" for infants. A recent report in *Pediatric* showed that some infants may actually be allergic to their own mother's milk if the mother is drinking cow's milk. It is known that substances the mother eats can pass through her breast milk to cause allergic reactions in the baby.

Physicians Irene Jakobsson and Tor Lindberg wanted to determine if the consumption of cow's milk on the part of the mother might be causing the problems in some babies with infantile colic. They found that when 66 breast-feeding mothers of colicky babies gave up cow's milk for one week, the symptoms of abdominal pain, gas, and excessive crying disappeared in 35 of the infants. When cow's milk was added back to the mothers' diets, 23 of the "cured" infants became sickly again. To see if whey, which contains the most allergenic of cow's milk proteins, was at fault, the mothers of about half of the reactive babies were challenged with whey protein capsules and placebo capsules. All but one infant became colicky in response to whey, while no reactions occurred when a placebo was used.

The researchers conclude that in one-third of the breast-fed infants with colic, the problems are related to cow's-milk consumption by the mother. Before switching to a commercial formula, they suggest that the mothers give up cow's milk to see how that works. (Reprinted with permission, *Tufts University Diet and Nutrition Letter*, 475 Park Ave. South, 30th Fl. New York, NY 10016.)

Evaluate your partner on the following points:
When reading:

1. I asked what the plan was for the passage.
2. I chose the main idea discussed by the plan.
3. I picked a plan.
4. I picked the problem/solution plan (even though the comparison plan is hinted at in the first sentence).

When retelling:

5. I told the name of the plan.
6. I said *problem/solution.*
7. I gave a main idea sentence.
8. I said something similar to:

The problem of colic in breast-fed babies was presented; some physicians did some studies to identify its cause as whey drunk by mothers in cow's milk; the proposed solution for many colicky babies was switching the moms off cow's milk.

RESULTS:

0   OH OH!
1–2   mmmmmmm!
3–4   Better than mmmmmm!
5–6   Much better, —good job!
7–8   You're there—great work!

The *five* common types of plans are:

description
sequence
causation
problem/solution
comparison

Which of these five is the easiest for you to pick? (If they're all easy, say so.)

_____

Why?

_____

_____

_____

Which of these five is the *most difficult* for *you* to pick? (If they are all difficult, write the hardest first, then the next, etc.)

_____

_____

_____

Why?

_____

_____

_____

Complete the following:

For passages muddled or not, long or short,

1. A strategy for remembering what I read has two parts. In reading, I will
_____.

In recalling (writing, speaking, or thinking about what I have read), I will
_____.

2. The strategy is called: Using _____.

As you leave today, think of what you might do to further improve how well you use the strategy. Look for the *five* types of plans in your reading outside our classroom. Please bring any passages you have found in your reading to the next session. These passages should have one of the *five* organizational plans that we have been discussing in the last four sessions. It doesn't matter what the passage is about, nor how short or long the passage is. Just bring the book, magazine or other material in which it is contained.

Session 5: Remediation of Difficulties and Use of the Strategy With Everyday Reading Materials

STUDENT'S PROGRAM FOR SESSION 5

1. Introduction to Session 5

Aim 1:   To update personal progress report.
Aim 2:   To remove difficulties in students' use of the strategy for particular writing plans.
Aim 3:   To have students identify examples of plans in reading materials that they read in their daily life.

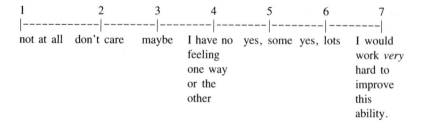

1	2	3	4	5	6	7
not at all	don't care	maybe	I have no feeling one way or the other	yes, some	yes, lots	I would work *very* hard to improve this ability.

At the beginning of our last session, you received a report of progress in acquiring the strategy. Since then you have made further progress and we have revised your personal report. Turn to your report and we will work through it. Notice the special comments beside numbers 9, 10, 11, 12, and 13. These indicate strengths you have in using each of the five plans as well as aspects to work on today.

Performance Check List

During the past sessions, you have found that:

1. To choose the organization in what you read is a key to understanding.

2. A strategy to improve memory is called *using the plan.*

3. The strategy has *two* parts—*to choose* the organization, and *to use* this organization.

4. *To choose* the plan needs your attention *before, while,* and *after* reading.

5. *To choose* the organizational plan, you **ask** two questions before reading:

What is the plan for this passage?
What is the main idea that fits this plan?

You **answer** these questions while you read, and **check** your answers after reading.

6. The five common plans are:

description
sequence
causation
problem/solution
comparison

7. Signaling words in the passage can help you to **pick** the plan.

8. Each of the plans has a **special way to pattern** the sentences in a passage.

9. The pattern of the *Description* plan is that most of the sentences are arranged to describe the person, place, things, event, or quality in the main idea.

_____

_____

_____

10. The pattern of the *Sequence* plan is that main idea sentences follow in a certain order.

_____

_____

11. The pattern of the *Causation* plan is that there is a cause and an effect organization. The main idea involves two main parts. In one part sentences tell about the **cause,** and in the other part sentences tell about the **effect.** In explanations we see the effect first followed by the cause, or explanation part.

_____

_____

12. The pattern of *Problem/solution* plan is that there is part of the passage that tells about a problem (question, puzzle, concern), and another that tells about its solution (answer, reply). In the question/answer version the answer must deal with the ideas discussed in the question and provide some answer. In the problem/solution version often the causes and effects of the problem are discussed first; then, a solution follows that should attempt to block or eliminate at least one of the causes of the problem.

_____

_____

13. The contrastive pattern of the *Comparison* plan is that different points of view are shown in different parts of the passage. It may be that one view tells what did happen and the other tells what did not happen; or, one might tell what exists and the other what does not exist; or each part might tell opposing arguments. Often when opposing views are compared they are compared on many of the same issues; for example, one political candidate's views on abortion, taxes, government spending, and defense, and then the other candidate's views on these same issues. Your memory will be improved if you remember that a comparison plan was used and the number and name of the issues compared; for the above example remember that the candidates were compared on four issues: abortion, taxes, government spending and defense.

_____

_____

_____

14. Once you have chosen the plan you must *use it to organize your written recall.*

15. *To use* the plan requires your attention *before, while,* and *after* you write your recall.

16. *While* you write put your ideas into sentences and paragraphs that follow the pattern of the plan identified.

17. *After* you write, check that you used the correct organization, correctly.

18. To *use it*— *write its name* on the top of the page where you'll be writing your recall (to help you get organized).
   — *write the main idea sentence* (to set up the plan)
   — *arrange sentences and paragraphs* to match the plan (keep thinking about how the plan works).
   — *check* that you've used it (Ask "Have I discussed the main idea the same way as in the passage?")
   — *write* down anything you've only just remembered (It often happens that you think of more information as you are checking).

Your skill in using this information has shown that you can:

(a) still learn more about using the strategy.
(b) find the main idea in a passage.
(c) choose the plan of the passage.
(d) use the same plan to arrange your recall.
(e) use the strategy effectively.

These seem to be your problem areas. (The numbers correspond to those on the above check list; check what the numbers mean and see if you agree with our analysis of your progress).

_____

_____

_____

_____

If you can fix these problems you will be able to use the strategy perfectly.

Today's Practice

I would like to have you work with the same partner that you worked with during the last session. We will come around and check you on problem areas.

You and your partner will be reading and recalling some passages. Then you will read each other's recall and fill out the **feedback** forms for each other; try to help each other with any problems; we will be available to consult with you about your questions.

First, fill out the test item below and check your answers with your partner and the progress report form. Then, work through the following set of passages to read, recall, and evaluate your progress.

Let's Check

Fill in the blanks:

For the plan strategy we *choose* it, _____ it, or _____ it!
Two questions to ask yourself before you read and write or tell what you remember are:

  1. What is the _____?
  2. What is the _____ that fits the _____?

Passage 1

Read and recall the passage and write down all you can remember from it. Each one of you should independently read and recall the passage. Then, work together with your partner evaluating your performance with the *Feedback* form; try to help each other in mastering the strategy. Let us help you when you have any questions.

The Steamboat

The steam boat came of age in the 1825–50 generation. Early steam vessels were built to operate on eastern rivers. They had deep hulls, and carried most of their cargo below decks. They were able to operate with low-pressure steam engines, and frequently carried sails also. Steamboats built for western rivers were considerably different. Their hulls were flat and shallow, and the superstructure—the part of the vessel above deck—sometimes was three stories high. Low-pressure engines could not be used: The far more powerful (and dangerous) high-pressure engines were installed above the waterline, and fuel, cargo, and passengers all were carried on the main deck and the superstructure. (From *The American Adventure: Expansion, Conflict, and Reconstruction (1825–1880)*. Copyright 1975, Allyn and Bacon.)

Write down as much as you can remember from the passage you have just read. Use complete sentences. You can use the words in the passage or your own words. Do not look back at the passage after you start writing.

_____

_____

_____

_____

_____

_____

_____

_____

_____

_____

_____

_____

Feedback

1. Did you pick out the organization as *comparison?*
    If so, _____ great!
    If not, _____ did you ask the two questions before reading?
    _____ did you look for the plan? (contrast between eastern and western steamboats)
    _____ did you find the main idea organized by the plan?
    (Differences in the eastern and western steamboats on the following aspects: hull depth, extent of superstructure, cargo location, type of pressure engine.)
2. Did you write the name of the plan at the top of the recall page?
    If so, _____ so far, so good!
    If not, _____ mmmmmmm!
3. Did you write down the main idea as the first sentence?
    If so, _____ keep it up!
    If not, _____ oh no!
4. Did you have two parts in arranging your sentences?
    If so, _____ not far to go now!
    If not, _____ tut, tut!
5. Were the two parts: one for the eastern steamboat and one for the western steamboat.
    If so, _____ I bet you remembered a lot!
    If not, _____ oh rats!
6. Did you check?
    If so, _____ double smiles!
    If not, _____ don't be so overconfident!

Passage 2

Hold the Eggs and Butter

This year began with the announcement by the Federal Government of the results of the broadest and most expensive research project in medical history. Its subject was cholesterol, the vital yet dangerous yellowish substance in the bloodstream. . . Among the conclusions: (1) Heart disease is directly linked to the level of cholesterol in the blood. (2) Lowering cholesterol levels markedly reduces the incidence of fatal heart attacks. Basil Rifkin, project director of the study, believes that research "strongly indicates that the more you lower cholesterol and fat in your diet, the more you reduce your risk of heart disease." (Copyright 1984 Time Inc. All rights reserved. Reprinted by permission from TIME.)

Write down as much as you can remember from the passage you have just read. Use complete sentences. You can use the words in the passage or your own words. Do not look back at the passage after you start writing.

_____

_____

_____

_____

_____

_____

_____

_____

_____

_____

_____

_____

Feedback

1. Did you pick out the organization as *causation?*
    If so, _____ great!
    If not, _____ did you ask the two questions before reading?
    _____ did you look for the plan? (cause: lower cholesterol, effect: less incidence of fatal heart attacks)

_____ did you find the main idea organized by the plan? (reducing cholesterol will result in less risk of heart disease)

2. Did you write the name of the plan at the top of the recall page?
    If so, _____ so far, so good!
    If not, _____ mmmmmmm!

3. Did you write down the main idea as the first sentence?
    If so, _____ keep it up!
    If not, _____ oh no!

4. Did you have two parts in arranging your sentences? (One part describing the cause: cholesterol, what it is and the study investigating it; the other part describing the effect on heart disease)
    If so, _____ not far to go now!
    If not, _____ tut, tut!

5. Did you check?
    If so, _____ double smiles!
    If not, _____ don't be so overconfident!

Passage 3

Caffeine and Birth Defects

Pregnant women needn't be as cautious about caffeine consumption as had been thought, according to a new study by the Food and Drug Administration. A 1980 study, in which caffeine was injected directly into the stomachs of pregnant rats, resulted in a high incidence of birth defects in the offspring. In the new study, caffeine was put into rats' drinking water—to more closely approximate the way humans ingest the stimulant—and few birth defects were found. (Copyright, 1984, U.S. New & World Report. Excerpted from issue of spring 1984.)

Write down as much as you can remember from the passage you have just read. Use complete sentences. You can use the words in the passage or your own words. Do not look back at the passage after you start writing.

_____

_____

_____

_____

_____

_____

_____

Feedback

1. Did you pick out the organization as *comparison?*
   If so, _____ great!
   If not, _____ did you ask the two questions before reading?
   _____ did you look for the plan? (contrast between old and new study on caffeine)
   _____ did you find the main idea organized by the plan? (the new more ecologically valid study didn't show a high incidence in birth defects from caffeine, while the older study did)
2. Did you write the name of the plan at the top of the recall page?
   If so, _____ so far, so good!
   If not, _____ mmmmmmm!
3. Did you write down the main idea as the first sentence?
   If so, _____ keep it up!
   If not, _____ oh no!
4. Did you have two parts in arranging your sentences?
   If so, _____ not far to go now!
   If not, _____ tut, tut!
5. Were the two parts: one for the old study and one for the new one?
   If so, _____ I bet you remembered a lot!
   If not, _____ Oh rats!
6. Did you check?
   If so, _____ double smiles!
   If not, _____ don't be so overconfident!

Passage 4

Infectious arthritis refers to the arthritis that some people develop as a complication of another disease caused by a virus, bacterium, or fungus. The infectious agent first causes one disease but then spreads into one or more joints, causing arthritis. For example, one common cause of infectious arthritis is the bacterium that causes gonorrhea. In some people, this bacterium escapes from the genital organs and gets into the bloodstream, which carries it into the joints and leads to arthritis.

Drug treatment to get rid of the infection usually clears up the arthritis completely, if it is begun soon after the joint symptoms began. After the swelling has gone down and the infection is gone, some people may need special exercises to rebuild strength in the affected area. (Arthritis Foundation booklet: *Arthritis, Basic Facts,* pp. 25–26).

Write down as much as you can remember from the passage you have just read. Use complete sentences. You can use the words in the passage or your own words. Do not look back at the passage after you start writing.

_____

_____

_____

_____

_____

_____

_____

_____

_____

_____

Feedback

1. Did you pick out the organization as *problem/solution?*
      If so, _____ great!
      If not, _____ did you ask the two questions before reading?
      _____ did you look for the plan? (the problem is infectious arthritis caused by a virus, bacterium, or fungus, and the solution is immediate drug treatment and for some exercise too)
      _____ did you find the main idea organized by the plan? (infectious arthritis can be cured with drug treattment)
2. Did you write the name of the plan at the top of the recall page?
      If so, _____ so far, so good!
      If not, _____ mmmmmmm!
3. Did you write down the main idea as the first sentence?
      If so, _____ keep it up!
      If not, _____ oh no!
4. Did you have two parts in arranging your sentences?
      If so, _____ not far to go now!
      If not, _____ tut, tut!

5. Were the two parts: one for the problem and one for the solution.
   If so, _____ I bet you remembered a lot!
   If not, _____ Oh rats!
6. Did you check?
   If so, _____ double smiles!
   If not, _____ don't be so overconfident!

Passage 5

Birding Tips: How to Tell the Difference between Geese and Ducks (From *Joy of Nature,* Copyright © 1977, The Reader's Digest Association, Inc., p. 187.)

Male and female geese have identical plumage. Large birds with long necks, geese are good walkers. Geese, which molt only once a year, look the same at all times of the year. Nests are placed in hollows on grassy or marshy ground. Geese usually feed on land, grazing on grass and grain; brant, a sea-going species, feed on ellgrass. Though geese are powerful swimmers, they do not dive. Geese are strong fliers. They often form precise V's or long, irregular lines. They are quite noisy in flight.

Male ducks are more colorful than females of the species. Small, plump birds with short necks, ducks have stubby legs and walk clumsily. Ducks molt body feathers twice a year. Most kinds have two plumages—breeding and nonbreeding. Males in eclipse (nonbreeding) plumage look like females. Ducks nest in various sites—some even in tree holes. All ducks can dive. Some species dive to obtain fish; others eat mollusks or aquatic plants. In flight, most ducks form loose flocks.

Write down as much as you can remember from the passage you have just read. Use complete sentences. You can use the words in the passage or your own words. Do not look back at the passage after you start writing.

_____

_____

_____

_____

_____

_____

_____

_____

_____

Feedback

1. Did you pick out the organization as *comparison?*
   If so, _____ great!
   If not, _____ did you ask the two questions before reading?
   _____ did you look for the plan? (contrast between geese and ducks in appearance and habits)
   _____ did you find the main idea organized by the plan? (geese and ducks differ in plumage between male and female and in breeding plumage in males, necks, walking ability, number of molting periods per year, location of nests, diet, diving ability, and flying behavior)

2. Did you write the name of the plan at the top of the recall page?
   If so, _____ so far, so good!
   If not, _____ mmmmmmm!

3. Did you write down the main idea as the first sentence?
   If so, _____ keep it up!
   If not, _____ oh no!

4. Did you have two parts in arranging your sentences?
   If so, _____ not far to go now!
   If not, _____ tut, tut!

5. Were the two parts: one for the geese and other for the ducks?
   If so, _____ I bet you remembered a lot!
   If not, _____ oh rats!

6. Did you check?
   If so, _____ double smiles!
   If not, _____ don't be so overconfident!

Use of Outside Reading Materials

Examine the materials that you have collected from outside reading materials. Select one sample to exchange with your partner. Have your partner read and recall the material; then give feedback on his or her performance.

After you each read and recall one selection, then examine and discuss the additional materials you collected. If you forgot to bring in materials, we have some available for you to examine.

Write down as much as you can remember from the passage you have just read. Use complete sentences. You can use the words in the passage or your own words. Do not look back at the passage after you start writing.

_____

_____

_____

_____

_____

_____

_____

_____

_____

_____

_____

_____

Recapitulation.   Many of you brought examples of writing organized with a plan now familiar to you. Others found such examples but forgot to bring them today. In any case, it is important to remember that what you learn *in* this class must be used in your reading and recall *outside* the class. Otherwise you will soon forget all that you have accomplished. When you read something that you want to remember—use the plan strategy. You can use the strategy to write down what you remember, to retell a friend what you remember about an article, or to think about the article by yourself.

Conclusion.   During the five sessions that we've been together you have done several things important to your role as a learner. Particularly, you have acquired a strategy which will help you better organize your memory for what you read. The work you have done in the sessions has shown how well you've learned the strategy. The next step is up to you. You must take what you have learned away from this setting and use it—otherwise our time together will have been wasted. Congratulations on your achievement in our class and best wishes for what's ahead.

Appendix

Example of a set of passages (506 words each) recalled and their content structures (193 idea units each) used in scoring. (The reactor and schizophrenia content structures and passages were published in Meyer (1975) and are included in the appendix with compliments of Elsevier Science Publishers B. V. (North-Holland), Information & Business Division.)

Fast Breeder Reactors

From (Fast Breeder Reactors by Seaborg, G. T. & Bloom, J. L.) Copyright © (1970) by Scientific American, Inc. All rights reserved.

The need to generate enormous additional amounts of electric power while at the same time protecting the environment is taking form as one of the major social and technological problems that our society must resolve over the next few decades. The Federal Power Commission has estimated that during the next 30 years the American power industry will have to add some 1,600 million kilowatts of electric generating capacity to the present capacity of 300 million kilowatts. As for the environment, the extent of public concern over improving the quality of air, water, and landscape hardly needs elaboration, except for one point that is often overlooked: It will take large amounts of electrical energy to run the many kinds of purification plants that will be needed to clean up the air and water and to recycle wastes.

A related problem of equal magnitude is the rational utilization of the nation's finite reserves of coal, oil, and gas. In the long term they will be far more precious as sources of organic molecules than as sources of heat. Moreover, any reduction in the consumption of organic fuels brings about a proportional reduction in air polution from their combustion products.

The breeder type of nuclear reactors holds great promise as the solution to these problems. Breeder reactors produce more nuclear fuel than they consume; they would make it feasible to utilize enormous quantities of low-grade uranium and thorium ores dispersed in the rocks of the earth as a source of low-cost energy for thousands of years. In addition, these reactors would operate without adding noxious combustion products to the air. It is in the light of these considerations that the U.S. Atomic Energy commission, the nuclear industry and the electric utilities have mounted a large-scale effort to develop the technology whereby it will be possible to have a breeder reactor generating electric power on a commercial scale by 1984.

Nuclear breeding is achieved with the neutrons released by nuclear fission. The fissioning of each atom of a nuclear fuel, such as uranium 235, liberates an average of more than two fast (high-energy) neutrons. One of the neutrons must trigger another fission to maintain the nuclear chain reaction; some neutrons are nonproductively lost, and the remainder are available to breed new fissionable atoms, that is, to transform "fertile" isotopes of the heavy elements into fissionable isotopes. The fertile raw materials for breeder reactions are thorium 232, which is transmuted into uranium 233, and uranium 238, which is transmuted into plutonium 239.

It has been mentioned that breeding occurs when more fissionable material is produced than is consumed. A quantitative measure of this condition is the doubling time: the time required to produce as much net additional fissionable materials as was originally present in the reactor. At the end of the doubling time the reactor has produced enough fissionalble material to refuel itself and to fuel another identical reactor. An efficient breeder reactor will have a doubling time in the range of from 7 to 10 years.

Content Structure of Fast Breeder Reactors

```
 1          ┌response
 2          ├problem
 3          ├collection
 4          ┌NEED TO GENERATE POWER
 5            ┌specific
 6          ┌ADD
 7              ┌agent
 8              └AMERICAN POWER INDUSTRY
 9              ┌patient
10              └1600 MILLION KILOWATTS OF ELECTRIC GENERATING CAPACITY
11              ┌benefactive
12            ┌PRESENT CAPACITY
13                ┌specific
14                └300 MILLION KILOWATTS
15              ┌setting time
16              └NEXT 30 YEARS
17            ┌ESTIMATED
18                ┌agent
19                └FEDERAL POWER COMMISSION
20          ┌PROTECT ENVIRONMENT
21            ┌specific
22          ┌IMPROVE QUALITY
23              ┌agent
24            └PUBLIC
25                ┌attribution
26                └CONCERN OVER IMPROVING ENVIRONMENT
27              ├patient
27              ├collection
29              ├AIR
30              ├WATER
31              └LANDSCAPE
32            ┌latter
33            ├collection
34            ├CLEAN AIR
35            ├CLEAN WATER
36            └RECYCLE WASTES
```

```
37    ⊢instrument
38    ⊾PURIFICATION PLANTS
39        ⌜attribution
40        ⊢MANY KINDS
41        ⊾RUN
42            ⌜FORCE
43            ⊾ELECTRICAL ENERGY
44                ⌜specific
45                ⊾LARGE AMOUNTS OF ELECTRIC ENERGY
46    ⊾RATIONAL UTILIZATION OF FINITE RESERVES
47        ⌜setting location
48        ⊾NATION
48    ⊢specific
50    ⊢collection
51    ⊢COAL
52    ⊢OIL
53    ⊾GAS
54    ⊢explanation
55    ⊾SOURCES OF ORGANIC MOLECULES
56        ⌜adversative
57        ⊾SOURCES OF HEAT
58        ⌜setting time
59        ⊾IN THE LONG TERM
60    ⊾REDUCE CONSUMPTION
61        ⌜patient
62        ⊾ORGANIC FUELS
63        ⌜latter
64        ⊾REDUCE AIR POLLUTION
65            ⌜manner
66            ⊾PROPORTIONATELY
67            ⌜former
68            ⊾COMBUSTION PRODUCTS
69    ⊢solution
70    ⊾BREEDER REACTORS
71        ⌜identification constituency
72        ⊾TYPE OF NUCLEAR REACTOR
73    ⊢explanation
74    ⊢covariance, antecedent
75    ⊢collection
76    ⊢PRODUCE
```

```
77   patient
78   FUEL
79   latter
80   MORE FUEL THAN CONSUME
81   specific
82   BREEDING = MORE FISSIONABLE MATERIAL PRODUCED THAN CONSUMED
83   explanation
84   QUANTITATIVE MEASURE IS THE DOUBLING TIME
85   specific
86   TIME AS MUCH NET + FISSIONABLE MAT. AS ORIGINALLY
87   explanation
88   PRODUCE
89   force
90   REACTOR
91   setting time
92   END OF THE DOUBLING TIME
93   latter
94   collection
95   ENOUGH FISSIONABLE MATERIAL TO REFUEL ITSELF
96      "    "    "        "     ANOTHER IDENTICAL REACTOR
97   attribution
98   DOUBLING TIME = 7 TO 10 YEARS EFFICIENT BREEDER REACTOR
99   USE
100  manner
101  ENORMOUS QUANTITIES
102  patient
103  collection
104  setting location
105  DISPURSED IN ROCKS OF THE EARTH
106  LOW-GRADE URANIUM ORE
107  LOW-GRADE THORIUM ORE
108  latter
109  LOW COST ENERGY
110  setting time
111  THOUSANDS OF YEARS
112  OPERATE
113  latter
114  WITHOUT ADDING NOXIUS COMBUSION PRODUCTS
115  benefactive
116  AIR
117  covariance, consequent (IN LIGHT OF THESE CONSIDERATIONS)
```

221

```
118    EFFORT MOUNTED
119        ┌agent
120        ├collection
121        ├U.S. ATOMIC ENERGY COMMISSION
122        ├NUCLEAR INDUSTRIES
123        └ELECTRIC UTILITIES
124        ├manner
125        └LARGE-SCALED
126        ├latter
127        ├GENERATE
128            ┌force
129            └BREEDER REACTOR
130            ├patient
131            └ELECTRIC POWER
132            ├range
133            └COMMERCIAL SCALE
134            ├setting time
135            └1984
136    ├attribution
137    NUCLEAR BREEDING OCCURS
138        ┌force
139        └NUCLEAR FISSION
140        ├patient
141        ATOM OF NUCLEAR FUEL
142            ┌explanation
143            └URANIUM
144                ┌specific
145                └(URANIUM)  235
146        ├latter
147        LIBERATES NEUTRONS
148            ┌specific
149            MORE THAN 2 NEUTRONS ON AN AVERAGE
150                ┌attribution
151                └FAST
152                    ┌explanation
153                    └HIGH-ENERGY
154        ┌collection
155        MAINTAIN
156            ┌agent
157            └ONE NEUTROL
```

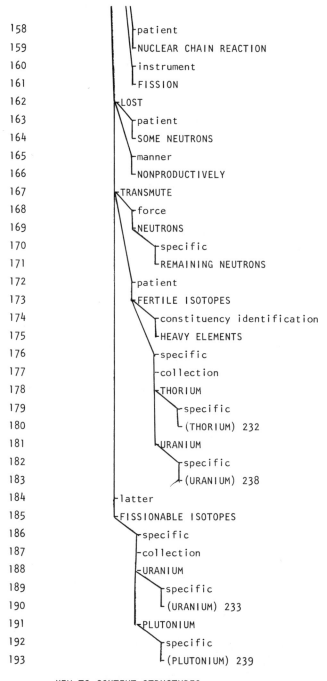

158	patient
159	NUCLEAR CHAIN REACTION
160	instrument
161	FISSION
162	LOST
163	patient
164	SOME NEUTRONS
165	manner
166	NONPRODUCTIVELY
167	TRANSMUTE
168	force
169	NEUTRONS
170	specific
171	REMAINING NEUTRONS
172	patient
173	FERTILE ISOTOPES
174	constituency identification
175	HEAVY ELEMENTS
176	specific
177	collection
178	THORIUM
179	specific
180	(THORIUM) 232
181	URANIUM
182	specific
183	(URANIUM) 238
184	latter
185	FISSIONABLE ISOTOPES
186	specific
187	collection
188	URANIUM
189	specific
190	(URANIUM) 233
191	PLUTONIUM
192	specific
193	(PLUTONIUM) 239

KEY TO CONTENT STRUCTURES

CAPITALIZED WORDS = CONTENT WORDS FROM THE TEXT

lower case words = relationships among the ideas in the text

Anti-s-proteins for Schizophrenics

The need to change the strange behavior of adult schizophrenics along with improving their ability to communicate is taking form as one of the major problems that psychiatrists must resolve soon. The American Psychiatric Association has proclaimed that psychiatrists must change adult schizophrenics by the end of this century. This action would benefit the largest proportion of hospitalized mental patients, two million schizophrenics. As for improving communication skills of adult schizophrenics, these confused schizophrenics must learn to stick to goals, state only important ideas, and listen for important ideas. Inhibition by schizophrenics will be needed to increase their use of goals, speaking skills, and listening skills. Inhibition is produced by the ability to prevent thinking about unimportant ideas; that is, the ability to maintain a set. Inhibition is lacking in schizophrenics.

A related problem of equal magnitude is the treatment of children in the nation's mental hospitals with schizophrenia. They need to be treated for their lack of responsiveness, their unusual body movements and their inability to differentiate between self and others. The schizophrenic child has made a fusion of himself with his mother. He is not like the autistic child that never becomes close to his mother after birth. Successful treatment of childhood schizophrenics would drastically reduce agony from their parents.

The anti-s-protein, an enzyme, holds great promise as the solution to these problems. Anti-s-proteins keep normal people sane. They are completely missing in the brains of adult and childhood schizophrenics, and this lack causes them to be mentally disturbed until the time when anti-s-proteins can be given to them. Proper doses could allow schizophrenics to function normally and return to society. It is in the light of these considerations that Dr. Gottlieb, Dr. Frohman, and Dr. Domino have mounted a concerted effort to develop the procedures whereby it will be possible to cure the nation's schizophrenics by 1987.

S-proteins are potent, unstable proteins called alpha-two-globulin. Anti-s-proteins control the production of the cork-screw shaped s-proteins. Cork-screw shaped s-proteins are the only type of s-protein found in schizophrenics, while the s-proteins of normals are mainly shaped like an accordion. The anti-s-proteins control the s-proteins by shutting off their production and preventing them from becoming abnormal. Anti-s-proteins could lessen the schizophrenic's confusion by stopping production of abnormal s-proteins, and dramatically curtail the schizophrenic's delusional state. Anti-s-proteins, the s standing for schizophrenic or stress, could stop the schizophrenic's hallucinogenic factory in his brain. This delusion factory over produces an essential amino acid for human metabolism, trytophan, and DMT, dimethyl tyrtamine. Thus, its use would result in a reduction in abnormalities in schizophrenics. It would reduce their strange behavior and trouble communication. It would eliminate their unrealistic fears and focus on the unimportant.

It has been mentioned that anti-s-proteins keep normal people from thinking and behaving bizarrely. The effect of anti-s-proteins on a normal person calms him down after a crisis. It reduces thoughts to a normal state. After a crisis anti-s-proteins inhibit extreme sensitivity to all noises and sights. Normal amounts of anti-s-proteins have this calming effect.

Content Structure of Anti-s-proteins for Schizophrenics

```
 1          ┌response
 2          ├problem
 3          ├collection
 4          ├NEED TO CHANGE STRANGE BEHAVIOR OF ADULT SCHIZOPHRENICS
 5              ┌specific
 6              ├CHANGE
 7                  ┌agent
 8                  └PSYCHIATRISTS
 9                  ┌patient
10                  └ADULT SCHIZOPHRENICS
11                  ┌benefactive
12                  ├LARGEST SINGLE PROPORTION HOSPITALIZED MENTAL PATIENTS
13                      ┌specific
14                      └TWO MILLION SCHIZOPHRENICS
15                  ├setting time
16                  └BY THE END OF THIS CENTURY
17              ├PROCLAIMED
18                  ┌agent
19                  └AMERICAN PSYCHIATRIC ASSOCIATION
20          ├IMPROVE ADULT SCHIZOPHRENIC'S ABILITY TO COMMUNICATE
21              ┌specific
22              ├INCREASE USE
23                  ┌agent
24                  ├ADULT SCHIZOPHRENICS
25                      ┌attribution
26                      └confused
27                  ├patient
27                  ├collection
29                  ├GOALS
30                  ├SPEAKING SKILLS
31                  └LISTENING SKILLS
32                  ┌latter
33                  ├collection
34                  ├STICK TO GOALS
35                  ├STATE ONLY IMPORTANT IDEAS
36                  └LISTEN FOR IMPORTANT IDEAS
37              ├instrument
38              ├INHIBITION
```

39	attribution
40	IS LACKING IN SCHIZOPHRENICS
41	PRODUCED
42	force
43	ABILITY TO PREVENT THINKING UNIMPORTANT IDEAS
44	specific
45	ABILITY TO MAINTAIN A SET
46	TREATMENT OF CHILDREN WITH SCHIZOPHRENIA
47	setting location
48	NATION'S MENTAL HOSPITALS
49	specific
50	collection
51	TREATMENT OF THEIR LACK OF RESPONSIVENESS
52	TREATMENT OF THEIR UNUSUAL BODY MOVEMENTS
53	" " " INABILITY TO DIFFERENTIATE BETWEEN SELF & OTHERS
54	explanation
55	CHILDHOOD SCHIZOPHRENIC MADE FUSION OF SELF WITH MOTHER
56	adversative
57	AUTISTIC CHILD THAT NEVER BECAME CLOSE TO HIS MOTHER
58	setting time
59	AFTER BIRTH
60	SUCCESSFULLY TREAT
61	patient
62	CHILDHOOD SCHIZOPHRENICS
63	latter
64	REDUCE AGONY
65	manner
66	DRASTICALLY
67	former
68	THEIR PARENTS
69	solution
70	ANTI-S-PROTEINS
71	identification constituency
72	AN ENZYME
73	explanation
74	covariance, antecedent
75	collection

```
76    KEEP
77         patient
78         NORMAL PEOPLE
79         latter
80         SANE
81         specific
82       KEEPS NORMAL PEOPLE FROM THINKING/BEHAVING BIZARRELY
83           explanation
84         CALMS A NORMAL PERSON DOWN AFTER A CRISIS
85             specific
86           REDUCES THOUGHTS TO A NORMAL STATE
87               explanation
88             CAUSES
89                 force
90               ANTI-S-PROTEINS
91                 setting time
92               AFTER A CRISIS
93                 latter
94               collection
95               INHIBIT EXTREME SENSITIVITY TO NOISES
96               INHIBIT EXTREME SENSITIVITY TO SIGHTS
97           attribution
98           NORMAL AMOUNTS OF ANTI-S-PROTEINS
99    MISSING
100        manner
101        COMPLETELY
102        patient
103       collection
104           setting location
105         BRAINS
106       ADULT SCHIZOPHRENICS
107       CHILDHOOD SCHIZOPHRENICS
108        latter
109       MENTALLY DISTURBED
110        setting time
111       UNTIL ANTI-S-PROTEINS CAN BE GIVEN TO THEM
112    GIVE PROPER DOSES
113        latter
114       NORMAL FUNCTIONING OF SCHIZOPHRENICS
```

```
115                    ┬benefactive
116                    └SOCIETY
117               ┬covariance, consequent (IN LIGHT OF THESE CONSIDERATIONS)
118               ┬EFFORT MOUNTED
119                 ┬agent
120                 ┬collection
121                 ┬DR. GOTTLIEB
122                 ┬DR. FROHMAN
123                 └DR. DOMINO
124                 ┬manner
125                 └CONCERTED
126                 ┬latter
127                 ┬CURE
128                   ┬force
129                   └INJECTIONS OF ANTI-S-PROTEINS
130                   ┬patient
131                   └SCHIZOPHRENICS
132                   ┬range
133                   └NATION
134                   ┬setting time
135                   └1987
136        ┬attribution
137        ┬CONTROL
138          ┬force
139          └ANTI-S-PROTEINS
140          ┬patient
141          └S-PROTEINS (PRODUCTION)
142          ┬explanation
143          └A-PROTEINS ARE POTENT, UNSTABLE PROTEINS
144            ┬specific
145            └ALPHA-TWO-GLOBULIN
146          ┬latter
147          ┬CONTROL OF THE PORUDCTION OF S-PROTEINS
148            ┬specific
149            └PREVENTS PROTEIN FROM GOING BAD & SHUTS OFF ITS PRODUCTION
150              ┬attribution
151              └CORKSCREW SHAPED PROTEINS
152                ┬explanation
153                └KIND FOUND IN SCH, NORMALS = ACCORDIAN SHAPE
154          ┬collection
155          ┬LESSENS CONFUSION
156            ┬agent
157            └ANTI-S-PROTEINS
```

229

```
158            patient
159            SCHIZOPHRENIC
160            instrument
161            STOP PRODUCTION OF ABNORMAL S-PROTEINS
162    CURTAILS
163            patient
164            SCHIZOPHRENIC'S DELUSIONAL STATE
165            manner
166            DRAMATICALLY
167    STOPS
168            force
169            ANTI-S-PROTEINS
170                specific
171                ANTI-SCHIZOPHRENIC OR STRESS PROTEIN
172            patient
173            SCHIZOPHRENIC'S HALLUCINOGENIC FACTORY
174                constituency identification
175                SCHIZOPHRENIC'S BRAIN
176            specific
177            collection
178            FACTORY OVERPRODUCE ESSENTIAL AMINO ACID METABOLIC
179                specific
180                AMINO ACID TYRTOPHAN
181            DMT FACTORY
182                specific
183                DIMETHYL TYRTAMINE
184            latter
185            REDUCTION IN ABNORMALITIES IN SCHIZOPHRENICS
186            specific
187            collection
188            REDUCTION IN STRANGE BEHAVIOR
189                specific
190                ELIMINATE THEIR UNREALISTIC FEARS
191            REDUCTION IN TROUBLE COMMUNICATING
192                specific
193                ELIMINATE THEIR FOCUS ON UNIMPORTANT
```

Trusts

The need to distribute your property while at the same time avoiding court costs is taking form as one of the major financial problems that you must resolve before your death. At your death you want your estate to go to chosen survivors as you desired. As for court costs, avoid the need for a probate court to distribute your estate. Proceedings of a probate court can be expensive. Probate courts distribute legacies, devises of real property, and residuary property to the spouse, descendants, and charities through an attested will made by the deceased in testamentary capacity.

A related problem of equal magnitude is the need to avoid obstacles in U.S. courts. These obstacles or hurdles in distributing your estate as you desire include delays in time, the management of your estate by the court, and state laws for equal distribution of your wealth. Proceedings of probate court have tied up estates for as long as six years, while the spouse lived without these funds. If you die without a will your estate is distributed to relatives equally.

The trust, a type of will substitute, holds great promise as the solution to these problems. Trusts avoid probate court to transfer title of ownership. Trusts avoid court costs and delays. In addition, they completely avoid payment to the government at death of gift taxes and estate taxes listed in the Economic Recovery Tax Act. Trusts enable you to control your property without legally owning it. In light of these assets of trusts, Lloyd Copenbarger, Pep Jackson, and others concerned with estate planning have systematically mounted an effort to distribute pamphlets to educate the public about trusts in the 1980s.

In establishing a trust the trustor divides the property into legal and benefical ownerships. The property transferred into a trust is called by a special term; it is called the corpus of the trust. Legal ownership is held by the trustee and beneficial ownership is held by the beneficiary. The trustee holds the legal title and the beneficiary uses the property. The trust merely divides the legal ownership from the benefical ownership. The trustor can change the trust with provisions of a revocable living trust. Property is distributed according to the wishes of the trustor. The trustee, such as the trustor's bank, can transfer a deceased trustor's farm, part of the trust's property, to new beneficiaries. The trustor as the former beneficiary would have had the rights to all benefits of the property, such as income, and the right to use the property, such as live on the farm. The trustee transfers the beneficiary rights to the farm to the new beneficiaries, such as the deceased trustor's spouse and the deceased trustor's children.

It has been mentioned that trusts avoid court costs and delays. A trust does not have a "life span." Trusts cannot die. Trusts provide transfer of property at your death to chosen individuals without court involvement. Trusts allow you to control the use of your property during your life and after your death.

Content Structure for Trusts

```
1        ┌─response
2        ├─problem
3        ├─collection
4        ┌DISTRIBUTE PROPERTY
5        │    ┌─specific
6        │    ├WANT TO GO TO
7        │    │    ┌─agent
8        │    │    └─you
9        │    │  ├─patient
10       │    │  └ESTATE
11       │    │    ├─benefactive
12       │    │    └SURVIVERS
13       │    │         ┌─specific
14       │    │         └─CHOSEN
15       │    │  ┌─setting time
16       │    │  └YOUR DEATH
17       │    │  └DESIRE
18       │    │       ┌─agent
19       │    │       └─YOU
20       ┌AVOID COURT COSTS
21       │    ┌─specific
22       │    ├AVOID NEED TO DISTRIBUTE
23       │    │    ┌─agent
24       │    │    ├PROBATE COURT
25       │    │    │    ┌─attribution
26       │    │    │    └─PROCEEDINGS CAN BE EXPENSIVE
27       │    │  ├─patient
28       │    │  ├─collection
29       │    │  ├─LEGACIES
30       │    │  ├─DEVICES OF REAL PROPERTY
31       │    │  └─RESIDUARY PROPERTY
32       │    │  ├─latter
33       │    │  ├─collection
34       │    │  ├─SPOUSE
35       │    │  ├─DECENDANTS
36       │    │  └─CHARITIES
37       │    │  ├─instrument
38       │    │  └WILL
39       │    │       ┌─attribution
40       │    │       ├─ATTESTED
```

```
41                        MADE BY
42                          force
43                        DECEASED
44                          specific
45                        DECEASED IN TESTMENTARY CAPACITY
46       AVOID OBSTACLES
47          setting location
48          U.S. COURTS
49          specific
50          collection
51         DELAYS IN TIME
52         MANAGEMENT OF ESTATE BY COURT
53         STATE LAWS FOR EQUAL WEALTH DISTRIBUTION
54         explanation
55         PROBATE COURT PROCEEDINGS HAVE TIED UP YOUR ESTATE
56           adversative
57           SPOUSE LIVES WITHOUT THESE FUNDS
58           setting time
59           6 YEARS
60         DIE WITHOUT WILL
61           patient
62           YOU
63           latter
64           IS DISTRIBUTED TO RELATIVES
65            manner
66            EQUALLY
67            former
68            YOUR ESTATE
69       solution
70       TRUST
71          identification constituency
72          TYPE OF WILL SUBSTITUTE
73          explanation
74          covariance, antecedent
75          collection
76          AVOID
77            patient
78            PROBATE COURT
79            latter
80            TRANSFER TITLE OF OWNERSHIP
```

```
 81      ─specific
 82      ─AVOID COURT COSTS AND DELAYS
 83           ─explanation
 84           ─TRUST DOES NOT HAVE A "LIFE SPAN"
 85               ─specific
 86               ─TRUST CANNOT DIE
 87                   ─explanation
 88                   ─PROVIDE TRANSFER TO PORPERTY
 89                       ─force
 90                       ─TRUST
 91                       ─setting time
 92                       ─YOUR DEATH
 93                       ─latter
 94                       ─collection
 95                       ─CHOSEN INDIVIDUALS
 96                       ─WITHOUT COURT INVOLVEMENT
 97               ─attribution
 98               ─ALLOW CONTROL PROPERTY DURING LIFE AND AFTER DEATH
 99      ─AVOID PAYMENT
100          ─manner
101          ─COMPLETELY
102          ─patient
103          ─collection
104              ─setting location
105              ─LISTED IN ECONOMIC RECOVERY TAX ACT
106          ─GIFT TAXES
107          ─ESTATE TAXES
108          ─latter
109          ─GOVERNMENT
110          ─setting time
111          ─DEATH
112      ─CAN ENABLE TO CONTROL
113          ─latter
114          ─USE OF YOUR PROPERTY WITHOUT LEGALLY OWNING IT
115          ─benefactive
116          ─PERSON
117      ─covariance, consequent (IN LIGHT OF THESE CONSIDERATIONS)
118      ─HAVE MOUNTED AN EFFORT TO DISTRIBUTE
119          ─agent
120          ─collection
```

```
121    ├LLOYD COPENBARGER
122    ├PEP JACKSON
123    ├OTHERS CONCERNED WITH ESTATE PLANNING
124    ┌manner
125    └SYSTEMATICALLY
126    ├latter
127    ├TO EDUCATE
128        ┌force
129        └PAMPHLETS
130        ┌patient
131        └PUBLIC
132        ┌range
133        └TRUSTS
134        ├setting time
135        ├1980s
136    ├attribution
137    ├DIVIDES
138        ┌force
139        └TRUSTOR
140        ┌patient
141        └PROPERTY
142            ┌explanation
143            ├PROPERTY TRANSFERRED IN TRUST CALLED BY SPECIAL TERM
144                ┌specific
145                └CORPUS OF THE TRUST
146        ├latter
147        ├LEGAL AND BENEFICIAL OWNERSHIP
148            ┌specific
149            ├TRUSTEE AND BENEFICIARY
150                ┌attribution
151                ├TRUSTEE HOLDS TITLE & BENEFICIARY USES PROPERTY
152                    ┌explanation
153                    └TRUST DEVIDES LEGAL FROM BENEFICIAL OWNERSHIP
154        ├collection
155        ├CAN CHANGE
156            ┌agent
157            └TRUSTOR
158            ┌patient
159            └TRUST
160            ├instrument
161            └PROVISIONS OF THE REVOCABLE TRUST
```

235

```
162    IS DISTRIBUTED
163      patient
164      PROPERTY
165      manner
166      ACCORDING TO THE WISHES OF TRUSTOR
167    TRANSFER
168      force
169      TRUSTEE
170        specific
171        DISIGNATED
172      patient
173      FARM OF DECEASED TRUSTOR
174        constituency identification
175        PROPERTY OF TRUST
176      specific
177      collection
178      RIGHT TO ALL BENEFITS OF PROPERTY
179        specific
180        INCOME
181      RIGHT TO USE PROPERTY
182        specific
183        LIVE ON FARM
184      latter
185    NEW BENEFICIARIES
186      specific
187      collection
188      SPOUSE
189        specific
190        DECEASED TRUSTOR'S SPOUSE
191      CHILDREN
192        specific
193        DECEASED TRUSTOR'S CHILDREN
```

References

Armbruster, B. B., & Anderson, T. H. (1980). *The effect of mapping on the free recall of expository text* (Tech. Rep. No. 160). Urbana-Champaign: University of Illinois, Center for the Study of Reading.

Armbruster, B. B., Anderson, T. H., & Ostertag, J. (1987). Does text structure/summarization instruction facilitate learning from expository text? *Reading Research Quarterly, 22,* 331–346.

Aristotle. (1960). *The rhetoric of Aristotle* L. Cooper. trans. New York: Appleton-Century-Crofts.

Aulls, M. W. (1982). *Developing readers in today's elementary school.* Boston, MA: Allyn and Bacon.

Baltes, P. B., Dittman-Kohli, F., & Kliegl, R. (1986). Reserve capacity of the elderly in aging-sensitive tests of fluid intelligence: Replication and extension. *Psychology and Aging, 1,* 172–177.

Baltes, P.B., & Willis, S. L. (1982). Plasticity and enhancement of intellectual functioning in old age: Penn State's Adult Development and Enrichment Project: In F. I. M. Craik & S. Trehub (Eds.), *Aging and cognitive processes* (pp. 353–390). New York: Plenum Press.

Barnett, J. E. (1984). Facilitating retention through instruction about text structure. *Journal of Reading Behavior, 16,* 1–13.

Bartlett, B. J. (1978). *Top-level structure as an organizational strategy for recall of classroom text.* Unpublished doctoral dissertation, Arizona State University.

Bartlett, B. J., & Briese, B. J. (1979). *Find the pattern: Improve the memory: A strategy to help mildly-intellectually handicapped readers remember text* (Research Report No. 5). Brisbane, Australia: Brisbane College of Advanced Education.

Bartlett, B. J., & Meyer, B. J. F. (1981). *A special plan for reading.* Unpublished materials. Tempe, AZ.

Bartlett, B. J., Turner, A., & Mathams, P. (1981, April). *Top-level structure: A significant relation in what fifth graders remember from classroom text.* Paper presented at the meeting of the American Educational Research Association in Los Angeles, CA.

Bartlett, B. J., & Turner, A. (1985). *Maintenance of learning about top-level structure: A three-year follow-up* (Research Report No. 12). Brisbane, Australia: Brisbane College of Advanced Education.

237

Bartlett, B. J., Turner, A., & Barton, B. M. (1987). *Knowing what and knowing how*. Melbourne: Thomas Nelson.

Beaugrande, R. de (1980). *Text, discourse, and process*. Norwood, NJ: Ablex.

Belmore, S. M. (1981). Age-related changes in processing explicit and implicit language. *Journal of Gerontology, 36,* 316–322.

Belsky, J. K. (1984). *The psychology of aging: Theory, research, and practice*. Monterey, CA: Brooks/Cole.

Berkowitz, S. J. (1986). Effects of instruction in text organization on sixth-grade students' memory for expository reading. *Reading Research Quarterly, 21,* 161–178.

Birren, J. E. (1974). Translations in gerontology—from lab to life: Psychophysiology and speed of response. *American Psychologist, 29,* 808–815.

Birren, J. E., Woods, A. M., & Williams, M. V. (1980). Behavioral slowing with aging: Causes, organization, and consequences. In L. W. Poon (Ed.), *Aging in the 1980's: Psychological Issues* (pp. 293–308). Washington, D.C.: APA.

Borgatta, E. F., & Corsini, R. J. (1964). *Manual for the Quick Word Test*. New York: Harcourt, Brace, and World.

Botwinick, J. (1959). Drives, expectations, and emotions. In J. E. Birren (Ed.), *Handbook on aging and the individual* (pp. 739–768). Chicago: University of Chicago Press.

Botwinick, J. (1967). *Cognitive processes in maturity and old age*. New York: Springer.

Botwinick, J. (1978). *Aging and behavior*. New York: Springer.

Britton, B. K., Glynn, S., Meyer, B. J. F., & Penland, M. (1982). Use of cognitive capacity in reading text. *Journal of Educational Psychology, 73,* 51–61.

Britton, B. K., Meyer, B. J. F., Hodge, M. H., & Glynn, S. (1980). Effect of the organization of text on memory: Tests of retrieval and response criterion hypotheses. *Journal of Experimental Psychology: Human Learning and Memory, 6,* 620–629.

Britton, B. K., Meyer, B. J. F., Simpson, R., Holdredge, T. S., & Curry, C. (1979). Effects of the organization of text on memory: Tests of two implications of a selective attention hypothesis. *Journal of Experimental Psychology: Human Learning and Memory, 5,* 496–506.

Burke, D. M.. & Light, L. L. (1981). Memory and aging: The role of retrieval process. *Psychological Bulletin, 90,* 513–546.

Burgess, B. A., Cranney, A. G., & Larsen, J. J. (1976). Effect on academic achievement of a voluntary university reading program. *Journal of Reading, 19,* 644–646.

Byrd, M. (1981). *Age differences in memory for prose passages*. Unpublished doctoral dissertation, University of Toronto.

Calfee, R., & Drum, P. (1986). Research on teaching reading: In M. C. Wittrock (Ed.), *Handbook of research on teaching* (pp. 804–849). New York: Macmillan.

Carrell, P. L. (1985). Facilitating ESL reading by teaching text structure. *TESOL Quarterly, 19,* 727–752.

Chall, J. S. (1983). *Stages of reading development*. New York: McGraw-Hill.

Chiesi, H., Spillich, G., & Voss, J. (1979). Aquisition of domain-related information in relation to high and low domain knowledge. *Journal of Verbal Learning and Verbal Behavior, 18,* 257–274.

Christensen, F. (1967). A generative rhetoric of the paragraph. In M. Steinmann (Ed.), *New rhetorics* (pp. 108–133). New York: Scribner's.

Cirilo, R., & Foss, D. (1980). Text structure and reading time for sentences. *Journal of Verbal Learning and Verbal Behavior, 19,* 96–109.

Cohen, G. (1979). Language comprehension in old age. *Cognitive Psychology, 11,* 412–429.

Cohen, G. (1981). Inferential reasoning in old age. *Cognition, 9,* 59–72.

Cohen, G. (in press). Age differences in memory for texts: Production deficiency or processing limitations? In L. L. Light & D. M. Burke (Eds.), *Language, memory and aging*. New York: Academic Press.

Cook, W. D. (1977). *Adult literacy education in the United States*. Newark, DE: International Reading Association.

Cook, L. K. (1982). *The effects of text structure on the comprehension of scientific prose*. Unpublished doctoral dissertation. University of California, Santa Barbara.

Cotman, C. W., & Holets, V. R. (1985). Structural changes at synapses with age: Plasticity and regeneration: In C. E. Finch & E. L. Schneider (Eds.), *Handbook of the biology of aging* (pp. 617–639). New York: Van Nostrand.

D'Angelo, F. J. (1979). Paradigms as structural counterparts of topoi: In D. McQuade (Ed.), *Linguistics, stylistics, and the teaching of composition* (pp. 41–51). Akron, OH: University of Akron Press.

D'Angelo, F. J. (1980). *Process and thought in composition*. Cambridge, MA: Winthrop.

Danner, F. W. (1976). Children's understanding of intersentence organization in the recall of short descriptive passages. *Journal of Educational Psychology, 68*, 174–183.

Dansereau, D. F., Brooks, L. W., Holley, C. D., & Collins, K. W. (1983). Learning strategies training: Effects of sequencing. *Journal of Experimental Education, 51*, 102–108.

Dansereau, D. F., Collins, K. W., McDonald, B. A., Holley, C. D., Garland, J., Diekhoff, G., & Evans, S. H. (1979). Development and evaluation of a learning strategy training program. *Journal of Educational Psychology, 71*, 64–73.

Davis, F. B., & Davis, C. C. (1956). *Davis Reading Test*. New York: The Psychological Corporation.

Dee-Lucas, D., & Larkin, J. H. (1986). Novice strategies for comprehending scientific texts. *Discourse Processes, 9*, 329–354.

Dee-Lucas, D., & Larkin, J. H. (1987). *Attentional strategies for studying scientific texts*. Pittsburgh, PA: Carnegie-Mellon University.

Denney, N. W. (1982). Aging and cognitive changes. In B. B. Wolman (Ed.), *Handbook of developmental psychology* (pp. 807–827). Englewood Cliffs, NJ: Prentice-Hall.

Diekhoff, G. M., Brown, P. J., & Dansereau, D. F. (1982). A prose learning strategy training program based on network and depth-of-processing models. *Journal of Experimental Education, 50*, 180–184.

Dixon, R. A., Hultsch, D. F., & Hertzog, C. (1986, August). *Twenty-five structurally equivalent texts for use in aging research*. Paper presented at the American Psychological Association Meetings, Washington, D.C.

Dixon, R. A., Hultsch, D. F., Simon. E. W., & von Eye, A. (1984). Verbal ability and text structure effects on adult age differences in text recall. *Journal of Verbal Learning Behavior, 23*, 569–578.

Dixon, R. A., Simon, E. W., Nowak, C. A., & Hultsch, D. F. (1982). Text recall in adulthood as a function of level of information, input modality, and delay interval. *Journal of Gerontology, 37*, 358–364.

Dixon, R. A., & von Eye, A. (1984). Depth of processing and text recall in adulthood. *Journal of Reading Behavior, 26*, 109–117.

Ekstrom, R. B., French, J. W., Harman, H. H., & Derman, D. (1976). *Manual for kit of factor referenced cognitive tests*. Princeton, NJ: Educational Testing Service.

Flavell, J. H. (1981). Cognitive monitoring. In W. P. Dickson (Ed.), *Children's oral communications skills* (pp. 35–60). New York: Academic Press.

Frederiksen, C. H. (1977). Structure and process in discourse production and comprehension. In M. A. Just & P. Carpenter (Eds.), *Cognitive processes in comprehension* (pp. 313–322). Hillsdale, NJ: Lawrence Erlbaum Associates.

Garner, R., Alexander, P., Slater, W., Hare, V. C., Smith, T., & Reis, R. (1986). Children's knowledge of structural properties of expository text. *Journal of Educational Psychology, 78*, 411–416.

Geva, E. (1983). Facilitating reading through flowcharting. *Reading Research Quarterly, 18*, 384–405.

Gillund, G., & Perlmutter, M. (in press). Episodic-semantic memory interactions across adulthood. In L. L. Light & D. M. Burke (Eds.), *Language, memory, and aging*. New York: Academic Press.

Glover, J. A., Zimmer, J. W., Filbeck, R. W., & Plake, B. S. (1980). Effects of training students to identify the semantic base of prose materials. *Journal of Applied Behavior Analysis, 13*, 655–667.

Glynn, S. M., Okun, M. A., Muth, K. D., & Britton, B. K. (1983). Adults' text recall: An examination of the age-deficit hypothesis. *Journal of Reading Behavior, 15*, 31–45.

Glynn, S. M., & Muth, K. D. (1979). Text-learning capabilities of older adults. *Educational Gerontology, 4*, 253–269.

Goetz, E. T., Reynolds, R. E., Schallert, D. L., & Radin, D. I. (1983). Reading in perspective: What real cops and pretend burglers look for in a story. *Journal of Educational Psychology, 75*, 500–510.

Gold, P. C., & Horn, P. L. (1982). Achievement in reading, verbal language, listening comprehension and locus of control of adult illiterates in a volunteer tutorial project. *Perceptual and Motor Skills, 54*, 1243–1250.

Golub, L. S. (1980). A computer assisted literacy development program. In L. S. Johnson (Ed.), *Reading and the adult learner* (pp. 47–54). Newark, DE: International Reading Association.

Gordon, C. J. (1980). *The effects of instruction in metacomprehension and inferencing on children's comprehension abilities*. Unpublished doctoral dissertation, University of Minnesota.

Gordon, S. K., & Clark, W. C. (1974). Application of signal detection theory to prose recall and recognition in elderly and young adults. *Journal of Gerontology, 29*, 64–72.

Graesser, A. C. (1981). *Prose comprehension beyond the word*. New York: Springer-Verlag.

Grimes, J. E. (1975). *The thread of discourse*. The Hague: Mouton.

Halliday, M. A. K., & Hasan, R. (1976). *Cohesion in English*. New York: Longman.

Harker, J. O., Hartley, J. T., & Walsh, D. A. (1982). Understanding discourse—a life-span approach. In B. A. Hutson (Ed.), *Advances in reading/language research* (vol. 1, pp. 155–202). Greenwich, CT: JAI Press.

Hartley, J. T. (1986). Reader and text variables as determinants of discourse memory in adulthood. *Psychology and Aging, 1*, 150–158.

Hartley, J. T. (1988). Memory for prose: Perspectives on the reader. In L. W. Poon, D. C. Rubin, & B. A. Wilson (Eds.), *Everyday cognition and adult and later life*. Cambridge, England: Cambridge University Press.

Hartley, J. T. (in press). Individual differences in memory for written discourse. In L. L. Light & D. M. Burke (Eds.), *Language, memory, and aging*. New York: Academic Press.

Hartley, J. T., Cassidy, J. J., & Lee, D. W. (1986, August). *Prior knowledge, processing load, and age in memory for prose*. Paper presented at the Annual Meeting of the American Psychological Association, Washington, D.C.

Hartley, J. T., Harker, J. O., & Walsh, D. A. (1980). Contemporary issues and new directions in adult development of learning and memory. In L. W. Poon (Ed.), *Aging in the 1980's* (pp. 239–252). Washington, D.C.: American Psychological Association.

Hasher, L., & Zacks, R. T. (1979). Automatic and effortful processes in memory. *Journal of Experimental Psychology, 108*, 356–388.

Heerman, C. E. (1983). Research on college reading programs and student retention efforts. *Reading World, 22*, 203–212.

Herber, H. L. (1978). Teaching reading in content areas (Second Edition). Englewood Cliffs, NJ: Prentice-Hall.

Hiebert, E. H., Englert, C. S., & Brennan, S. (1983). Awareness of text strsucture in recognition and production of expository discourse. *Journal of Reading Behavior, 15*, 63–79.

Holley, C. D., Dansereau, D. F., McDonald, B. A., Garland, J. C., & Collins, K. W. (1979). Evaluation of a hierarchical mapping technique as an aid to prose processing. *Contemporary Educational Psychology, 4*, 227–237.

Horn, J. L. (1982). The theory of fluid and crystallized intelligence in relation to concepts of cognitive psychology and aging in adulthood. In F. I. M. Craik & S. Trehub (Eds.), *Aging and cognitive processes* (pp. 237–278). New York: Plenum Press.

Horn, J. L., & Cattell, R. B. (1966). Refinement and test of the theory of fluid and crystallized intelligence. *Journal of Educational Psychology, 57,* 253–270.

Huff, K. H. et al. (1977). *A job oriented reading program for the Air Force: Development and field evaluation* (US AFHRL technical report, No. 77-34).

Hulicka, I. M., & Grossman, J. L. (1967). Age-group comparisons for the use of mediators in paired-associate learning. *Journal of Gerontology, 22,* 46–51.

Hulicka, I. M., Sterns, H.. & Grossman, J. (1967). Age-group comparisons of paired-associate learning as a function of paced and self-paced association and response times. *Journal of Gerontology, 22,* 274–280.

Hultsch, D. F., & Dixon, R. A. (1983). The role of pre-experimental knowledge in text processing in adulthood. *Experimental Aging Research, 9,* 17–22.

Hultsch, D. F., & Dixon, R. A. (1984). Memory for text materials in adulthood. In P. B. Baltes & O. G. Brim, Jr. (Eds.), *Life-span development and behavior* (vol. 6, pp. 77–108). New York: Academic Press.

Hultsch, D. F., Hertzog, C., & Dixon, R. A. (1984). Text recall in adulthood: The role of intellectual abilities. *Developmental Psychology, 20,* 1193–1209.

Hunt, E. (1978). Mechanics of verbal ability. *Psychological Review. 85,* 109–130.

Johnson, R. E. (1970). Recall of prose as a function of the structural importance of the linguistic units. *Journal of Verbal Learning and Verbal Behavior, 9,* 12–20.

Just, M. A., & Carpenter, P. A. (1980). A theory of reading: From eye fixations to comprehension. *Psychological Review, 87,* 329–354.

Kieras, D. E. (1980). Initial mention as a signal to thematic content in technical passages. *Memory and Cognition, 8,* 345–353.

Kieras, D. E. (1985). Thematic processes in the comprehension of technical prose. In B. K. Britton & J. Black (Eds.), *Understanding expository text* (pp. 89–107). Hillsdale, NJ: Lawrence Erlbaum Associates.

Kintsch, W. (1974). *The representation of meaning in memory.* Hillsdale, NJ: Lawrence Erlbaum Associates.

Kintsch, W., & van Dijk, T. A. (1978). Toward a model of text comprehension and production. *Psychological Review, 85,* 363–394.

Labouvie-Vief, G., & Gonda, J. N. (1976). Cognitive strategy training and intellectual performance in the elderly. *Journal of Gerontology, 31,* 327–332.

Labouvie-Vief, G., Schell, D. A., & Weaverdyck, S. E. (1981). *Recall deficit in the aged: A fable recalled.* Unpublished manuscript, Wayne State University.

Larson, C. O., & Dansereau, D. F. (1986). Cooperative learning dyads. *Journal of Reading, 29,* 516–520.

Lehnert, W. G. (1981). Plot units and narrative summarization. *Cognitive Science, 5,* 293–331.

Light, L. L., & Anderson, P. A. (1985). Working-memory capacity, age, and memory for discourse. *Journal of Gerontology, 45,* 737–747.

Light, L. L., Zelinski, E. M., & Moore, M. (1982). Adult age differences in reasoning from new information. *Journal of Experimental Psychology: Learning, Memory, and Cognition, 8,* 435–447.

Lorch, R. F., Lorch, E. P., & Matthews, P. D. (1985). On-line processing of the topic structure of a text. *Journal of Memory and Language, 24,* 350–362.

Mandel, R. G., & Johnson, N. S. (1984). A developmental analysis of story recall and comprehension in adulthood. *Journal of Verbal Learning and Verbal Behavior, 23,* 643–659.

Mandler, J. M. (1987). On the psychological reality of story structure. *Discourse Processes, 10,* 1–29.

Mandler, J. M., & Johnson, N. S. (1977). Remembrance of things parsed: Story structure and recall. *Cognitive Psychology, 9.* 111–151.

McGee, L. M. (1982). Awareness of text structure: Effects on children's recall of expository text. *Reading Research Quarterly, 17,* 581–590.

Meyer, B. J. F. (1971). *Idea units recalled from prose in relation to their position in the logical structure, importance, stability, and order in the passage.* Cornell University, M.S. thesis.

Meyer, B. J. F. (1975). *The organization of prose and its effects on memory.* Amsterdam: North Holland.

Meyer, B. J. F. (1981). Basic research on prose comprehension: A critical review. In D. F. Fisher & C. W. Peters (Eds.), *Comprehension and the competent reader: Inter-specialty perspectives* (pp. 8–35). New York: Praeger.

Meyer, B. J. F. (1983). Text structure and its use in studying comprehension across the adult life span. In B. A. Hutson (Ed.) *Advances in reading/language research* (vol. 2, pp. 9–54). Greenwich, CT: JAI Press.

Meyer, B. J. F. (1984). Text dimensions and cognitive processing. In H. Mandl, N. Stein, & T. Trabasso (Eds.), *Learning from texts* (pp. 3–52). Hillsdale, NJ: Lawrence Erlbaum Associates.

Meyer, B. J. F. (1985a). Prose analysis: Procedures, purposes, and problems. In B. K. Britton & J. Black (Eds.), *Understanding expository text* (pp. 11–64; 269–304). Hillsdale, NJ: Lawrence Erlbaum Associates.

Meyer, B. J. F. (1985b). *Practice makes perfect.* Prose Learning Series, Department of Educational Psychology, Arizona State University.

Meyer, B. J. F. (1987). Reading comprehension and aging: In K. W. Schaie (Ed.), *Annual review of gerontology and geriatrics* (Volume 7, pp. 93–115). New York: Springer.

Meyer, B. J. F., & Bartlett, B. J. (1985). *A plan for reading: A strategy to improve reading comprehension and memory for adults* (Prose Learning Series #14). Tempe, AZ: Arizona State University.

Meyer, B. J. F., Brandt, D. M., & Bluth, G. J. (1980). Use of the top-level structure in text: Key for reading comprehension of ninth-grade students. *Reading Research Quarterly, 16,* 72–103.

Meyer, B. J. F., & Freedle, R. O. (1978). *The effects of different discourse types on recall.* Princeton, NJ: Educational Testing Service.

Meyer, B. J. F., & Freedle, R. O. (1984). The effects of different discourse types on recall. *American Educational Research Journal, 21,* 121–143.

Meyer, B. J. F., & Rice, G. E. (1981). Information recalled from prose by young, middle, and old adults. *Experimental Aging Research, 7,* 253–268.

Meyer, B. J. F., & Rice, G. E. (1983a). Learning and memory from text across the adult life span. In J. Fine & R. O. Freedle (Eds.), *Developmental studies in discourse* (pp. 291–306). Norwood, NJ: Albex.

Meyer, B. J. F., & Rice, G. E. (1983b). *Effects of discourse type on recall by young, middle, and old adults with high and average vocabulary scores.* Paper presented at the National Reading Conference, Austin, TX.

Meyer, B. J. F., & Rice, G. E. (1984). The structure of text. In P. D. Pearson (Ed.), *Handbook of research in reading* (pp. 319–352). New York: Longman.

Meyer, B. J. F., & Rice, G. E. (1988). Prose processing in adulthood: The text, the reader and the task. In L. W. Poon, D. C. Rubin, & B. A. Wilson (Eds.), *Everyday cognition in adult and later life.* Cambridge, England: Cambridge Press.

Meyer, B. J. F., Rice, G. E., Knight, C. C., & Jessen, J. L. (1979). *Effects of comparative and descriptive discourse types on the reading performance of young, middle, and old adults* (Prose Learning Series #7). Arizona State University.

Meyer, B. J. F., Rice, G. E., Bartlett, B. J., & Woods, V. (1979). *Facilitative effects of passages with the same structure and different content on prose recall.* Unpublished manuscript, Arizona State University.

Morholt, E., & Brandwein, P. F. (1972). *Biology Patterns in the Environment* (Teaching-Learning Strategies). New York: Harcourt Brace Jovanovich.

Moscovitch, M. (1982). A neuropsychological approach to memory and perception in normal and pathological aging. In F. I. M. Craik & S. Trehub (Eds.), *Aging and cognitive processes* (pp. 55–78). New York: Plenum Press.

Mosenthal, J. H. (1984). *Instruction in the interpretation of a writer's argument: A training study.* Unpublished doctoral dissertation, University of Illinois at Urbana-Champaign.

Nelson, N. J., & Denny, E. C. (1973). *Nelson Denny reading test.* Boston, MA: Houghton Mifflin.

Niles, O. S. (1965). Organization perceived. In H. H. Herber (Ed.), *Perspective in reading: Developing study skills in secondary schools.* Newark, DE: International Reading Association.

Okun, M. A. (1976). Adult age and cautiousness in decision: A review of the literature. *Human Development, 19,* 220–233.

Okun, M. A., & Elias, C. S. (1977). Cautiousness in adulthood as a function of age and payoff structure. *Journal of Gerontology, 32,* 451–455.

Otto, W. (1970). Reading and ABE: What we know, what we need to know. In W. S. Griffith & A. P. Hayes (Eds.), *Adult basic education: The state of the art* (pp. 110–128). Washington, D.C.: U.S. Government Printing Office.

Overall, J. E., & Woodward, J. A. (1975). Unreliability of difference scores: A paradox for measurement of change. *Psychological Bulletin, 82,* 85–86.

Overall, J. E., & Woodward, J. A. (1976). Reassertion of the paradoxical power of tests of significance based on unreliable difference scores. *Psychological Bulletin, 83,* 776–777.

Pachtman, A. B. (1977). The effects of a reading and language arts program on the critical thinking and critical reading of the first-year law student. *Dissertation Abstracts International, 38-A,* 2431–2432.

Palincsar, A. S., & Brown, A. L. (1984). Reciprocal teaching of comprehension-fostering and monitoring activities. *Cognition and Instruction, 1,* 117–175.

Pastore, R. E., & Scheirer, C. J. (1974). Signal detection theory: Considerations for general application. *Psychological Bulletin, 81,* 945–958.

Pearson, P. D. (Ed.). (1984). *Handbook of research in reading.* New York: Longman.

Pearson, P. D., & Gallagher, M. C. (1983). The instruction of reading comprehension. *Contemporary Educational Psychology, 8,* 317–344.

Perfetti, C. A. (1985). *Reading ability.* New York: Oxford University Press.

Perlmutter, M. (1978). What is memory aging the aging of? *Developmental Psychology, 14,* 330–345.

Petros, T., Tabor, L., Cooney, T., & Chabot, R. J. (1983). Adult age differences in sensitivity to semantic structure of prose. *Developmental Psychology, 19,* 907–914.

Plemons, J. K., Willis, S. L., & Baltes, P. B. (1978). Modifiability of fluid intelligence in aging: A short-term longitudinal training approach. *Journal of Gerontology, 33,* 224–231.

Prescott, G. A., Balow, I. H., Hogan, T. P., & Farr, R. C. (1978). *Metropolitan achievement tests, advanced 2, forms JS and KS.* New York: The Psychological Corporation.

Propp, V. (1958). *Morphology of the folktale* (L. Scott, trans.) Bloomington: Indiana University Research Center in Anthropology, Folklore, and Linguistics, Pub. 10.

Poon, L. N., Krauss, I. K., & Bowles, N. L. (1984). On subject selection in cognitive aging research. *Experimental Aging Research, 10,* 43–49.

Rattanavich, S. (1987). *Using top-level structure instructional modules in teaching English to Thai secondary school students.* Singapore: SEAMEO Regional Language Center.

Reese, H. W., & Rodeheaver, D. (1985). Problem solving and complex decision making. In J. E. Birren & K. W. Schaie (Eds.), *Handbook of the psychology of aging* (2nd edition) (pp. 474–499). New York: Van Nostrand Reinhold.

Reutzel, D. R. (1985). Story maps improve comprehension. *The Reading Teacher, 38,* 400–404.

Rice, G. E. (1986a). The everyday activities of adults: Implications for prose recall—Part I *Educational Gerontology, 12,* 173–186.

Rice, G. E. (1986b). The everyday activities of adults: Implications for prose recall—Part II *Educational Gerontology, 12,* 187–198.

Rice, G. E., & Meyer, B. J. F. (1985). Reading behavior and prose recall performance of young and older adults with high and average verbal ability. *Educational Gerontology, 11,* 57–72.

Rice, G. E., & Meyer, B. J. F. (1986, April). *The relation of everyday activities of adults to their prose recall.* Paper presented at the meeting of the American Educational Research Association, San Francisco, CA.

Robertson-Tchabo, E. A., Hausman, C. P., & Arenberg, D. (1976). A classical mnemonic for older learners: A trip that works! *Educational Gerontology, 1,* 215–226.

Rogosa, D., Brandt, D., & Zimowski, M. (1982). A growth curve approach to the measurement of change. *Psychological Bulletin, 92,* 726–748.

Rosenshine, B., & Stevens, R. (1984). Classroom instruction in reading: In P. D. Pearson (Ed.), *Handbook of reading research* (pp. 745–798). New York: Longman.

Rumelhart, D. E. (1975). Notes on a schema for stories. In D. G. Bobrow & A. M. Collins (Eds.), *Representation and understanding: Studies in cognitive science* (pp. 211–236). New York: Academic Press.

Rybash, J. M., Hoyer, W. J., & Roodin, P. A. (1986). *Adult cognition and aging.* New York: Pergamon Press.

Salthouse, T. A. (1982). *Adult cognition: An experimental psychology of human aging.* New York: Springer-Verlag.

Sanders, R. E., Murphy, M. D., Schmitt, F. A., & Walsh, K. K. (1980). Age differences in free recall rehearsal strategies. *Journal of Gerontology, 35,* 550–558.

Sanders, R. E., Sanders, J. A. C., Mayes, G. J., & Sielski, K. A. (1976). Enhancement of conjunctive concept attainment in older adults. *Developmental Psychology, 12,* 485–486.

Sanders, J. A. C., Sterns, H. L., Smith, M., & Sanders, R. E. (1975). Modification of concept identification performance in adults. *Developmental Psychology, 11,* 824–829.

Schaie, K. W., & Hertzog, C. (1985). Measurement in the psychology of adulthood and aging: In J. E. Birren & K. W. Schaie (Eds.), *Handbook of the psychology of aging* (2nd edition) (pp. 61–92). New York: Van Nostrand Reinhold.

Schaie, K. W., & Willis, S. L. (1986). Can decline in adult intellectual functioning be reversed? *Developmental Psychology, 22,* 223–232.

Schank, R. C. (1975). *Conceptual information processing.* Amsterdam: North-Holland.

Schmitt, F., Murphy, M., & Sanders, R. E. (1981). Training older adult free recall rehearsal strategies. *Journal of Gerontology, 36,* 329–337.

Seaborg, G. T., & Bloom, J. L. (1970). Fast breeder reactors. *Scientific American, 223,* 13.

Shearin, C. W. (1976). An evaluation of a program to teach critical reading skills to adult volunteers. *Dissertation Abstracts International, 37-A,* 1355.

Shipley, W. C. (1940). A self-administering scale for measuring intellectual impairment and deterioration. *Journal of Psychology, 9,* 371–377.

Short, E. J. (1982). *A self-instructional approach to remediating less skilled readers' use of story schema, causal attributions, and expectations for success.* Unpublished doctoral dissertation: University of Notre Dame.

Simon, E. W., Dixon, R. A., Nowak, C. A., & Hultsch, D. F. (1982). Orienting task effects on text recall in adulthood. *Journal of Gerontology, 31,* 575–580.

Singer, H., & Donlan, D. (1982). Active comprehension: Problem-solving schema with question generation for comprehension of complex short stories. *Reading Research Quarterly, 17,* 166–186.

Slater, W. H. (1985). Teaching expository text structure with structural organizers. *Journal of Reading, 28,* 712–718.

Slater, W. H., Graves, M. F., & Piche, G. L. (1985). Effects of structural organizers on ninth-grade students comprehension and recall of four patterns of expository text. *Reading Research Quarterly, 20,* 189–202.

Smith, K., & Brown, G. (1987, January). *Helping children to understand content-based text at the upper primary and early secondary level.* Paper presented at the Oceania Congress on Reading in Hobart, Tasmania, Australia.

Smith, S. W., Rebok, G. W., Smith, W. R., Hall, S. E., & Alvin, M. (1983). Adult age differences in the use of story structure in delayed free recall. *Experimental Aging Research, 9,* 191–195.

Spilich, G. J. (1983). Life-span components of text processing; structural and procedural differences. *Journal of Verbal Learning and Verbal Behavior, 22,* 231–244.

Spilich, G. J., & Voss, J. F. (1982). Contextual effects upon text memory for young, aged-normal, and aged memory-impaired individuals. *Experimental Aging Research, 8,* 45–49.

Spiro, R. J., & Taylor, B. M. (1980). *On investigating children's transition from narrative to expository discourse: The multidimensional nature of psychlogical text classification* (Technical Report No. 195). Urbana-Champaign: University of Illinois, Center for the Study of Reading.

Stein, N. L., & Glenn, C. G. (1979). An analysis of story comprehension in elementary school children. In R. O. Freedle (Ed.), *Discourse processing: Multidisciplinary perspectives* (pp. 53–120). Norwood, NJ: Albex.

Sterns, H. L., & Sanders, R. E. (1980). Training and education in the elderly. In R. E. Turner & H. W. Reese (Eds.), *Life-span developmental psychology: Intervention* (pp. 307–330). New York: Academic Press.

Sticht, T. G., & James, J. H. (1984). Listening and reading. In P. D. Pearson (Ed.), *Handbook of reading research* (pp. 293–318). New York: Longman.

Stine, E. L., Wingfield, A., & Poon, L. W. (1986). Speech comprehension and memory through adulthood: The roles of time and strategy. In L. W. Poon, D. C. Rubin, & B. A. Wilson (Eds.), *Everyday cognition and adult and later life.* Cambridge, England: Cambridge University Press.

Surber, J. R., Kowalski, A. H., & Pena-Paez, A. (1984). Effects of aging on recall of extended expository prose. *Experimental Aging Research, 10,* 25–28.

Taub, H. A. (1979). Comprehension and memory of prose materials by young and old adults. *Experimental Aging Research, 5,* 3–13.

Taub, H. A., & Kline, G. E. (1978). Recall of prose as a function of age and input modality. *Journal of Gerontology, 33,* 725–730.

Taylor, B. M. (1980). Children's memory for expository text after reading. *Reading Research Quarterly, 15,* 399–411.

Taylor, B. M. (1982). Text structure and children's comprehension and memory for expository material. *Journal of Educational Psychology, 74,* 323–340.

Taylor, B. M. (1985). Toward an understanding of factors contributing to children's difficulty summarizing a textbook material. In J. A. Niles (Ed.), *Issues in literacy: A research perspective* (pp. 125–131). Rochester, NY: The National Reading Conference.

Taylor, B. M., & Beach, R. W. (1984). The effects of text structure instruction on middle grade students comprehension and production of expository text. *Reading Research Quarterly, 19,* 134–146.

Taylor, B. M., & Samuels, S. J. (1983). Children's use of text structure in the recall of expository material. *American Educational Research Journal, 20,* 517–528.

Thompson, D. N., & Diefenderfer, K. (1986, April). *The use of advance organizers with older adults of limited verbal ability.* Paper presented at the meeting of the American Educational Research Association.

Thorndyke, P. W. (1977). Cognitive structures in comprehension and memory of narrative discourse. *Cognitive Psychology, 9,* 77–110.

Trabasso, T., & van den Broek, P. (1985). Causal thinking and the representation of narrative events. *Journal of Memory and Language, 24,* 612–630.

Treat, N. J., Poon, L. W., Fozard, J. L., & Popkin, S. J. (1978). Toward applying cognitive skill training to memory problems. *Experimental Aging Research, 4,* 305–319.

Turner, A., (1984). *Learning effects of an instruction to utilize text organization.* Brisbane, Australia: Brisbane College of Advanced Education.

Usher, M. (1981). *Using top-level structure in high school.* Brisbane, Australia: Brisbane college of Advanced Education.

van Dijk, T. A., & Kintsch, W. (1983). *Strategies of discourse comprehension.* New York: Academic Press.

Vincent, J. P. (1985). *Effects of discourse types on memory of prose by young, middle-age, and old adults with average vocabularies.* Unpublished doctoral dissertation, Arizona State University.

Vincent, J., Meyer, B. J. F., & Rice, G. E. (1985, April). *Effects of discourse tyupe on recall by young, middle, and old adults with high, high-average, and average vocabulary scores.* Paper presented at the meeting of the American Educational Research Association in Chicago. IL.

Walker, C. H., & Meyer, B. J. F. (1980). Integrating different types of information in text. *Journal of Verbal Learning and Verbal Behavior, 19,* 263–275.

Wechsler, D. (1955). *Manual for the Wechsler Adult Intelligence Scale.* New York: Psychological Corporation.

Williams, J. P., Taylor, M. B., & Ganger, S. (1981). Text variations at the level of the individual sentence and the comprehension of simple expository paragraphs. *Journal of Educational Psychology, 73,* 851–865.

Williams, S. L. (1985). Towards an educational psychology of the older adult learner: Intellectual and cognitive bases. In J. E. Birren & K. W. Schaie (Eds.), *Handbook of the psychology of aging.* (2nd edition) (pp. 818–847). New York: Van Nostrand Reinhold.

Willis, S. L., Blieszner, R., & Baltes, P. B. (1981). Intellectual training research in aging: Modifications of performance on the fluid ability of figural relations. *Journal of Educational Psychology, 73,* 41–50.

Yesavage, J. A. (1985). Nonpharmacologic treatments for memory loses with normal aging. *American Journal of Psychiatry, 142,* 600–605.

Yekovich, F. R., & Thorndyke, P. W. (1981). An evaluation of alternative functional models of narrative schemata. *Journal of Verbal Learning and Verbal Behavior, 20,* 454–469.

Young, C. J. (1983). *Integration of facts across textual distances by young and old adults.* Unpublished masters thesis, Arizona State University.

Zabrucky, K., Moore, D., & Schultz, N. R. (1987). Evaluation of comprehension in young and old adults. *Developmental Psychology, 23,* 39–43.

Zelinski, E. M., & Gilewski, M. J. (in press). Memory for Prose and Aging: A Meta-analysis. In M. L. Howe & C. Brainerd (Eds.), *Cognitive development in adulthood.* New York: Springer-Verlag.

Zelinski, E. M., Gilewski, M. J., & Thompson, L. W. (1980). Do laboratory tests relate to self-assessment of memory ability in the young and old? In L. W. Poon, J. L. Fozard, L. S. Cermak, D. Arenberg, & L. W. Thompson (Eds.), *New directions in memory and aging: Proceedings of the George Talland Memorial Conference* (pp. 519–544). Hillsdale, NJ: Lawrence Erlbaum Associates.

Zelinski, E. M., Light, L. L., & Gilewski, M. J. (1984). Adult age differences in memory for prose: The question of sensitivity to passage structure. *Developmental psychology, 20,* 1181–1192.

Author Index

Subject Index